S I X
MONTHS
O F F

Also by Lamar Alexander

STEPS ALONG THE WAY

FRIENDS: JAPANESE AND
TENNESSEANS
(with Robin Hood)

S // I // X
MONTHS
O // F // F

AN AMERICAN FAMILY'S
AUSTRALIAN ADVENTURE

L A M A R
ALEXANDER

WILLIAM MORROW AND COMPANY, INC.
NEW YORK

#18070903

Copyright © 1988 by Lamar Alexander

Endpaper map copyright © 1988 by Markie Hunsiker and Jim McClelland.

Library of Congress Cataloging-in-Publication Data

Alexander, Lamar.
  Six months off: an American family's Australian adventure / Lamar Alexander.
    p. cm.
  ISBN 0-688-07417-0
  1. Alexander, Lamar—Journeys—Australia. 2. Tennessee–
–Governors—Biography. 3. Australia—Social life and customs.
I. Title.
F440.3.A44A3 1988
919.4'046—dc 19   88-17719
CIP

Printed in the United States of America

      7 8 9 10

BOOK DESIGN BY JAYE ZIMET

Excerpts from "Little Gidding" in *Four Quartets,* copyright © 1943 by T. S. Eliot, renewed 1971 by Esmé Valerie Eliot. Reprinted by permission of Harcourt Brace Jovanovich, Inc.

Excerpt from *Alexander and the Terrible, Horrible, No-Good, Very Bad Day,* by Judith Viorst, copyright © 1972. Reprinted by permission of Atheneum Publishers, an imprint of Macmillan Publishing Company.

Excerpt from *Pat Nixon: The Untold Story,* by Julie Nixon Eisenhower, copyright © 1986. Reprinted by permission of Simon & Schuster.

Excerpts from *Memories, Dreams, Reflections,* by C. G. Jung, edited by Aniela Jaffe and translated by Richard and Clara Winston, copyright © 1965. Reprinted by permission of Pantheon Books, a division of Random House, Inc.

Excerpt from *All the King's Men,* by Robert Penn Warren, copyright © 1946, 1974. Reprinted by permission of Harcourt Brace Jovanovich, Inc.

Excerpt from *A Death in the Family,* by James Agee, copyright © 1967. Reprinted by permission of Grosset & Dunlap.

Excerpt from *The Music of Man,* by Yehudi Menuhin and Curtis Davis, copyright © 1979 by Irwin Publishing. Reprinted by permission of Methuen Publishing, Toronto, Ontario.

Excerpt from "A Windy Afternoon" by A. D. Hope, from *A Late Picking: Poems 1965–74,* copyright © 1975 by A. D. Hope. Reprinted by permission of Angus & Robertson Publishers.

Excerpt from *Robinson Crusoe,* by Daniel Defoe. Used by courtesy of Bantam Books, a division of Bantam, Doubleday, Dell Publishing Group, Inc.

Excerpts from *Thoughts in Solitude,* by Thomas Merton, copyright © 1956, 1958 by the Abbey of Our Lady of Gethsemani. Reprinted by permission of Farrar, Straus and Giroux, Inc.

Dedicated to the
thirty always changing
relationships within our
family of six

CONTENTS

BOOK I: ENDING

BOOK II: SEARCHING

BOOK III: NEW BEGINNING

B O O K I

ENDING

What we call the beginning is often
the end. And to make an end is to
make a beginning. The end is
where we start from.

—T. S. ELIOT,
Four Quartets

C H A P T E R 1

''A W - *S T R A Y* -
U L - Y U H ! ? ''

//

I think I'll move to Australia.
—Judith Viorst
Alexander and the Terrible, Horrible,
No Good, Very Bad Day

It just came up one night at supper. I remember that the sun was still hot through the big windows, even though it was six o'clock so it must have been midsummer, and it must have been 1985.

We were sitting at our places around the breakfast-room table in the Mansion. I was at the head. Honey commanded the other end, guarding the only exit to the television set. The children sat two on each side, their chairs slightly turned toward their mother, their backs slightly toward me. *Sat* is not the right word. The children *perched* on their chairs, as if a McDonald's drive-in window might magically appear, pop open, and supply a box of Chicken McNuggets and a reprieve from the steady dripping torture of family dinner. Instead, the kitchen door swung open and in marched the chef and the assistant chef, Eric Hathaway and Philip Morris, each balancing three precisely decorated plates of food, which they placed in front of each of us.

"What's this?" asked Will, who was six then.

"Good veal," answered his mother, alert to the challenge.

"I don't eat veal."

"Tonight you do."

Kathryn, who was eleven, said, "I'd rather have fried chicken."

Leslee asked sweetly, "Could I please have steak?" Leslee had just arrived at thirteen years of age.

Her mother said, "Only if you go and cook it, and wash the pans and the dishes and then turn out the lights because Eric and Philip will be gone by then and I don't want Ida coming in here at six in the morning to a dirty kitchen." Ida Finch cooked at the Mansion in the mornings.

I studied this conversation from my end of the table and experimented with what seemed to be perfectly adequate-tasting veal (although I did wish once again that the chefs would cook fried ham and biscuits and red-eye gravy and white beans and cornbread, the kind of country cooking I grew up with), and I watched while Honey led the children in conversation in the same practiced way a circus ringmaster performs when all the spotlights are on all the rings. Once I had asked Leslee whether the children's chairs actually *were* always slightly turned toward their mother, with their backs slightly toward me, or was I just imagining things.

"I guess they are, Dad. It's because you're always daydreaming, spaced out. You're always tuning in after everything's over. But we love you anyway." She leaned over and kissed my cheek and returned to the center of her ring at the circus.

Suddenly Honey ceased ringmastering, looked down the table squarely at me, and said in Honey's calm but measured, direct way, "We've got to get out of here."

I sensed I should join the conversation.

I said, "No need to worry about that. The state constitution *kicks* us out automatically, at noon on a cold day in January, maybe a year and a half from today."

Six-year-old Will slipped from his seat nearest his mom and edged toward the door.

Honey helped him back into his chair. "No TV until you eat some beans, or at least some potatoes," and she turned again toward me. "I mean *really* out of here, a long way away and for a long time, not just two or three weeks, maybe for six months."

"Six months!" shouted Will. "Ho boy! Six months off from school!"

"Wrong," I said. "If we stay six months you can enjoy going to school in another country."

"I hate school," Will said.

"You're not allowed to say hate," said Drew, who was almost sixteen.

"*I'd* go to Norway," offered Leslee.

"You don't know where Norway is," Drew said.

"It's where aha is," countered Leslee.

Her mother said, "Rock groups like aha are usually on tour. I was thinking of Paris, where you could improve your French, or Switzerland, or maybe even Australia, where it's warm and friendly, where kangaroos and koala bears live, where it's too far away for anybody to come find Daddy. I was thinking of a place where we could get a clean break and a rest."

Drew said, "I've never heard of *one other family* taking a six-month *family* vacation. It's embarrassing just to think about it. Besides, it would be my junior year, my most important year. I can't go."

"Kangaroos are boring," Will chimed in, working hard to keep up. "Plus, I'd have to take a six-months supply of Coke."

"Why is that?" I asked, realizing immediately I shouldn't have.

"Because they might not have Coke in Australia and I'll forget what it tastes like and I don't want to forget what Coke tastes like or I might hate it when I get back."

A most troubled wail arose on my right: "Aw-STRAY-ul-yuh!? You-all are *serious*. I can't go to Aw-STRAY-ul-yuh for six months!"

"Well, the couch potato's alive," observed Drew.

Kathryn kicked Drew, and continued the wail: "Australia's too far away. I might like to go to Africa for two weeks. That would be fun—as long as we can stay away from France where they blow people up. But Aw-STRAY-ul-yuh!? I'd be away from my friends for six months and I'd come home talking weird. Torie went to *Oregon* for *two weeks* and came home talking weird. I'd rather take ten exams than go to Australia for six months."

Will had slipped under the table and out the door. I could hear his three-wheeler roaring down the black-and-white-squared marble floor toward the television set in my office. He shouted back over his shoulder, "I ate three beans," but his mother by then had surrendered.

I resumed daydreaming. But instead of imagining how to outwit legislators and prison rioters and nuclear-waste dumpers and teachers' union leaders—I dreamed a new and wonderful dream. *There I was—in floppy shorts, faded T-shirt, and old tennis shoes, walking alone on a white sand beach. My arms were tanned and there had not been one worry wrinkle on my face when I had shaved that morning. The sky was the brightest blue I had ever seen. The ocean breezes dried drops of sweat as quickly as they appeared on my forehead. It had been a very long walk but I felt no urgency. I had no destination in mind, no appointed time to stop. There was no three-by-five-inch card apportioning my life into fifteen-minute segments. No yellow pad waited with a list of things to do. No one asked me for a job. No one challenged me to remember his name. No one even recognized me.*

There was a mailbox. I thought, "It must take two weeks, maybe three, for United States mail to reach Australia. Nothing urgent could ever reach me in time to do anything about it." That made me wildly, irresponsibly happy. It was almost impossible to imagine. In Australia there would be nothing to do, nothing at all for six months.

Harsh background music—chairs scraping the floor —jerked me back to reality. Drew, Leslee, and Kathryn were preparing *their* escape. "Take your dishes to the kitchen first," their mother directed.

Now Honey and I were alone. She moved from her end of the still cluttered table to Leslee's chair, which was next to mine, and sat leaning forward on her elbows, her chin cupped in her hands. These moments after dinner—moments when just the two of us could talk—were precious. I tried hard to be home every night for supper. My friends who were governors in other states professed astonishment at this, even said they were a little jealous. I would assure them, "A few minutes of 'quality time' with the children is much more important than some after-dinner speech." But after eight years of my "quality time" spent pretty much only at the supper table, the children's chairs seemed, if anything, to be a little more turned toward their mother's end of the table, and their backs turned even more toward mine.

Honey's hand touched mine, and she said softly, "We *do* need a rest. We need some space and some reflection time, to see ourselves from another perspective. We need to get to know each other again." She got up and began to clear the table and then stopped and looked back. "And you need some time to think about what to do with the rest of your life."

"And what about you?"

She sighed. "Well, I guess for a while it'll be enough for me if we're a family again."

CHAPTER 2

THE MANSION

//

"Oh, no thank you Judy. I have to
keep doing things for myself. I tell
my girls that if you become
dependent on others and let them do
everything for you, you soon become
ugly."

—Mrs. Richard M. Nixon
in *Pat Nixon: The Untold Story*,
by Julie Nixon Eisenhower

Honey left to help Kathryn with math and I sat there with the rest of the dirty dishes thinking of my very first meal at that breakfast room table. It was when I was nineteen and my girlfriend Jane's father had taken me with him for breakfast with the Governor. "Mr. Mac"—which was what I very respectfully called Jane's father—was an important executive at the Alcoa aluminum plant in my hometown of Maryville.

He was so important that he knew the way to the state capitol in Nashville almost without having to look—which was sort of the way he drove that day, slumped low behind the steering wheel of his new 1959 '98 Oldsmobile, inhaling Winstons and ruminating in bass tones, and occasionally waving one arm and instructing me on some crucial Rule of Life.

When we reached the gate outside the Mansion, Mr. Mac shifted the Oldsmobile into neutral, and we paused to admire the three-storied Georgian house on ten well-shrubbed, tall-treed, blue-grassed acres that today in our state still symbolizes political victory, the prize of battle, the real spoils. Today on that same gate a bronze plaque announces: EXECUTIVE RESIDENCE, but only the First Ladies and society writers call it that. To everyone else, it is now what it was then: the Mansion. So, having contemplated it once again, Mr. Mac jerked into low gear and aimed the '98 Oldsmobile up a long, winding driveway until the car lurched to a stop at wide double front doors where a state trooper stood. Just before the trooper came around to open the door on the driver's side, Mr. Mac said to me in that low growl he loved to practice and I always envied, "I expect you'll live here one day."

The trooper led us to the breakfast room by the kitchen where the Governor was sitting in his place at the head of the table, reading the morning newspaper. Mr. Mac and I took seats on either side of him, facing one another. Mr. Mac lit a Winston. The Governor was smoking a "DFT," a Dual Filter Tareyton. That impressed me. I had never met anyone who actually *smoked* "DFTs." But what impressed me even more was the way the two of them carried on.

The Governor and Mr. Mac were soul brothers, two Mississippi white boys grown up. Once they'd both been skinny, creek-smart, sweaty, scratching out a rock-hard, barefoot living at the bottom of the heap in black-and-white cotton-quilted little delta towns. Now they were fleshed out, street-smart, air-conditioned, luxuriating in '98 Oldsmobile, cleated-rubber-golf-shoe, high-powered-fishing-boat Tennessee living—happily splashing in pleasant new ponds where the Governor was the biggest frog of all and Mr. Mac had a pretty nice-sized lily pad for himself in a smaller pond. ("Be the big frog in the smaller pond," was one Mr. Mac Rule of Life.) But no big lily pad in *any-sized* new pond can cause a Mississippi-born-and-raised white boy to forget his rock-hard, barefoot scratching-out days. No Mississippi white boys ever forget that, which is one reason they have such a good time getting together and which is what they talk about when they do.

Even before the prisoners who worked at the Mansion could bring out ham and eggs and grits and toast and coffee, the Governor and Mr. Mac started talking Mississippi, a language of growling and nudging and elbowing and foot stomping (if standing) and shuffling around in your chair and table slapping (if sitting down, as we now were) and undulating belly laughs and good-natured cussing and hugely glorified stories about happiness in the rock-hard, barefoot scratching-out days.

This manner of speaking is more than an accent. It is sui generis, a complex symphony of sound and feeling that can only be learned in Mississippi before you are six. It involves swallowing some words in the way English aristocrats do—except that the British don't say *hunnnhhh* and *hawwnhhh* nearly so much. Then other words must be regurgitated in full-throated, deep-breathed grunts and snorts, words like *heee-unnh* (as in where we were) and *theah-unh* (as in where we were going) and *bums* (as in bombs) and *hay bo-ahh!* (as in hello boy, which, in this language, is said to both blacks and whites).

I was inexperienced and from a law-abiding small town and seeing the prisoners at the Mansion made me uneasy. The "outside" prisoners clipped the putting green, cleaned the paddock and stable, raked leaves, tended the azaleas, washed the cars of the Governor's political supporters, and shot basketball at a hoop above one of the doors of the six-car garage. The "inside" prisoners cleaned the nine bathrooms, changed the sheets in the six bedrooms, rubbed the black-and-white marble floor in the foyer, and oiled the walnut rail on the carved wrought-iron banister that curved along the edge of the great, elliptical, free-standing carved-stone stairway that led upstairs to the private rooms. Some inside prisoners played cards in the basement, and still others cooked and served our ham and eggs and grits and coffee and toast.

There were many other interesting people about. State troopers sat in chairs in the foyer, stood by the front doors, and paced the grounds. Tour guides arrived early on many days to await the scheduled busloads of the Mansion's real owners, Tennesseans who would be anxious to inspect "their" house.

I had read that there could be political club women meeting in the library, staff members playing pool in the sun room,
while ambassadors or even the vice-president of the United
States might be occupying the guest bedrooms on the second
floor at the top of the stone staircase. There were whispers that
Elvis Presley had come from Memphis to court the Governor's
tall blond daughter. Living in the Mansion must be like living
in a *museum*, I thought then, as a visitor of nineteen.

The Governor left before eight A.M. to go to his capitol
office, where, according to the newspapers, he was often able by
noon to have the state on such an even keel that he could spend
the rest of the day on the golf course, sometimes with his old
buddy Mr. Mac. Mr. Mac and I also drove to the capitol to look
around, and on the way I pondered what the Governor had told
us about the prisoners: "Murderers are the best, better than
thieves. Murderers' crimes are crimes of passion."

As it turned out, Mr. Mac was right. Nineteen years later,
in November 1978, I was at the Mansion again, this time inspecting my new living quarters, a traditional visit for newly elected
Governors. The very best class of murderers still frequented the
place. My host, who was technically still the Governor until I
was officially sworn in, had decided that I should meet the prisoners, so he shouted over his shoulder to the state troopers,
"Bring 'em in and line 'em up around the wall."

This governor and I were sitting in the same breakfast
room by the kitchen where Mr. Mac and I once sat. The Governor, of course, was at the head of the table. I sat at one side where
I had sat nineteen years before and considered what was on my
plate. The Governor explained, "It's an African egg dish. One
of the prisoner cooks invented it." And then he said, "You
know, murderers are the best," and his voice, like an echo from
the past, resonated as out from the kitchen, up from the basement, down the great elliptical freestanding carved stone staircase, in from the tennis court, and from the stable and the
paddock, and from the putting green came white-uniformed
black men, all eager to please the only man who could send them
home with a pen's stroke. Exhibiting the most pleasant of dispo-
sitions, they stood erect, shoulder to shoulder, along three sides
of the small breakfast room.

The Governor barked, "Tell the new governor your name, your age, where you're from, what you did, and how long you got for it."

I cannot now remember the names. I do remember wondering whether any women and white people ever murdered anyone well enough to earn a position at the Mansion. But things proceeded something like this:

"Grover Thomas Washington, thirty-four, Dyersburg, triple murder with an ax, one hundred ninety-nine years . . ."

"Lincoln Grant Jefferson, twenty-seven, Nashville, cut wife's throat with scissors, two hundred fifteen years . . ."

"Harrison Alexander Brown, twenty-four, Chattanooga, murder with a hacksaw, two consecutive life sentences . . ."

And so it went until all the murderers had introduced themselves.

As the prisoners filed out, I said to the Governor, "You didn't have to do that."

The Governor smiled and said, "Aw, they like it," and turned his attention to what remained of the African egg dish on his plate.

A few weeks later, the day before our family moved into the Mansion, I ordered that all the prisoners be returned to the main state prison. The state troopers who sat in the foyer moved their desk to the basement. Honey asked the new *paid* cooks and staff not to come on weekends. We were determined that while I was governor even though we would be living in the Mansion, our three children—and a fourth, who was on the way—would grow up in a "normal" environment. We wanted no spoiled children.

Two nights later, our Leslee, who even at six had become instantly at ease in her new surroundings, telephoned from her second-floor bedroom at the top of the carved stone staircase all the way to the troopers' desk in the basement. "Will one of you-all bring me up a hamburger, a Coke, and some french fries—large, please—to my room?" And if one of the troopers had not checked with Honey—who went immediately to Leslee's room and recited a lesson on the value of doing things for oneself—Leslee would have arranged for her own regular room service at the Mansion.

CHAPTER 3

WILDLIFE REFUGE

//

... how difficult it is to be simple.

—C. G. Jung

Memories, Dreams, Reflections

It was January 9, 1987, eight days before my term as governor expired, five days before we would move out of the Mansion. The friend standing with Honey and me in the receiving line asked, "When did you decide to do this, to take the whole family and move to Australia for six months?"

I replied, "I'm not sure we ever actually sat down and *decided* it. Somehow it just sounded right the first time Honey mentioned it and when people asked where we'd be living we started saying, 'Oh, we're thinking of taking six months off, maybe in Australia,' and then we made some plans and it sounded even better. What surprised me was how many other families were thinking about the same kind of thing."

Honey said, "A lot think about it but not very many seem to ever manage to do it." Her eyes were darting often to the double front doors where guests were pausing to read the sign and then hurrying on in from the cold. "Maybe it was easier for us because we had to move *somewhere*. In a way it's easier to pack for six months in Australia than for whatever we'll be doing next in Tennessee. We're only taking two suitcases apiece. Everything else goes to storage."

None of the three hundred invited guests crowding in could miss the sign or the word RULES scrawled across its top. The sign had been masking-taped onto the double front doors that opened onto the black-and-white-squared marble floor of the Mansion's foyer.

This was the same black-and-white marble floor that had served as a speedway for Will's daily three-wheeler races. For eight years it had been the setting for state banquets, a reception area for heads of state and Japanese investors, a gathering place for citizens. And it had been a basketball court for Drew, who, until he was fourteen, hung a goal on the walnut railing of the great elliptical free-standing carved stone staircase that led to our upstairs living quarters.

But no guest tonight would reach those upstairs living quarters. Not only was a purple cord stretched across the bottom of the stairs—a normal precaution—there was a state trooper at either end of the cord. Several downstairs rooms, usually open, were closed and their doors were locked. As the evening progressed, the residence manager, his two student assistants, and Honey's administrative assistant found reasons to visit at least every ten minutes the few open rooms remaining.

Two overcoated troopers with walkie-talkies guarded the iron gate at the foot of the winding entrance driveway, their checklists making certain that no uninvited guest slipped in. Inside the Mansion every chandelier rheostat was turned up. Outside the floodlights had never burned brighter. The tennis court and swimming pool lights were all on. Troopers in the basement stared at three television monitors that were receiving images from infrared cameras whirring monotonously in every downstairs room and at every outside corner of the house.

Plainsclothesmen waving flashlights paced the iron fence sur-
rounding the estate.

"There is more security here tonight than there is at the
main prison," I whispered to Honey as we greeted guests.

"There needs to be," she said, smiling at the newest arrival.

Two more troopers stood at the front steps on either side
of the double front doors. To each guest they suggested that he
or she might wish to read the RULES on the sign.

RULE NUMBER ONE: *No sex, drugs or alcohol (do this and
you will probably get busted).* (The word "sex" had been crossed
out.)

"You didn't say anything about sex, Daddy," Leslee explained. "But don't worry. We're having fun." It was Leslee's
farewell party at the Mansion. She had invited her best
friends—three hundred seventh, eighth, and ninth graders from
every corner of Nashville. Her mother—who was state chairman of the "Just Say No" campaign to discourage teenage use
of drugs and alcohol—had discussed with Leslee some very specific requirements before the party was allowed.

RULE NUMBER ONE was a grand success. Of course,
only a professional criminal could have violated it in the face of
the armed garrison Honey had assembled. It helped even more
when, early in the evening, two of the sturdier troopers found
a couple of reckless fifteen-year-old boys sampling beer in the
shadows by the horse barn. This sobering news tore through an
already sober crowd: The beer had been poured on the ground,
the boys sent home, and it was even rumored that their parents
had been called. No one messed with RULE NUMBER ONE.

RULE NUMBER TWO was *You must dance,* and it was a
dismal failure. This was not the fault of the girls. They shim-
mied by themselves, danced with each other, horsed about in
groups, tempted and teased and encouraged and finally yanked
and shouted at the boys, most of whom stood along the walls of
the party tent behind the Mansion as if they had never seen
girls. In the boys' defense, most of them were in the eighth
grade, and even eighth-grade boys who know how to dance
don't on principle. And second, what eighth-grade boy would
want to dance *with girls* in front of the governor and his wife,

plus what looked like half the Tennessee highway patrol in the middle of a tent so flooded with lights that it might as well have been Ringling Brothers Barnum and Bailey center ring.

At ten the troopers ushered the guests into their parents' lined-up cars, except for a few girls who raced with Leslee up the carved-stone staircase to the third-floor attic for the Last Slumber Party. Honey went upstairs to check on Kathryn and Will, and I went to my downstairs office to read tomorrow's schedule card. I found a note on my desk. "Dad, what do you think about what I have written for my school application? Love, Leslee."

I slumped in a stuffed chair by the fire to read what she had written. My eyes were heavy, and hurt around the rims, as if smoke had gotten in them. My legs felt heavy, too. This morning, when I was shaving, I didn't like what I'd seen in the mirror. Tired eyes. Fatter face. Deeper lines. Lately I had been realizing that my eyeglasses were thicker than ever—and more of my hair in front was disappearing. And all of my pants were tight. Leslee had said at breakfast, "You'd be on the most eligible bachelor list, Dad, if you'd lose twenty pounds, except for Mom, of course."

I didn't want Leslee to go away to school. Leslee was fourteen and pretty and adventurous and, best of all, nice to her daddy. In Australia she and I would have six months to spend more time together. I looked forward to that. But somehow I knew I would be disappointed. Leslee had become a teenager, ready to spend time with someone other than her dad or mom. We had moved into this cavernous place when she was only six, chubby and cute with blond ringlets. I thought, Ever since our second night here, when she ordered the troopers to bring a hamburger and french fries to her room, she has done maybe the best job of any of us of living an abnormal life normally. She has survived the unnaturalness of everyone knowing her name, of being driven to school by highway patrolmen, of living in a house that is constantly full of other people and more like a museum than a home, and of having a father constantly thinking about the complications of his job. One night, when I was already in bed, Leslee, then about age eight, had wandered into our room and asked me to carry her to bed. I said I was too tired. She said, "Pretty soon, Daddy, I'll be too big for you to carry."

Leslee's school application form said, "In reading your application, we hope to gain as complete a picture of you as possible. Please use this space to tell us something more about you. You could write about your family."

I had encouraged her. "Use your imagination."

On the application she had written:

Many teenagers might call their family a zoo, but I think the description particularly fits my family's situation. Perhaps a more specific view would be a wildlife refuge. We are different animals, wandering and discovering quietly but being observed constantly. We have lived in a fishbowl viewed by everyone from every angle for the past eight years.

It has not been easy with my father as Governor. The entire family has been thrust into the public eye. We have learned a lot though. We are all unique.

My younger brother Will reminds me of a kangaroo. He is feisty and very assertive.

Kathryn, who is twelve, asks for attention by being flashy but she leads those who choose to follow her. These qualities remind me of a peacock.

My older brother Drew is a panther, a loner. At the age of 17 he does things as he wishes and gets away with everything.

I see myself as a brash monkey, asserting her will where she can and sometimes not knowing where to stop.

I characterize my father as an egret, standing on one leg and viewing the world. Although powerful in government, he is withdrawn in family life.

My mother is the lioness who keeps the family in hand and allows us to live and grow.

The assortment of personalities in my family is great. I am looking forward to spending time in Australia with my family under normal circumstances.

(signed) Leslee Taylor Alexander, age 14

January 9, 1987

C H A P T E R   4

O N E   T W E N T Y - O N E   R U T H   S T R E E T

//

. . . the Boss said, "Put the old white thunder-mug under the bed and it'll look just like home."

—ROBERT PENN WARREN

All the King's Men

I never could say "Ruth Street" right.

I would say the word "Ruth," and my tongue would still be out like a snake's when "Street" rushed out. This would all happen before I could pull in my tongue and *hiss,* which is the sound you should start with when you say "street." You try to say Ruth Street *fast.* It's easier just to say, "Corner of Ruth and Oak Park," which is what I said whenever anyone wanted to know where I lived, which was not often, because in a small town like Maryville almost everybody knew where you lived anyway. They knew at least *that* about you.

Ruth Street runs from the Blount County Fire Hall on Broadway to Pistol Creek at the bottom of the hill. The fire hall was the best place for lobbing snowballs at the cars of tourists speeding toward the Florida sun. In my hometown, Maryville, only one adventure gave us more of a thrill than lobbing snowballs at Ohio tourists (there were so many of these that we concluded that there must be nothing fun to do in Ohio). We loved to lob one and then watch the driver skid to a stop on the icy highway. Almost always he would roll down his fogged window and scream in some unusual accent, "You blasted little hillbillies. You've hit my windshield!" which is exactly what we were and what we aimed to do.

But our supreme adventure in Maryville occurred in the summers. At the other end of Ruth Street, at the bottom of the hill by Pistol Creek, the woods provided a hospitable and private den for hiding bikes and for smoking Indian "see-gars." It also provided a good supply of the see-gars themselves. Indian see-gars, of course, didn't grow as see-gars, and you could not buy them at the Broadway Food Market. They had to be cut at some considerable risk from grapevines hanging high in the poplars and oaks. The highest-growing grapevines naturally were the top quality and well worth the trouble it took to cut them with a pocket knife while you stood on a branch. When I was ten years old, nothing was more satisfying on a lazy June afternoon than lying on the grassy banks of Pistol Creek with my best friends, protected by the scrub and tall trees, cutting and smoking a dozen or so of these top-quality Indian see-gars, lighting one on the end of the last one.

I never smoked an Indian see-gar *before* I was ten. I did once try a chaw of Red Man tobacco, but that was in a cave, where it was fifty-six degrees, and when I crawled out into the suddenly hot July sun, I puked so much I have never wanted to try another chaw. The only *smoking* I ever did before age ten was limited to picking up and finishing off cigarette butts—Camels, when I could find them, because my granddad, R. R. Rankin, smoked Camels. I had to rewrap most of those Camel butts because the first smokers usually had dropped them lighted, then stepped on them, leaving them smushed in sorry shape. This was not so much of a problem since cigarette paper for rewrapping was available at the Broadway Food Market. We pooled our allowances, and one of the other boys would buy the cigarette paper, explaining to Mr. Nicely that the paper was for a father who rolled his own. My allowance was fifteen cents a week—a nickel for my bank, a nickel for the church, and a nickel for me, for such things as I might purchase at the Broadway Food Market.

The most cigarette smoking I ever did was when I was six and visiting in Newton, Kansas, where my granddad was a Santa Fe railroad engineer, and therefore to me one of the most important men in all of Kansas. While Granddad was railroading and Grandmother was cooking and singing in the kitchen, I would go to his second-floor study where his tobacco was and, after opening all the windows, would puff away until my mouth began to taste like burned cardboard and then I would stop smoking for the day.

Then I still thought that Granddad's initials, R. R., stood for "Rail Road" Rankin. Granddad Reu Raymond Rankin took me to the roundhouse, where steam locomotives turned around and were repaired, and sat me next to him in the cab of one of the last of those belching monsters. He gave me a watch that worked and showed me a one-hundred-dollar bill. He let me see and hear him dicker with a salesman about the price of a new 1946 Packard ("Probably the last car I'll ever buy," he said, fishing for sympathy and a lower price.), and he instructed me on the Rules of Life. "Aim for the top, there's more room there" was one I remember. "Whistling girls and crowing hens always come to some bad ends" was a rule I didn't quite grasp. On the Fourth of July, at 427 East Fifth Street in Newton, we lit sparklers and rockets and even blew up some cherry bombs.

Cherry bombs were specifically prohibited at the corner of Ruth and Oak Park in Maryville, as were a number of other things, such as drinking more than one Coke a week, swearing, telling racial jokes, missing Sunday school or church or choir practice, and having nothing to do. There were a great many other things that were never mentioned but were generally understood to be prohibited. Smoking Indian see-gars and chewing Red Man tobacco, for example, would fall in this category. Picking up and finishing off Camel cigarette butts would not only have been prohibited, but would have never even *been imagined* by the rulemakers at our house.

It was not really necessary to prohibit much on Ruth Street because there was a built-in system of mischief control: There was always something to do and always someone watching. Not only watching but encouraging and helping and clapping and trying to put your picture in the paper almost anytime you did anything that amounted to something. This was all done with great enthusiasm and seriousness by almost everyone in town.

By the time I was ten, the alarm clock in my second-floor bedroom was set to ring at four each morning. Usually I would reach over and turn it off just before it rang, so it would not wake my sisters, Ann and Jane. In the dark I pulled on jeans, tennis shoes, and flannel shirt, stepped carefully down the squeaky stairs, tossed a newspaper bag in the front basket of my Sears Schwinn bike, and raced to the Broadway Food Market. There I picked up a packet of about seventy-five Knoxville *Journals,* threw them into my bicycle basket, rode down Broadway, turned left at the fire hall, and pitched the first *Journal* on the front porch of one-aught-seven Ruth Street, which was Mr. White's little brick house behind the Watts tourist court. (Mr. White himself pronounced it that way, *one-aught-seven,* when I collected from him each week.)

With one hand I could fold and pitch a *Journal*—always on the porches, never in the yards—and steer with the other hand. It meant I never stopped until about 5:00 A.M., when I climbed back up the squeaky stairs and crawled under the rumpled quilt for another hour's sleep. The only time it took me more than one hour to deliver papers were when it rained, and then each paper had to be wrapped in plastic. Several times a mean collie on Sterling Avenue slowed me down, but one morning I slowed *him* down with a water gun filled with ammonia water, and after that he left me alone. And once I was very late with the papers, almost late to school, because there was a cow in Mrs. P. H. Allen's front yard and I debated with myself for a considerable time before I told her about it. Would you wake up your sixth-grade teacher at 4:30 in the morning to tell her there was a cow in her yard when it might not be *her* cow?

I was up again at six to practice the piano because I liked

it, because it left the afternoons free for sports, and because I had
to. While Mother's kitchen produced smells of bacon and the
strong coffee that Dad liked, I sat in the next room at our third-
hand upright Kimball piano that mother had bought with her
schoolteacher's savings. My piano lessons began when I was
three, at experimental classes at Maryville College (and stopped
when I enrolled at Vanderbilt University when I was eighteen).
I played well enough to win "superior" ratings at spring festi-
vals as well as first-place cups at two statewide piano competi-
tions. Piano playing was how my mother interpreted for me the
First Catechism of the Presbyterian Church. She would say,
" 'Man's chief end is to glorify God,' and the reason you play
with so much music is because God gave you that gift."

One of Mother's gifts was handing down her Rules of Life,
something she had apparently inherited from her father, R. R.
Rankin. But in pronouncing these Rules, she had a habit of
improvising too much, I thought. For example, on sunny October afternoons—when the maples, oaks, sweet gums, and poplars along Ruth and Oak Park were red and golden and the
neighbors' burning leaf piles scented the air—Mother would
rule, "God gave us this beautiful day to rake leaves." Such rul-
ings led me also to see God as responsible for making the hedge
grow high, so I could cut it, and for making the white paint peel
off our frame house, so I could paint it. I did not argue with
either Mother or God, but I thought one or the other or both
were taking unfair advantage of their positions.

Mother was also very good at announcing Rules that meant
more than they seemed to mean. For example, the point of
"Finish what you started; your dad always does," was not that
you should finish something, but that you should *start* something—and respect your dad. Or, take "If you don't eat breakfast
you won't amount to anything"; the message here was that it is
important to amount to something.

Dealing with these extra Rules—and sideyard football and
softball—kept my afternoons busy and full until 5:30, when I
would rush to the Broadway Food Market for my package of
afternoon *News-Sentinels*. While it was still daylight I could run
the Ruth Street route in half the time it took to deliver the
morning *Journals* and arrive home just in time for supper at six.
Then by 6:30, on Mondays, Wednesdays, and Fridays, Dad and

I would be flopped on the floor in the living room in front of the tall mahogany Zenith radio, eager for the staccato trumpet that announced the beginning of another adventure of *The Lone Ranger*. On warm autumn Saturday afternoons we'd carry the radio to the front porch and turn it up so we could hear University of Tennessee football games while we worked in the yard. Bringing our radio outside always seemed to me a waste of time because everyone else on Ruth Street had their radios outside, too, turned up so loud that we could have heard the game anyway. In the winter, the radio was also inside on Saturday afternoon, so we could hear Milton Cross and the Metropolitan Opera, which was something I never got used to.

If God blessed me with a gift of music, he transmitted it through my gentle, wavy-black-haired dad, Andrew, who possessed a pure tenor voice. Dad grew up on a farm, with a piano in the parlor and summer camp meetings in the back fields. These weeklong meetings featured determined preaching and strong singing "like we're getting the clothes off the line in a hard shower." Dad had a collection of relatives who sang in church choirs all over the county. One singing cousin, the Reverend Charles M. Alexander, the son of one of our county sheriffs, warmed up revival crowds from England to Australia. "Charles M. was the world's greatest song leader at the turn of the century and no one has ever inspired me more," Cliff Barrows, Billy Graham's song leader, told me once.

If music was my first notion of what to do with God's gifts, it was Miss Lennis Tedford, with whom I spent a half hour each week, who showed me how to apply discipline to a gift. Miss Lennis would decree "Stop the monkey business. You've been playing Jerry Lee Lewis. Your left hand is jumping. Play nice and even. Keep the piece under control. Play it slower than you *can* play it. And use the metronome."

The metronome became my steady friend, its beat my closest companion. Its quiet *tick-tock tick-tock tick-tock* became a part of me, measuring my struggle with Bach's counterpoints, and Rachmaninoff's *hard* left hand, and Mozart's runs, and especially with Czerny's arpeggios. Mastering those Czerny exercises with the metronome made me feel better prepared for almost anything. Above all, amid the busyness of life on Ruth Street, music resonated within me, gave me peace, especially

Mozart's sonatas and the gospel songs of Alfred E. Brumley.

Our New Providence Presbyterian Church, also on Broadway, was the center of a good part of our lives. In addition to choir on Sunday, there was Fellowship on Sunday night, Boy Scouts on Monday night, choir practice on Tuesday, prayer meeting on Wednesday, weekend rallies and vacation Bible school and church camp in the summer. And, of course, there was Sunday school. Sunday school at New Providence Church was where I tried out for the first time a new word—a word that some of the smoking boys at Pistol Creek *guaranteed* would produce a sure-fired reaction, although none of them had said what the word meant.

The word was "shit," and when there was a break in the Old Testament lesson I said it. It got an even better reaction than the boys had promised, so I said it again and better this time—"sheee-IT!"—exactly the way I had heard it said on Pistol Creek—and then I watched with wonder as Aunt Betty Banks dismissed the class, summoned the preacher, dragged me to the parking lot, and found my mother, all within what seemed like sixty seconds. It seemed unusual to me that in all of their ensuing discussions neither Aunt Betty nor Mother nor the preacher would actually repeat to each other or to anyone else the word that had provoked such consternation. And in it all, they forgot to punish me, which took part of the fun out of it.

I walked every day to West Side Elementary School (where my father had been principal until he took a job at the aluminum plant to support the family better). There I received a vigorous education as well as 105 black marks in Mrs. Jackson's fourth grade (five black marks meant you were in serious trouble), for which I was given two licks with the paddle. The paddling smashed two Milky Way candy bars in my back jeans pocket, to the delight of the eagerly witnessing class. The next morning during first-period class, when each of us said out loud a one-sentence prayer, classmate Bill Earnest's sentence was "Dear God, please forgive Lamar Alexander for all his sins."

In high school, elections were important and a big part of the system of mischief control. Almost everyone was elected to something and accorded the applause of the community. There was something about growing up in this small town that encouraged achievement and, occasionally, adventure, that limited the damage of mistakes, but still wound you up, and thrust you on your way, still too naïve to know what was impossible to achieve.

I was paddled again. In the ninth grade this time. The paddling was given by the principal, J. P. Stewart—even though I was class president and my father was vice-chairman of the town's school board. I had been caught once too often leading a chorus of windlike *whooooshing* noises whenever the ninth-grade English teacher turned her back to open a window. Having gotten in trouble at school, I got in trouble at home, which is the way things used to work in American public education. My poor deportment must have been especially embarrassing for my mother, who was one of the town's two preschool teachers. Every morning in a converted garage in our backyard, she taught 25 three- and four-year-olds and in the afternoon, 25 five-year-olds. She discovered gifted children before many of their parents did. Mother eventually put herself out of business by harassing the school board on which my father served to build a kindergarten classroom for every new school building long before our state had public kindergarten. She must have spent every penny of her earnings on my sisters and me. "Your dad did the tithing," Mother told me later. "I never thought about tithing with that money then. There was never enough and I just assumed God gave it to me to help you children."

Dad kept his finances to himself, but it was clear he never had money to waste. Despite Mother's working, we still had no television in 1955 when I was fifteen. We had no car until I was ten, and when we got it—a white 1940 two-door Chevy—a couple of my classmates, whose fathers had newer and bigger cars, smirked. But nobody in Maryville smirked much because it was hard to tell who was poor or rich. Most people had some money because of the thousands of jobs for aluminum workers at the Alcoa plant, or because of farming, or both. But people who were rich, relatively speaking, were careful not to act rich, and most people who were poor did their best neither to feel or act poor. This included my black friends, whose grandfathers had been recruited from Alabama in 1917 to come to our all-white mountain town to help build the aluminum plant. These black grandfathers therefore received their first good jobs about the same time the plant gave the white grandfathers *their* first good jobs. Three generations of good jobs created a basic self-esteem and respect for one another among blacks and whites that (I discovered later) was unusual.

Probably the thing that stirred up my dad the most was when Eleanor Roosevelt, and then Lyndon B. Johnson, came to East Tennessee to pronounce us Appalachian-poor. Talking about this so upset Dad that the veins in his throat would swell and turn blue, the way the veins in his Quaker mother's throat had looked during the years I knew her, when she lay dying in our front bedroom. The *real* reason Dad's veins turned blue was that Eleanor Roosevelt and Lyndon B. Johnson were Democrats, and we were Republicans. Dad practiced his Republicanism the way I practiced the piano, systematically—he practiced it over coffee at Byrne Drugstore, in the courthouse on Saturday mornings, and as a member of the local Republican party executive committee. I was led to believe that almost everyone worthwhile was a Republican except for a couple of Democratic bankers and store owners, and one lawyer, and one plant foreman, who lived on Willard Avenue. Even the officers of the local aluminum workers' union were often Republicans.

There was good reason for such Republicanism. When Tennessee seceded in the Civil War, our part of eastern Tennessee tried not to go along and it fought on the Union side. As a result, ever since Abraham Lincoln was elected president of the United States, our congressional district had never (and still has not) sent a Democrat to Congress. Republicans have worked hard to keep this tradition strong. Farther up in the mountains from Maryville, on Saturday mornings old Republicans would haul a conspicuous drunk to the town square, round up the children, and tell them the drunk was a Democrat, "Just to get the young-uns off on the right foot." Granddad Rankin once said, "There are plenty of people around here who have never spotted their ballot with a vote for any Democrat."

By the time I was a teenager, Granddad had retired to a farm near Cassville, in the southwest corner of Missouri where Grandmother had grown up. He was comfortable there because in the 1840s that part of Missouri had been settled by descendants of the same wild and ornery Scotch-Irish frontiersmen—like the Rankins and the Alexanders—who pioneered

Tennessee, fought hand-to-hand with the Cherokees for thirty years, and then moved west, looking for more fights.

At this time Granddad could only whisper. The same year he retired from railroading, doctors in Kansas had cut out his voicebox. "Cancer of the larynx, too many cigarettes," was what they had told him. After that, he whistled hymns in church, called his dog, Sandy, with a whistle I still keep on my desk, and rasped at Grandmother when she didn't suit him. My best summers as a teenager were spent on my grandparents' farm—enjoying the fresh taste of raw milk and butter every day, scything grass beneath the hot Missouri sun, and helping Granddad type up the genealogical records of his Scotch-Irish ancestors way back to 1688 in County Derry, Ireland.

Granddad's correspondence with relatives helped to found the Rankin reunions at Mt. Horeb Presbyterian Church in Dumplin Valley in Jefferson County, where our ancestors settled in 1783, thirteen years before Tennessee became the sixteenth state. Sometimes at those reunion services I played the old upright piano while relatives sang "God Be With You Till We Meet Again," which was written by Jeremiah Rankin in 1880. After a covered-dish dinner-on-the-grounds of fresh yellow corn and red tomatoes and fried chicken and biscuits and all anybody could eat, we would follow Granddad Rankin as he stepped cautiously from beneath the big white oaks into the hot sun. Our little parade always would stop at the same place behind the church and wait for Granddad to raise his cane and point toward a row of gravestones. As in every mountain graveyard, all the stones still standing faced east (because the Bible teaches that Jesus will come again from the East and no family wants its loved ones facing the wrong way when he comes). Granddad would then lengthen his six-feet-four-inch frame (as much as age would permit) and pause for silence, and then, looking down at us children, intone: "I am the fifth, your mother standing here is the sixth, you are the seventh, and your children will be the eighth generation. No one except the Cherokees goes further back than that in East Tennessee."

Grandmother died in 1967. Granddad sold his farm and moved home to East Tennessee. "You can't take the mountains out of a mountain boy," he pronounced—another Rule of Life.

He bought Mr. White's little house at one-aught-seven Ruth Street, where Mother could keep an eye on him and he could keep his independence. When, with his one good eye, he would aim his Hudson up Ruth Street and down Broadway, even the Ohio tourists seemed to know to get out of the way.

He had not lived in Tennessee since 1897, when as an eleven-year-old with sixteen brothers and sisters, he ran away from home and from a life so hard that he was never willing to describe it to me. He had stopped for a while in Decatur, Alabama, to visit his younger brother, Marvin, who had run away earlier. Granddad had then drifted to Texas, where he found his first railroad job. Now at the end of his life he was back home in the mountains again. He got married again, this time to Mae Brotherton, whose ancestors had come to Dumplin Valley at about the same time as his. As children Reu and Mae had both attended Mt. Horeb Presbyterian Church. Now, both in their eighties, they were together again.

"Well, what are you going to do, Lamar?" Granddad asked me, in one of our last conversations. He was rocking on the front porch at one-aught-seven Ruth Street.

"Maybe someday run for governor," I answered.

He whispered, "I wouldn't. Politics is too hard. But if you do, aim for the top. There's more room there."

C H A P T E R 5

LOSING

//

"I don't think it's the kind of thing
that can be prepared for; it just has to
be lived through."

—JAMES AGEE
A Death in the Family

Kathryn's kicking in Honey's stomach announced an imminent arrival one hot June night in 1974. I was in our living room having a campaign meeting. About 11:00 P.M., Honey appeared in her robe at the bottom of the stairs.

"It's time," she said.

There was a firehouse scramble. Political savants disappeared nervously into the night. I ran to bring the car to the end of the sidewalk. Two hours later, Kathryn Rankin Alexander, wet and wiggling, was bawling in her mother's arms at Vanderbilt Hospital.

Good news followed good news. Six weeks later I won the Republican nomination for governor of Tennessee. But three months later, as the 1974 general election approached, I was losing. I could feel it, losing, but at first I ignored it. I ignored blank faces and grim stares that told me voters were mad at all Republicans about Watergate. I challenged reporters who wrote me off. "It's close," I told them, and the more I said it, the more I believed it. But Honey felt the campaign was sinking. Others felt it, too.

"How's it going?" I would ask—which is what politicians say when they meet.

"Hard to tell."

"Maybe pickin' up," someone else would say.

"People are quiet," would say another.

It wasn't winner's talk.

Campaigns always break, for the winner. I kept hoping, waiting, for the campaign to break *for* me—and then I felt it, an unmistakable, heavy, nauseating loneliness as my opponent's campaign rushed on by, running free-form, and I began to understand the glaze in the eyes of people who would rather not say anything than have to say, "No, I don't think I'll vote for you."

At first I was angry. Then, by the last few days of the campaign, I had lost the incandescence that everyone sees in a candidate who knows where he is, knows where he is headed, and knows he is winning. I looked and felt like a loser, tired and unconvincing and hollow and empty. By election day I didn't have to hear the early absentee ballot returns on the car radio to know that I had lost.

I received the first official bad news in that 1974 election by flipping the dial on the car radio. I was driving slowly with Honey en route to our "victory" party, not wanting to miss any of the early news, when an announcer reported that the voting was close in mountain counties where I should have been winning big. Bad news on election night usually arrives early and as fast and hard as a gunshot. By 7:30, when we reached the Grand Ballroom at the Rodeway Inn, the TV stations were all agreeing: Ray Blanton, the Democrat, would be the winner.

The ballroom we had rented was too big for a funeral. Our cheerful blue and yellow decorations seemed left over from someone else's party. The band members were sorting and resorting music, as if they felt reluctant to disturb the stillness. Bartenders gossiped quietly. The stench of losing hung in the air.

"Know anything?" I asked the first person I saw.

"It's over," said my father-in-law, who had flown up from Texas for the celebration. He was direct, like his daughter.

A red-faced car dealer who had driven from the mountains was reporting his call home to the election commission. "The dangdest thing. The first nine county boxes all went for Blanton."

He reported this to a group of other political sages who stood along the wall, and they all chewed it over.

"Can't figure it."

"You could smell it coming."

"They'd uv stolen it if they hadn't won it."

One of the group walked over and touched my shoulder, and said, "Sorry."

A young campaign worker joined the group and said, "Them votes ain't all in yet," then waited to see if any of the sages thought that made a difference. None did.

"It didn't rain," said an older one of the group. His right hand twitched steadily in his front pants pocket, creating a steady jingling of loose coins.

"Wouldn't have mattered," said another. "They came out of the hills, people we hadn't seen voting in fifteen years. It was too many Democrats, mad about Watergate."

"It's been a long day. Maybe we ought to go in," said somebody, looking at one of the dozen television sets we had stationed around the ballroom so we could see ourselves winning. The TV screens showed pandemonium and sweet victory all right but it was sweet victory filling a crowded ballroom at Democratic headquarters in the Continental Inn. The noise of their happiness was as grating as a siren's shriek outside a funeral.

A county chairman's wife said loudly, "We should have turned around. I *told* you we should have turned around, right when we heard it on the radio."

Her husband said, "We can't leave now. Someone has to stay here with *them.*"

She said, "But staying too long's worse than not coming at all. *They* feel like *they* have to stay."

One of the sages along the wall observed, "You could see it comin'. Them mountain Republicans wasn't talking. They was gettin' ready to vote wrong."

"Well, at least we won the primary," said another one, jingling the change in *his* pocket. "That was something."

So many additional nervous hands had joined in the twitching and exploring of change within pants pockets that a jingling little symphony quickened along the wall—as did the pace of commentaries. But the stories trailed off quickly and the twitching of hands eventually slowed and the change-jingling symphony became barely noticeable again.

A receiving line formed. The loyal drifted by and shook hands and touched and kissed us.

"There'll come a time," said a man. "You're young. There's four years from now. Maybe the Senate someday. We'll help put you in."

"There'll come a day," agreed his wife.

"Don't kid yourself," an experienced voice behind me said to someone else. "It'll be fifty years before we elect another Republican governor."

"You're better off." The woman talking put her worn face close to Honey's. "God didn't want you to win. Things work out for the best, don't they? That political life would have been no good for that family of yours. Those sweet children would have grown up without a daddy. You look around and see what politics does to people. It's a mean business. I know what I'm talking about."

The woman moved to me and reached for my coat lapel, and breathed on me.

"A fellow like you wasn't meant to be in politics in the first place. Blanton called you a 'choirboy' didn't he? Politics ain't for choirboys. You're all better off. God knows best. You see if I'm not telling you right."

Many in the receiving line tried to say something like, "Glad to see you, sorry it's under these circumstances." One mumbling voice after another would emphasize the three words, *under these circumstances,* in the way parents and grandparents had emphasized them at funeral parlors when it had been necessary to visit a family after a death.

We were home by nine, sitting with a few friends, trying

to think òf something upbeat to say. But we were drained, our eyes hurt, and our arms and legs were heavy. There was not enough energy to coax even one healing laugh from the pits of our stomachs. We were struggling to celebrate a political life that had ended, but mainly we reminisced about how it might have been lived differently.

"You spent too much time at Republican meetings, Rotary clubs, convincing people already for you," Honey said.

"You should have busted him. You should have taken him on, early, hit him harder, shown him for what he was, split the Democrats," the finance director said.

"But what difference would it have made?" asked the campaign manager.

I thought about the long night drives in the snow, such as one to Erwin in the mountains to see seven Young Republicans; to Tracy City to pick up five hundred dollars. I thought about the volunteer who waited with her baby at the foggy airport until midnight; about the college classmate who had given twenty-five dollars each month since January. I had let them all down. And what was there to show for it? I was drained, sick. I had never felt worse.

"We'll just have to pull ourselves together and go on, pick up where we were or start something new. It may take a while," Honey said. She had campaigned hard, but still somehow had attended the piano recitals, the home-room meetings, the school plays that I had missed; had encouraged me, defended me, loved us all, and borne another child, all in an enterprise that was mine, really an inconvenience to her—and now *she* was the strong one at the end of the day, the one calmly philosophical and hopeful. And she was drained and tired, too. Conversation ran down and the last friend left early. Honey and I walked together slowly upstairs and went to bed, but not to sleep until long after midnight had ended the day.

CHAPTER 6

WINNING

//

Success is counted sweetest
By those who ne'er succeed . . .

—Emily Dickinson
"Success"

Win or lose, the campaign ends. Either way is sudden death, an ordeal, and in each case the new beginnings that follow are untidy, like the endings. The difference is that when you win, a new life is sitting up there like a polished apple waiting for you to bite it. When you lose you don't know where to go from where you are, and the hardest thing is that there seems to be nothing to deal with but the end. The winner at least knows what the new life will be. The loser must somehow *discover* a new life.

The loser, who ends without an obvious new beginning, must seek one, and that usually involves wallowing; at least it did for me in 1974 when I lost the governor's race. *Wallowing* is just the right word for the process which became uncomfortably long for the wallower—me—and uncomfortably messy for those who had to watch. I began by trying to rebuild my law practice, which took months, and which I found to be no fun. I bought and sold houses to make extra money to pay my debts, even dealing once with a seller whose son had been keeping a horse in the downstairs bathroom. There wasn't much sense of mission about moving a horse out of a bathroom. I tried debating a Democratic friend twice a week on a television news segment, which was more fun than I expected. Every few months I would arrange a small dinner with my remaining supporters—mostly those who had co-signed my bank note—to talk about paying off the campaign debt. That was fun, too. But usually the only result was that the cost of the dinner was added to the debt.

In the midst of my thrashing around, Senator Howard Baker called, on January 4, 1977, when Honey and I were enjoying our eighth-anniversary dinner. He had been elected Republican leader of the United States Senate. Senator Baker wanted me to come to Washington to help organize his new office. Honey encouraged me to go. She said, "You can get back home to us on weekends. It's obvious to me that you need to get away, to try something different, get some space from us." She also meant, I think, that the family would be glad for a while to have some relief from my wallowing.

When I returned to Nashville for good, Honey said, "You're ready to run again for governor."

"How did you know?"

"It's peanut butter. All anyone has to do to understand you is to go back to Ruth Street. Your mother fixed you peanut butter sandwiches with lettuce and mayonnaise; you eat them today. You grew up in the mountains; you like to be there today."

I said, "I'm afraid maybe I'm fooling myself."

"But maybe you learned something about losing," Honey said. "If you run the way you did before, you'll lose again. You flew around in little airplanes, seeing the same people. You weren't all that easy to approach. You weren't yourself. And you were never able to say really why you wanted to be elected."

"The truth is, I'm not sure I know that now," I admitted. "I feel like I'd be doing what I'm supposed to be doing . . ."

". . . what you're *expected* to be doing," she interrupted. "I hope you don't run again unless you can tell yourself and then

me and everybody why you want to be governor, what you hope
to accomplish. And you need to find some way to be yourself
and be comfortable. People will know in a minute if you're not."

Knowing deep down why you seek the office is the first
thing and the main thing a candidate can do to help himself or
herself win. *Why do you want to be alderman, sheriff, mayor, judge,
or governor?* Stand up in front of the mirror and say it, out loud:
"What do you hope to accomplish?" It's not easy to say why. But
saying it clearly is not always necessary, thankfully. Voters *sense*
whether or not a candidate has a purpose. For years Howard
Baker's popularity in Tennessee puzzled me because sometimes
when he'd finished speaking and telling funny stories, I couldn't
remember what his point was. But that had made no difference
to his listeners, the voters. He seemed just to *resonate* with them.

It was the same with Tennessee's legendary Senator Estes
Kefauver. A county judge once told me, "You couldn't always
tell what Estes was trying to say but you could tell he was trying
to say something *good.*" People can feel whether you know who
you are, and where you want to go, and why you want to go
there. People tend to vote for leaders who seem to have a sense
of purpose because people want help finding a purpose for
themselves.

In 1978, I found my purpose walking one thousand miles
across Tennessee, trying to shake at least a thousand hands a
day, spending the nights in people's homes along the way, saying grace before supper tables piled high with boiled fresh yellow corn and turnip greens, and hot buttered biscuits and fried
or baked chicken and country ham, and fried okra and chocolate
pies or apple-butter cakes, and great big glasses of lemonade and
iced tea.

When I began my walk in Maryville on January 26, 1978,
from my parents' front porch at 121 Ruth Street, it was so cold
that the television cameraman's batteries froze. And when more
than five months later, on July 6, I stuck my feet into the Mississippi River at Memphis, the First Tennessee Bank's big moving
display sign read 106 degrees.

At first my walk embarrassed quite a few establishment
Republicans: playing my old high-school trombone—or sometimes the washboard—in "Alexander's Washboard Band," a rag-
tag collection of four University of Tennessee band members

and me! Wearing the same red-and-black flannel shirt each and every day, even to dinners, even in the summer, even on TV! (I packed extra ones—which we auctioned off along the way to raise campaign money; one way I could tell I was winning was that the bids for autographed shirts kept going higher, even up to five hundred dollars in Columbia one April night.) Walking along the side of the highway waving at every car and truck! Never available for campaign meetings!

"He's acting a fool," some of these Republicans said.

Honey was absolutely my number one chief defender. She would tell them, "It's Lamar, through and through. Let him be."

In the losing 1974 election four years earlier, when Kathryn was born, Drew had been five and Leslee two. So for Honey, the main difference between the 1974 and 1978 elections was that now she had Kathryn on her hip instead of Leslee, and had to drive Drew to third grade instead of to kindergarten. But for me, the main difference was that in 1974 I lost, and now I sensed that I was winning.

The thousand-mile walk, day after day after day, became my metronome, a practiced discipline that infused me with the music of the lives of the people I sought to serve. Living in their homes put me better in tune with myself and with them. I knew I had found my mission. I knew I was in my groove—or was it their groove? For the first time since the 1974 primary election, I began to radiate the glow of a winning candidate. For the first time ever, I possessed that incandescence that voters see in a candidate with a sense of purpose.

This time I learned about winning, that there can come a time in a campaign when you *know* you'll win. It's not that early stage when the talk gets right—although hearing it get right surely does help because politics is still a word-of-mouth enterprise. The right talk helps a candidate more than slick ads and computer polling and telephoning technology, all of which cost plenty but don't win elections. The problem is, getting the talk right usually only means getting the *leadership* to talk right, and how the leaders talk doesn't win elections.

You know you are winning when down deep you can feel your campaign setting in with the people. This setting-in feeling happened for me in 1978 on an October evening after the first frost in Overton County, a rural hilly area. I have a very warm spot in my heart now for the people of Overton County because in 1978 nearly a majority of them voted for me; but historically it had been the kind of place that a Republican tried to avoid at night, much less tried to carry on election day. (Even George McGovern carried Overton County.) But there I stood, blaring my slide trombone with "Alexander's Washboard Band," in the center of the stage in the elementary school auditorium. First with our music and then in my speaking, I tried phrasing and cadences practiced and polished on stump after stump. The heat of the crowd fogged the glass of the windows, which had been opened when people took off their warm coats.

I could feel myself sweating rivulets inside my red-and-black lumberjack shirt—the shirt that had become the public symbol for my thousand-mile campaign walk across the sovereign state of Tennessee. I explored the rhythm of the crowd, and the crowd explored mine, and it was the same rhythm, and in that warm and crowded Overton County school auditorium developed a rare reciprocal emotion, a real and unexpected excitement—especially delicious because it was forbidden excitement *for a Republican* in a nest of Democrats.

It was five days before election day when the tide shifted and the campaign just broke wide open. The Overton County crowd's excitement told me that it had felt it, too, even as other people, in other places, told me later they had felt it, too, and at just about the same time.

It may seem unlikely that a candidate can feel this so precisely, so let me try to describe it. My race for governor in 1978 was against Democrat Jake F. Butcher, a wealthy and powerful Knoxville banker. For two weeks solid, up until that night in Overton County, the race had been like two stock cars at the Saturday night Speedway, straining all-out, throbbing, pulsating, at 110 deafening miles per hour, side by side, neck and neck, front wheels grinding, almost touching. I had never felt such pressure, and when the release suddenly came I had rarely felt such joy. Statewide, my campaign slipped on past Jake Butcher's, the way one race car finally slips ahead, never to be really challenged again in the stretch. A winning candidate can feel this.

Still, there was one thing that eluded me. When my walk across Tennessee ended—I honestly still couldn't have expressed, just in so many words, *why* I wanted to be governor, or what I hoped to accomplish. I could feel that my motivation was more than just wanting to do my best at some challenging public service job. Something else inside of me must have known why I wanted to be governor—and the voters must have sensed it. I hoped it would articulate itself along the way. I wanted to be able to *say* it to myself as much as I felt it.

C H A P T E R 7

T R A N S I T I O N

//

"Who are you?" said the Caterpillar....

"I hardly know, Sir, just at present," Alice replied rather shyly. "At least I know who I *was* when I got up this morning, but I think I must have been changed several times since then."

—Lewis Carroll
Alice's Adventures in Wonderland

There is nothing worse than listening to a politician tell why he won an election. The politician, of course, has no earthly idea why this happened. All he or she really knows is that things shifted in his favor. Probably the smartest thing that the politician ever did was to start the campaign and hang on to the finish, which, in more cases than you might imagine, is all it takes to win. There is no need to make much more of it than that, because in America a voter who for years has been enjoying the flavor of vanilla might say on election day, "Let's see, I think I'll try chocolate."

"What's wrong with the vanilla?"

"Nothing. I just think I'll try chocolate."

And that will be that.

Politicians and their advisers scheme and plan campaigns for years. But for the people who vote and therefore decide such things, most elections turn out to be basically simple affairs. After months of speeches and dinners and fund raising and conflicts and polls and pushing and shoving—then finally, about three weeks out, the people, the big eternal question-mark public, start to tune in, trying to get an idea of what all the noise is about, and of which candidate knows best who he or she is, and which one knows best why he or she is running. The public watches the opposing candidates on television and listens to all the talk, and then the public starts to make up its collective mind.

Minds change. Sometimes, minds change several times during an election campaign's last weeks—while the old and sick and absent are mailing in their early ballots—but sooner or later, certainly by the final week, one candidate will begin to fall, usually of his or her own weight, as it seems that everything is breaking right for the other candidate, and finally the voter will have that crucial private conversation with the voting machine, "I'd rather have this candidate than that one."

Some candidates will tell you that the best thing about winning an election is the thrill of election night. It was not so for me. I felt like daughter Leslee must have felt turning thirteen. Most of the joy of the moment had been used up in anticipation of the event. After so many years of hoping and pushing and shoving—and especially after gazing so longingly at winning on the night I lost—winning in 1978 became less of an event. The joy had been used up, for example, in incredible moments like that night in Overton County, when the campaign shifted and broke and I slipped on by to win.

Years later I was reminded of this during a break in one of the governors' conferences in Washington, D.C. We took our youngest child, Will, to the Smithsonian Institution to see

Tyrannosaurus rex. Will was disappointed. *Tyrannosaurus* was not "really big." It could not possibly have grown as big as it had in Will's dreams, after Honey read to him story after story about immense dinosaurs. Honey assured him that when *Tyrannosauruses* were alive, they "were bigger than all these bones strung together in the Smithsonian and, Will, this room we are in is after all a very big room, which makes the dinosaurs look smaller." It did no good.

"They would only be a *little* bigger," Will said. The experience was not as good as he anticipated because he had expected too much.

What *is* good about winning is that there is a transition to a new life—in my case a new life as governor, set to begin on a certain date in January, only two months away. Everyone had agreed that there should be a transition time, a formally established period when I could clean up the end of my campaign, say my good-byes. Such a transition was official permission to flounder for a while. I know it gave me time to think about what was really important to me, as I realized that my new administration was not an extension of the campaign but a totally different, new beginning. There would even be an inauguration to celebrate this new beginning as well as the end of what had gone before.

Some who are elected never pause long enough to discover the transition, never separate themselves from the campaign, never become even a little disenchanted with its rawness and selfishness and the premium it places on manufactured media events and on tactics and issues that sound good and mean little and upon power for power's sake; they never find a creative purpose for their new adventure. Instead, they plunge ahead, dragging into their new lives the habits and mind-sets of their old adventures. Their busyness delays the chance to make a new beginning, sometimes until it is too late.

Most Americans do not mind that most elected officials plunge ahead so self-confidently, wasting the opportunity for transition. Most of us don't notice this because we ourselves are so busy plunging ahead from thing to thing, always in motion on our way from job to job, from one diversion to the next. We have never taken much time to become very good at dealing with endings or seeing the need for transitions. Perhaps one reason we stay so busy is to avoid what comes *with* the transitions—the uneasiness of keeping still while others watch us and expect action, and the uncomfortable and inconvenient questions we must ask ourselves before the real new beginnings. So, like us, most of our elected representatives plunge ahead, carrying the vestiges of their previous existence awkwardly into their new lives.

Still it is sad when officials waste the formal transition process between the end of a campaign and the beginning of an administration, because it is one of the few formally sanctioned transitional stages Americans know about and tolerate. When an elected official raises his or her right hand and puts the left hand upon a Bible and swears an oath—that is a moment in America when everyone stops and watches, a long moment that everyone remembers. Who can forget the fire while Robert Frost read poetry at John F. Kennedy's inauguration; or the chill of the black-and-white photograph of Jackie Kennedy, Judge Sarah T. Hughes, and Lyndon B. Johnson, with his right hand raised, on Air Force One in Dallas; or the throaty burst of male cheers, sounding more like a fraternity election, at Gerald Ford's swearing-in in the East Room of the White House; or the tears even in Dan Rather's eyes when the Marine Band played the "The Star-Spangled Banner" at Ronald Reagan's inauguration, or even a mayor's swearing-in or an alderman's. Everybody stops and thinks for a moment. An inauguration in America is one of the few times in our busy lives when we pause to celebrate the happy coincidence of an end with a beginning.

C H A P T E R 8

PRELUDE IN D MINOR

//

The major chord is . . . happy. The
minor chord is sad. And what is
sadness? It is a division, a sense that
things are not right, that you want
what you cannot have, lament what
you have not done. You bewail the
loss of something, you are not at one
with yourself or the world. . . . That
minor chord . . . wants to rise, to
become major, to unite again with its
natural series.

—YEHUDI MENUHIN
The Music of Man

The familiar black Lincoln appeared at the state capitol
after dark, gleaming in the streetlights. It stopped

where the word GOVERNOR was lettered on the curb, by the high marble steps at the east entrance. This was Monday, January 15, 1979, and the rain was coming down cold.

The corridors of government were deserted except for one reporter and two aging capitol policemen. The reporter laughed to himself at such good luck. No one had expected the governor to be at the capitol at this hour, on such a miserable night, only five days before the end of his term.

The state trooper who had been driving now stood by the limousine. He squinted in the rain, looking from side to side. Another trooper, who had been riding, opened the right rear door and Governor Ray Blanton stepped into the wet. He walked cautiously up the first few slick marble steps, and when he saw the reporter, he paused to wish him a cordial good evening.

The reporter asked, "Will you sign any clemency papers tonight?"

Governor Blanton replied, "That remains to be seen." The governor's cordiality had vanished. His voice had no inflection. It was his poker-hand reply.

Then, with troopers ahead and behind, the governor hurried up the remaining three dozen steps and disappeared behind the columns through a private back entrance into his first-floor office. When one of the troopers closed the door behind him, it was 8:10 P.M.

Inside the governor's office, the new legal counsel—the old counsel had been indicted three weeks earlier and had resigned—had spread stacks of files on the governor's desk, on the oak conference table, some even on the carpet.

The lawyer said, "I suppose you'll want to start with this case," and handed over a thick file from the table.

"Well, I've given this one more consideration than you can imagine. I've made up my mind," Governor Blanton announced, and he pardoned Roger Humphreys, who had reloaded a two-shot derringer nine times in order to shoot eighteen bullets into his former wife and her lover.

The secretary of state had been summoned to authenticate the governor's signature on the document.

"This takes guts," said the governor to the secretary of state.

"Yeah, well, some people have more guts than brains," the secretary of state replied.

This was only the beginning. That night Governor Blanton signed all in all fifty-two pardons and commutations for some of Tennessee's most notorious prisoners, murderers, rapists, and robbers, some of whose crimes were so atrocious they had been condemned to death. One was a triple murderer. One had poisoned her husband and mother, and was suspected of poisoning her father.

The unexpected lights in the governor's office attracted reporters the way porch lamps draw moths in the summer. When he left his office by the back entrance at 11:30, reporters waited at every exit. In the rain the high marble steps glistened in the flood of television lights. Reporters tripped over themselves stumbling down the slick steps and nearly tripped the governor.

Without a word, the governor stepped into the rear of the black Lincoln, and it vanished into the night. The corrections commissioner rushed Roger Humphreys's clemency papers to the state prison in Nashville.

"Am I dreaming?" Humphreys asked the warden as he walked out of his cell at 11:50 P.M., exactly eleven minutes before I could have raised my right hand, sworn the oath, and become the governor of Tennessee—at least that was what the state attorney general's office said in a surprising legal opinion released earlier that same Monday.

Across town in the federal building, the United States attorney was also working late. He was convinced that the state attorney's opinion had triggered the governor's mass release of prisoners. The U.S. attorney believed that Governor Blanton knew of the talk around Nashville about the possibility of an early swearing-in of the new governor. He was convinced that Governor Blanton badly wanted to push these fifty-two criminals, including Humphreys, out of prison before midnight, before *he* was pushed out of office. And the U.S. attorney thought he knew why. He had a source in the governor's office. The source had warned in advance that clemency documents were being prepared for a Monday night mass release. The FBI told the U.S. attorney that fourteen of the fifty-two who were part of the mass release were targets of the FBI's cash-for-clemency investigation.

This, of course, was a startling conclusion—that a governor, the state's chief law-enforcement officer, or someone acting for him, might be receiving cash to release some of the state's worst criminals! But the FBI investigation had been proceeding deliberately for months. Just three weeks before the Monday night mass release, a federal grand jury had indicted the governor's counsel, the governor's chief of security detail, and the governor's extradition officer for selling clemencies for cash in twenty instances. The FBI had told the court it had marked the money and had videotapes of the exchange.

You could almost hear the explosions of anger popping, house by house, as Tennesseans awoke to Tuesday morning's news. GOVERNOR IN MIDNIGHT MASS RELEASE OF PRISONERS, the headlines screamed. The storm of protest was unmatched since the Civil War. "He makes Nixon look like a choirboy," said one Democrat state senator. Choirboys, I thought, seemed suddenly in demand.

This was not Governor Blanton's first meeting with trouble. He grew up tough in a rural county on the Tennessee-Mississippi border where "Walking Tall" Buford Pusser was sheriff. Growing up in Pusser country sometimes meant hand-to-hand combat. Blanton had knife scars on his back and bullet scars on his neck from rough nights after daytime construction work.

"We were so poor growing up that we would lift a board in the morning to steal eggs from cackling hens—and when it snowed there were wet streaks across the homemade quilts we slept under. I know what hard times are," Blanton told one reporter.

When his overseas phone calls to a lady friend showed up as a state expense, Governor Blanton challenged the Capitol Hill press corps: "Do you want a eunuch or a third-generation scion of a rich family who doesn't understand the problems of the poor?" Finally he told reporters he would refuse to answer "negative questions."

But Governor Blanton's biggest trouble had come from his promise on television to pardon Roger Humphreys, who was the son of a Blanton patronage chief. That on-again off-again promise helped make Humphreys the most famous double murderer in Tennessee history and helped make me Blanton's successor.

On Tuesday afternoon, the day after the fifty-two clemency orders were signed, the new legal counsel told reporters that the governor might pardon at least eighteen more people before he left office, including "one big name." Rumors spread that the "big name" was James Earl Ray, who had killed Martin Luther King, Jr. The U.S. attorney's source provided the names of the eighteen; the list included several more inmates who the FBI and the grand jury believed had paid their way to freedom.

Wednesday morning was cold and rainy. I was happy to be in my hideaway office writing my inaugural address. The telephone rang a little before noon. It was the United States attorney who said, "The governor is about to release some state inmates who we believe have bought their way out of prison. Will you take office, as soon as you can, to stop him?" It was January 17, 1979, three days before the scheduled inauguration.

There had been previous suggestions of an early swearing-in, but at the time I had refused to consider it. I could not imagine such a thing, had never heard of it happening in America. I had always marveled at how the nation stopped to admire the most important transfer of power in the world at the presidential inaugurations. Nothing could stop or tarnish the regular renewal of democracy at inaugurations, not bitter election contests or even an assassination or a presidential resignation. In the United States the torch is always passed peacefully and with grace. It is a celebration of our right to change governments. It is something that makes us different from a lot of other countries. No matter how bad things had gotten, I could not destroy an inauguration. Surely everyone could wait just three more days.

Governor Blanton had baited FBI agents who were investigating the cash-for-clemency rumors. "It is nothing but a vendetta by a Republican U.S. attorney," the governor said on the same television broadcast when he announced the Humphreys pardon. But the United States attorney who had phoned me was, like the governor, a Democrat. Not only that. Governor Blanton had once appointed him a circuit judge—and in addition he was the former college roommate of the governor's old, now indicted, legal counsel.

I recalled an earlier conversation I had had with the state attorney general.

I had asked, "Could the governor *really* empty the prisons, turn them all out?"

"He could."

"And what could anyone do about it?"

"Under the state constitution, nothing."

I did what I thought then was the right thing to do. I still think I did the right thing. I had no other choice. I let the U.S. attorney's phone call to me set in motion a swift and secret coup to deprive the governor of his office three days early. I wondered, would it be constitutional? No one had ever heard of such a thing. Where would the ceremony be held? And when? Would the Democrats approve? Would they participate? What about the legislature? Didn't it have to be a legislative ceremony, a public ceremony? Should Governor Blanton be told? But if he were told, wouldn't he release prisoners anyway and make all the secret efforts futile?

Who should attend the ceremony? Who would tell them, and when? What if Blanton orders the highway patrol or the National Guard to surround the capitol to secure it, to keep out the premature pretenders? There would be two governors, each issuing orders to the same armed forces, contending for the same job at the same time! Tennessee would look even worse than it would have with Blanton pardoning even more murderers who had bought their freedom!

What about my parents? They would be at Wednesday evening church services in Maryville, and would miss the swearing-in; they wouldn't even know about it ahead of time. And the campaign supporters who had saved their money and paid for their hotel rooms and bus tickets and for the inaugural balls on Saturday. What about them? And the inaugural parade marching bands from McMinnville and Milan and Memphis and everywhere who had been practicing in the cold until their lips were blue. Even the campaign staff would not all be able to attend. And they had worked so hard.

And our family? It was moving day for us. Everything we owned had been boxed, sent to storage, or to the fifteen-thou-sand-square-foot Mansion with an iron fence around it that for a few years would be our home. Honey was waiting for me now at our empty old home in Green Hills. It must have been as cold and depressing as a morgue. Leslee had stayed home from school, sick. Kathryn was crying; everything that was important to her had been packed and sent away.

So when I telephoned Honey to tell her about the possibility of an early swearing-in, she was understandably impatient. "Are you sure you can do that, that it is legal?" And she reminded me, "None of us have anything to wear to an inauguration this afternoon. The clothes are all in boxes at the governor's residence. Why doesn't somebody make up his mind? What are you going to do?"

I would not make up my mind because the Democratic leaders and I could not agree on who would go first. I was not about to take office on my own initiative. That would be no better than a guerrilla general in a junta takeover. And the legislative leaders were not about to take the first step. The governor, after all, was *their* governor, a Democrat. For three hours on Wednesday afternoon, the Democratic leaders and I exchanged telephone messages through the state attorney general and procrastinated.

The coup, which needed to be swift to be effective, stalled—until the United States attorney and the state attorney general became advocates instead of merely counselors. The state attorney general ruled that such an action would be constitutional under the circumstances. The Chief Justice, who was a Democrat, agreed to leave his hospital bed to swear me in. The Democratic legislative leaders then consented to a statement that I would read at the early swearing-in, and they promised to attend. The ceremony would begin at 5:30 P.M. in the courtroom of the Supreme Court building near the capitol. No one would be told until five o'clock, when the Democratic leaders would walk to the Supreme Court building from their offices in the Legislative Plaza. The attorney general would call Governor Blanton just before five-thirty.

At 5:15 the attorney general announced to reporters waiting in the legislative office building that in twenty-five minutes the governor-elect would become the governor. The reporters had been clamoring all afternoon for just this news, but when it came, at first it was almost impossible for them to accept. Stunned, the reporters joined a solemn procession that wound its way along the darkening halls of the Legislative Plaza offices and gradually lengthened as legislative aides and lobbyists and hangers-on joined it up the escalator, then through the tunnel under the capitol and out onto Charlotte Avenue and down the hill to the Supreme Court building.

Lumbering along at the head of the procession were the speaker of the Senate and the speaker of the House. They said little, but their tired faces spoke for them, faces drained of color and of energy, exhausted by the pressure of the afternoon of conspiracy. Traffic halted respectfully, and the procession meandered across Seventh Avenue toward the Supreme Court building, its lights burning brightly in winter's early darkness.

At about that time, our family was saying an unexpected second good-bye to an old friend, our home in Green Hills. We had raced there to put on whatever clothes we had found and some we had borrowed.

"The most important celebration in your life is more like a funeral," Honey mourned as we five, plus a staff member and a state trooper, packed ourselves into a single patrol car. Leslee was coughing. Kathryn clung to Honey. Drew tried to understand why all this was happening on Wednesday when it was supposed to happen on Saturday. Ten minutes later we arrived at the basement entrance to the Supreme Court building. We walked quickly up the back stairs. The halls and stairs were filled with people with anxious faces rushing to the first floor. Most of them had no idea what they were rushing to see.

The ceremony began at 5:56 and ended six minutes later. The legislative leaders and I and our family stood crowded into an open area just in front of the bench in the middle of the mahogany-paneled room. Friends and reporters, and a few others who had found out about the service stood silently, most with arms crossed, facing us behind a wood railing. Except for the whirring and clicking of the television cameras there was an odd silence, as if people were holding their breaths.

The ceremony began, a solemn prelude in a minor key, sad and disturbing. There was no purity in the chords of the melody that afternoon. Things weren't right; something had been lost. It was a wake without the wailing. Everyone there knew the difference between what they were seeing and hearing and what they should have been seeing and hearing. There was also a deep

feeling of discontent and a knowledge that this discord could
not last, that things would somehow have to be put right in the
right way.

The Chief Justice spoke. "Are you ready to take the oath
of office?"

Honey had somehow managed to remember to bring the
family Bible. She stood between the Chief Justice and me holding it open to my father's favorite verse, 2 Timothy 2:15. I raised
my right hand and placed my left on the Bible.

Everytime I see a certain black-and-white photograph of
that oath-taking I think of the tension and the sadness. There is
Drew, only nine then, peering straight ahead, his nose barely
peeking above the open Bible. There are Leslee and Kathryn,
small, on their tiptoes, reaching up to imitate me, trying to place
their hands on the Bible, too. In the photograph Honey looks
resolute but tired, and there are the faintest signs of tears on her
cheeks. The Chief Justice and I have our right hands raised. The
Democratic pallbearers surround us, looking down, their faces
betraying what the speaker of the House later said he'd felt,
"You have to do what you think is right, but this made me
half-sick."

After the oath-taking there was a prayer for the people and
a prayer for our family. Those assembled collectively and nois-
ily expelled their breaths, and a sort of relieved applause
erupted.

It was over.

And suddenly it was quiet again. I said, "These have not
been happy days for me," and, for the first time that afternoon,
I mentioned the now former governor, explaining that he had
brought this untimely demise upon himself and that its sudden-
ness meant that others would have to tidy things up. "We will
therefore secure the capitol, turn all of the old records over to
the FBI, lock the prison gates, and review all pardons he has
granted," I explained.

Ray Blanton's first reaction to the end of his life as gover-
nor was to send his lawyer to the capitol to retrieve his papers.
My new staff refused to release the papers. Blanton telephoned
Lewis Donelson, the state's new finance chief, and asked quietly,
"You mean I'm not allowed to come get my papers?"

"That's right," said Donelson.

"By whose authority?"

"By the governor's authority."

"I am the governor."

"Not anymore."

After the service, some of the reporters drove to the former governor's home. Blanton stood in the misting rain on his front porch staring into the television lights.

"I didn't know a governor could do that," he said.

"How did you find out about it?"

"The attorney general called just before it happened but I had already heard it on Cronkite's show."

He paused and then added, "There is such a thing as courtesy. I thought they would have the courtesy to tell me. This was not necessary. Why didn't the U.S. attorney call me? I am saddened for the people of Tennessee."

At the capitol where the FBI was sorting and wrapping and tying up boxes of papers, a few of the former governor's top aides and secretaries stayed on, laughing and drinking in a macabre farewell party. The party ended by ten o'clock. All the Blanton aides were finally gone, forever, from the capitol by ten-thirty, when one returned sheepishly to retrieve two bottles of bourbon left in an office cabinet.

College bands marched in metronomic cadence, their lines correct and their music fit for a celebration. Elected officials occupied their proper chairs. National Guardsmen stood at attention. My parents sat in the front row. Ten thousand bundled well-wishers huddled shoulder to shoulder on the plaza. Most were shivering, but they were glad because they knew that what they were hearing and seeing was what we should be hearing and seeing and it created a satisfying conclusion. Even the freezing rain stopped before the ceremony began at noon.

For those of us looking from the special scaffolding to the plaza, the well-wishers' umbrellas below us formed a brightly colored sea. Beside us loomed the solemn old capitol, witness during the last three days to unprecedented scenes of turbulence and intrigue.

It was Saturday, January 20, 1979. For the first time in our state's history, the retiring governor did not pass the torch at the inauguration. The symbol of the ending we were celebrating was not there. But all of the other rituals and symbols proceeded in happy natural intervals toward an orderly new beginning.

The minister from Mountain City offered a prayer.

The Dayton College student whom I had met on my walk across Tennessee sang.

The Chief Justice asked for the second time in three days if I was ready to take the oath of office.

Honey held the family Bible open again to 2 Timothy 2:15: "Study to show thyself approved unto God, rightly dividing the word of truth, a workman who needeth not to be ashamed."

And when I raised my right hand and swore to defend the constitution, so help me God, I experienced an overpowering sense of gratitude and responsibility and relief. Finally, I could begin!

Still Honey said, "There's a bittersweet taste, a little taint. It's not really like the end of a long campaign and the launching of a new dream."

But when the twenty-one-gun salute frightened the youngest children and stung their parents' ears, it put a series of exclamation points at the end of a campaign and the end of an administration, and gave the natural lift to the new administration that I had been hoping and waiting for.

Honey was four months pregnant with Will, but we danced until almost all the inaugural parties had wound down and did not crawl into bed until late. I will always remember how happy she was to wake up on Sunday to see six inches of snow. "It is clean, sweet snow. Everything is washed clean again. It is so white and pretty and sparkling," she said.

CHAPTER 9

ONE DAY STOLEN

//

The governor and his council faintly
remember the pond . . . but now they
are too old and dignified to go
a-fishing, and so they know it no
more forever. If the legislature
regards it, it is chiefly to regulate the
number of hooks to be used there, for
they know nothing about the hook of
hooks with which to angle for the
pond itself. . . .

—HENRY DAVID THOREAU
Walden

It was October 1986. Brown cornstalks waited broken in
the fields, and the sun rode high over Chilhowee Moun-

tain. We turned onto Miller's Cove Road, and Corfe, the cocker spaniel, lifted his long nose from the briefcase beside me and scrambled into the front seat with the trooper who was driving. The dog's black-and-white underside quivered, his clipped tail circled and wiggled, and his front paws pushed at the closed window. He was searching desperately for a way to thrust that long nose outside.

Corfe scratched the window so wildly that he tumbled backward into the seat beside me. He righted himself and scrambled back into the front, where he stood again on his back legs, front paws on the window, scratching, whimpering, until finally his anticipation disturbed me, so I leaned up and rolled the window halfway down. Out the window in triumphant frenzy extended the nose, a periscope with a sense of smell!

The car drew closer and the dog's quivering increased and his whimpering became frantic. When we turned down the gravel road, I opened the door and let him go, and watched him follow his nose as he ran with the car, too close to the wheel, watched him splash through the creek, race up the hill, and finally, wet and snorting and quivering in ecstasy, scramble into the rail-fenced yard, wildly pawing the ground of his favorite place to be and I wondered how much of life I must be missing without such a nose.

The trooper and I unloaded the car, and then he drove quickly away, leaving me with Corfe in splendid loneliness. I hurried into the log cabin to change clothes. I had only my coat and tie to get rid of. This morning, in my eagerness for this stolen day, I had put on my walking boots and khaki pants, had worn them to the technical institute dedication on the Oak Ridge Corridor. (Television news only shows head shots of a governor, never pants and boots.) That way I had saved a few more minutes for my day in my place in my mountains, mine and Corfe's.

I quickly constructed a peanut butter, mayonnaise, and lettuce sandwich, grabbed a box of raisins and an apple, and walked outside to the bluebird box by the rail fence. Last month there had been five dead baby birds in the box, but there was nothing new today. The white oak leaves were still green—their leaves always come down last—but acorns were thumping fast on the cedar shingles. The dogwoods had red berries and some red leaves. The walnut trees had no leaves and green walnuts hung exposed on the branches. The first frost had been late. Winter would come suddenly.

I followed a cow path behind the cabin. It had become a colored carpet of autumn leaves—butter-yellow tulip poplar, blood-red sourwood, yellow-green silver bells, red and orange and yellow maple. Corfe followed the path, too—in a manner of speaking—ranging and sniffing back and forth across the trail and up the slopes until he was breathing hard. His genes told him he should be looking for something, but too much city life had made it hard for his nose to remember what.

Thick laurel and rhododendron and blueberry bushes and mountain myrtle and briars made the going harder. Corfe's shaggy coat had begun to accumulate briars and stickers by the time the ridge we were climbing intersected another ridge, less steep, where there was a hunter's trail. The trail led to a clearing up higher where I had not been before. There I collapsed and lay back on the pine needles and twigs and envied the floating sweet gum and maple leaves. Three weeks later anyone sitting here could see valleys and mountains all around, but now the branches were still full enough and seemed to close in around me. The breeze was warm and smooth. I looked up through to the dried blue October sky. The extra T-shirt I had put on this morning was wet and cool on my back. The dog lay on his side, legs stretched out in the sun.

I was as secure as I had ever felt. There might still be copperheads around, poisonous, maybe a rattler. They, too, liked to stretch out in the autumn sun. But these were my mountains—I had hiked in them, slept in them, gotten lost in and found my way out of them since I was a boy. I knew that snakes wouldn't bother me if I didn't bother them. Snakes had their place there, too.

Somewhere near there would be black bears. That frightens some people. Once, one had frightened me: It had crawled into my trail shelter while I slept, pulled out all the cans of food, ripped them apart. But there were so many white oak acorns on the ground now that it felt like walking on marbles. With so much to eat, the bears would stay deep in the safety of the national park.

I thought about the number of things in the mountains that

might get you. Wild hog: Once one had walked right across my sleeping bag. But hogs roam at night. Black widow spider: You'd have to be pretty unlucky to be bitten by a black widow spider. Hornets: The first frost had killed them. Deer: Only problem with deer is they attract hunters with rifles. But hunters have never bothered me. How safe I felt in the isolation of this place. Because I knew what there was to be afraid of, I was not afraid. I fit here. The only sounds were the acorns bouncing and the birds and chipmunks and squirrels—and an occasional snort from a sleeping cocker spaniel.

I am tired. I had not realized how tired. Tired in every bone. Tired behind my eyes. In the mornings my legs hang like millstones. Eight years of piled-up tiredness. Eight years of creating and pushing ideas to try to help a state find itself, move itself. Still pushing. "Have you never heard of a lame duck?" the reporters ask.

Still, I feel guilty stealing this day. There are projects to lock in place. There are things that I wish I had thought of earlier, like a network of bike trails, or a better way to help people who lose their jobs and who can't deal with change because they can't read and write and compute.

Every day some brand-new idea bubbles up, but it is harder now for the ideas to bubble out. *Maybe someone will do them later, if the ideas are good. I can hope for that. The state is moving better than it ever has. My pushing must have helped, helped get things started and on the way for sure, maybe helped a lot, but after a while it was not so much my doings. After a while it became something like a stream rushing, just swept me ahead with it. The state was becoming itself and I was merely an instrument to help that happen. Then the best thing I could do was to help people struggling to bring their own lives into order, and I learned that you start that by helping people where they live, help them to know and be comfortable with who they are. When I was elected I understood almost nothing about that, had absolutely no idea that would be my job.*

Those faces this morning at the dedication of the new twenty-five-million-dollar technical institute on the Oak Ridge Corridor—I could read those faces. They were as tired of my speech as I was.

Better Schools. Better Schools. Push. Push. A few more people hear it every time I say it. It's good some things end naturally. Over the waterfall in three months, and gone, and then what?

Peace, I hope. That's really why I want to go to Australia. For some peace. But everyone seems so uncomfortable with the notion of my having nothing to do there. How uncomfortable they became just with the notion of someone ending something!

"You're throwing it all away," one friend said.

"Get off the political track and you'll never be able to get back on," a governor warned.

After my speech at a National Press Club luncheon in Washington, D.C., one reporter asked, "What's next?"

I said, "Moving to Australia," and there was a huge laugh.

Then, afterward, a reporter grabbed me and said, "The others are running for president and you're running for the other side of the world!"

"I thought he was kidding about going to Australia," Laurance Rockefeller told the president of the National Geographic Society after we had talked about my heading a National Committee for Americans Outdoors.

President Reagan suggested: "Run for the Senate."

It was coming from all sides:

"We'll start paying you now and you can start practicing law when you come back from Australia."

"Come with us for a year and make a million dollars."

"Hit while you're hot, while you can get the big bucks."

"What's wrong with him?"

I shivered awake. The sun had dropped below Chilhowee Mountain. I hurried down the hunter's trail to the first ridge, then down the color-carpeted cow path to the cabin, where I built two fires and murdered three wasps. I discovered one piece of country ham in the freezer, fried it, ate it, and by eight o'clock was reading in bed. Corfe, the cocker spaniel, had beat me to it, had already laid his nose on the railing of the wicker chair by the fire, arranged the rest of himself in the lap of the chair, and was sleeping.

The wasps had been aroused by the same Indian summer warmth that put me to sleep. All night I twisted and grabbed for the quilt, first for protection from wasp zooming and finally for protection from the morning, which was cold and made me wish for the summer's stickiness again. I dressed reluctantly, waited for the sound of driveway gravel popping, and walked out to meet the unmarked patrol car. Thick fog spread down the cove, leaving saucer spots among the trees. Mountain mist blotted out the sky. I tossed my briefcase into the car's backseat and climbed in after it.

The trooper said, "It'll burn off by ten," and turned the car down the gravel road. Green tomatoes with brown split marks were about all that was left in the garden at the bottom of the hill. We bumped across the slat bridge. Hesse Creek was so low the water was barely moving. Orange maple leaves plugged the gaps in the rock dam Will and I had built in August.

When I rolled down the car window to wipe off the outside dew, the air stung. Corfe lay beside me, nose on my briefcase, not stirring. Either his nose was satiated with mountain smells or the sadness of leaving had overcome him. We rode for a while behind a yellow bus full of bundled-up waving children, and when it turned off we picked up speed by porches put to bed for the winter, by farms where the only garden flowers left were plastic and the mist hung so low it touched the ponds.

The morning newspaper lay next to me. I scanned the front page, then the front of the second section, then the editorials, and then relaxed. I thought about what the just-retired governor of Delaware had told me. "It took six months to quit worrying about what went wrong yesterday. It was August before I could enjoy the morning newspaper."

It all depends on what goes
after the comma.

"We've got to get out of here."

The Governor's Mansion

What the mansion marble floor was best for

Looking out the window of Base Camp Sydney

Potato sacks, gray socks,
and black shoes

"I don't think I'm going to
like it."

Lonsdale Smith

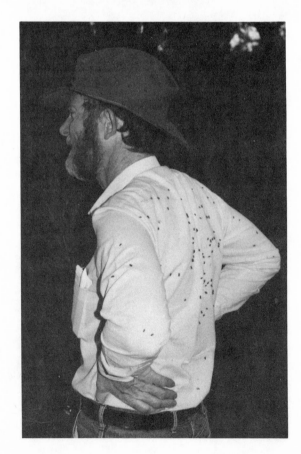

Buzzing, biting black flies
layer the ranger's shirt at
Nocoleche Sheep Station.

The idea was first to hunt and see the trout, then to present him a tasty-looking fly for breakfast.

Tasmania—about as far from Nashville as you can go and still be on earth.

Leslee

The boy from Snowy River

CHAPTER 1 0

"YOU'RE NOT GOVERNOR ANYMORE"

//

Rooster today. Featherduster
tomorrow.

—Australian adage

From my notebook:
     Tues., Nov. 4, 1986: Election Day—It was raining.
Honey and I stopped at Kathryn's soccer game on the way home
from voting.

A friend asked, "You must feel a little emotion today? The
beginning of the winding down."

"I don't feel it," I said, too defensively.

Honey left. The trooper drove me through our old neighborhood in Green Hills, by our old house, and we stopped at the
new house we were buying on the same street. I walked in the
rain by the old house trying to remember how the big maple tree

in its front yard had looked before the leaves fell. Drove home, switching dials on the car radio for early election news.

At dinner I asked, "Anyone want to go to the new governor's victory party?"

"Got a test," Leslee said.

"I've got homework," Will said, who didn't.

"I don't have homework; I'm just not interested," Drew said.

"Kathryn?"

"Just a minute. I'm thinking of an excuse."

Trooper car and backup car were waiting. Honey and I left for victory party at 6:45. Same route we took in 1974 when the car radio startled us early with bad news. It did it again. Republican Winfield Dunn had lost absentee ballots in Republican Carter County. At 7:32, CBS declared Democrat Ned McWherter the winner.

Wed., Nov. 5—Day after the election. Woke up at five A.M., wondering how to pay for new house. Reached for Honey and found Will. "If I had a pouch, he'd be in it," she said, still half-asleep. My head hurt. The kind of hurt that usually stays all day and makes other things hurt, too. I told Honey, "My eyes and head and bones are tired." She said, "It's what happens when you suddenly stop going 100 miles per hour." Defeats make it worse, I thought. It has been a long time since I had felt a defeat. Reached in the dark for my glasses. Didn't need them when we moved in eight years ago. Stumbled toward door, tried hard not to step on dogs, who have become so accustomed to my early rising that they don't move.

In downstairs office, curtains shut (by troopers last night), morning paper on desk (troopers), schedule taped to door (troopers did that, too). Made yellow pad "to do" list. Paid bills until five-thirty. At six-ten, said into speaker phone, "Going running," and two patrol cars appeared at front door, I ran out in the dark, and they followed. Only other lights were Honey typing in her office.

Kids to school. Nothing scheduled for morning.

Honey: "I feel disorganized. I have a lot to do but I can't get it done."

I couldn't get my ducks in a row, either, but it wasn't an all-bad feeling. Felt same way I felt riding bus home after first year of New York University Law School, like a sack of potatoes was being lifted from my shoulders. I had been heading full steam. Now someone else could worry. I sensed the disorientation that comes when you move off a secure and busy track toward an unknown one.

Fri., Nov. 7—Slept from nine to six A.M. Still drained. Must be the way you feel in shock. Honey not much enjoying luxury of transition, either.

Kathryn: "At school they want me to keep a journal of our trip. I don't want to because Dad will publish it."

Honey: "By the way, the morning paper says George Ariyoshi is taking driving lessons."

I said, "George Ariyoshi has been governor of Hawaii for sixteen years, almost his whole life. He probably has forgotten what the steering wheel is for. I don't need driving lessons. Most people don't need driving lessons."

She said, "Most people don't put on their blinkers when they go around a curve, either," Honey said. "Just thought I'd mention it."

Mon., Nov. 17—Letter from Bill Garrett, *National Geographic* editor: "1988 is Australia's bicentennial." I hadn't known that.

Governor-elect came by at 11:00, left at noon, and his cigar smoke stayed until late afternoon.

Kathryn broke her ankle playing soccer. Will hit his head with karate board showing off for the governor of Delaware, who was spending the night. The governor got right in the swing of things by chipping his tooth.

Tues., Nov. 18—Warm day, stiff wind. Yellow leaves still on maple and poplars. People sitting on benches, taking walks. Leaves raked into piles or stuffed into many green plastic bags in most yards. First physical examination in two years. 100/68. Very good pulse. 182 pounds, up from 176. Too much. Getting too big for my britches. The doctor said, "Your trip is something a lot of people would like to do. We'd go to France. There are so many places *not* to go these days." I said, "We thought of France, but it's cold there between January and June, when we're going, and Kathryn read about people getting blown up in the Paris metro and I worried about it being so close that someone might call me and pull me back home."

Wed., Nov. 19—The sun was so warm that the four of us, who had worked together for eight years, left our jackets at the lunch table and—probably for the last time ever—moved lawn chairs onto the crab orchard stone patio, my favorite outdoors place at the Mansion. We lunged ahead, as we always did, reviewing a long list of projects. This time I was racing to put into concrete what I had helped to start—chairs of excellence at the universities, bicentennial parkways, higher pay for master teachers, programs for gifted children—and I even had a few new things in mind, when one of the four interrupted: "May I say this gently? You're not the governor anymore. Oh, technically you are, but you're really not. It's time to let McWherter be the governor."

It began to sink in. All the attention was now on the *new* governor. In meetings I noticed how everyone sat around talking only about, "Will *he* do this or that, or how does so-and-so get along with *him?*" The world seemed immobilized waiting for a word from *him.* Did people actually once talk that way about me?

The patio discussion lost its energy, and our meeting ended as the sun drifted behind the magnolias and the afternoon grew cool. I felt a new emptiness. My crusades, projects that for eight years seemed so crucial, now seemed less so. But the closer I came to the finish line, the busier I was. It was the same for Honey and the children. I thought, we are all so busy with wrapping things up that we barely speak, barely notice each other. We have thought nothing about the life ahead. Life now has become a frenzied ride to the finish, a wild roller-coaster ride faster and faster and up and down a track that everyone knows suddenly will end in black-midair. What an odd way to prepare for whatever comes next, but it seems like the only way to do it. We keep hurrying faster and faster so that we can leap off the end of the track into the unknown.

Had some extra time this morning and just used it, enjoyed it. Retied my shoes. Brushed my teeth twice. Gave Honey a longer-than-usual hug (which surprised her). I usually didn't do these things because there was always something else I could be doing to try to change the world.

Sat., Dec. 6—Woke up early, read *Walden.* Thoreau: "Morning is the alive time." That must be why I'm always up early.

To catch more of the morning. It *is* when I am more awake—I never yawn before breakfast. In Australia some days I will just wake up and read all morning. What a luxury that will be! 8:00 A.M. Briefcase lost. I had put it by the front door. Found it in backseat of trooper car, with folded newspaper on top, courtesy trooper. Such service will end soon. Former North Carolina governor says his biggest problem out of office was that he kept bumping into doors. Flew to Memphis. Girl said: "Look, Jodie, there's Lamar Alexander. That *was* the governor." Next someone will say, "Weren't you Lamar Alexander?"

CHAPTER 1 1

ROLLER COASTER

//

I'm nobody! Who are you?
Are you nobody too?
Then there's a pair of us!—don't tell!
They'd banish us, you know.

How dreary to be somebody!
How public like a frog
To tell your name the livelong day
To an admiring bog!
—EMILY DICKINSON
"Real Riches"

un., Dec. 7, 1986—Mansion. Honey was upstairs in her bathroom after church. This was no ordinary bathroom. It was big, with marble floors and drawers and closets everywhere. Big windows welcomed the morning light. One governor's wife had used this bathroom as a sewing room. It had been that lady's favorite room, safely removed by several doors from the constant flow of troopers, staff, docents giving tours, and clubs meeting. And it was Honey's retreat, too, her only really private place in this fifteen thousand-square-foot monster Mansion.

Both cocker spaniels were pawing to get in Honey's private retreat. They could sense when she was getting ready to go running and they would go crazy to go, too. I waited a decent moment and opened the door. Corfe romped in, took the best chair, and laid his nose on the armrest. His running mate, Lady, pawed and scratched for a while and then sat, panting.

Honey's hair was piled up, which made her neck look straight and her as cute as a button. I thought about how much time I had missed with her during the last eight, maybe twelve years. Her birthday dinners usually had been celebrated at county Republican dinners. Australia was coming none too soon.

She put on running shoes. Kathryn arrived, dragging her still broken right foot, wanting to try on several in different ways, for her mother's approval, Honey's pink sweater and a new dress.

Honey said to Kathryn, the dogs, and me, "Most people close the door to the bathroom to keep people out."

"I am here on business," I said.

"Why do you always have business when I'm about to do something I like to do, which isn't so often?"

I sat on the floor with the new house contract and with visas to sign.

"At least you're not visitors," she said, and signed the visas and began to read the contract. On another morning, when she was half dressed, two Tennessee citizens had wandered right into the bathroom. They had climbed over the rope at the bottom of the carved-stone staircase and come on up, and discovered Honey and asked her for directions to the kitchen. It was, after all, *their* house and they wanted to see "where they cook."

Mon., Dec. 8: Republican governors' meeting in New Jersey—My last governors' conference, this one on trade and politics. I watched more than participated. I thought, some Washington

TV reporters have more gall than governors. They will stand up anywhere in the room, put lights on their own faces, and begin loud talking, recording their segments of the evening news, all this right in the middle of someone's speech. They seem to *prefer* to do it in the middle of someone's speech.

I introduced to the other governors author David Halberstam, who said about Japanese car makers, and Japanese manufacturers in general, "Less goes in and more comes out." The next speaker said, "We're coming to the end of the dream that children will have a better life than their parents. There *is* a sense among many that there is a better life coming, but it's a different definition of better life."

Tues., Dec. 9: Still in New Jersey—Former Treasury Secretary Bill Simon told us he will sail his 125-foot yacht around the north of Australia. He will carry a phone and Thermofax so he can stay in communication with rest of world. Doesn't want to miss a thing. "What will you *do* in Australia?" he asked me, everyone asked me. The idea in America is that what you do is what you are. So if you are doing nothing, you are nothing.

Vice-president George Bush called. "See you this afternoon at the White House with the president. Tell him whatever you think about the Iran-contra business. Give him an outside-the-beltway view. Still going to Sydney? That still on?"

Richard Nixon spoke, first time to the governors since 1974. Baritone California voice, same stand-up with no mike, no stand, no notes, young aide to the side. All said, "Mr. President." Blue suit, black hair combed back. Lines accumulating in face. Hands together with long, piano player's fingers knitted. A fifties tie. "Khrushchev did his homework. Brezhnev liked Cadillacs and women. U.S. and USSR can't be friends, can't afford to be enemies. China uses capitalist tools to achieve Communist ends. In Middle East, we want peace, Soviets want the Middle East. We are the leaders of the free world; without us, everyone else would have to surrender." He swayed back and forth, ski nose in the light, eyes sunk in shadows. All forehead and some gray hair. Presentation so compelling that it reminded me how much he needed strong-willed and broad-gauged advisers with the experience to help him select the best ideas and discard the worst ones. He had that in his first term, not in the second.

In the afternoon, airplane to Washington, D.C. I was sitting next to the governor of New Jersey, who once taught history and who said: "How many people get to see two historic presidents of the United States in one day, in the midst of a crisis?" President Reagan and staff met us in Cabinet room. I had practiced what I would say and when it came my turn I said it: "Mr. President, I was a candidate in 1974. Watergate helped to defeat me. People were spitting on Republican candidates they were so mad. None of us want your last two years destroyed by this Iran business. Haven't we learned from experience that you should stop whatever else you are doing, find out what happened, announce it, clean house, apologize and get on with it? People trust you. They understand you can make a mistake, too."

"Lamar, it's more complicated than that," the president said.

"Enjoy Australia," Chief of Staff Don Regan said as we left. Back to New York for dinner with *Reader's Digest* editor.

Next Day—Virginia. On Pat Robertson's television show. My first time to meet him. He wore a blue suit, yellow tie. Pleasant face. Intelligent manner. He knows why he wants to be president, what he hopes to accomplish. Vastly underestimated, I thought. He said: "The liberal press doesn't like traditional Christians or conservatives; put them together and it's tough. And what will you do when you leave office? Australia? Really? Why?"

Home to Nashville in time for last press party. Capitol Hill reporters gave me a boomerang and a Crocodile Dundee poster with my face pasted where Paul Hogan's was supposed to be.

Sat., Dec. 13, after supper—Honey: "Do you think you'll ever get over your aversion to washing and drying dishes and putting them up?"

"In Australia, I'm going to be an ideal husband."

"It's better to let people know what you are really going to do. Then they're not disappointed."

"I really am going to try to be an ideal husband."

Her eyes questioned mine and while I was thus disarmed, she handed me a tray of dishes from the washer.

I said, "But this isn't Australia."

"I thought you might want a head start."

It seemed like the whole state was going to Australia with us, in spirit anyway. Bob Walden in Murfreesboro: "I stayed in Nam eleven extra months just so I could go to Sydney for six days in 1974. You're going to like it."

Mon., Dec. 15—Walking again, this time to Ooltewah. Junior high-school principal asked, "The students would like to know, what has the eight years been like for your family?"

I said, "We have four children. Last month Leslee's horse stepped on Drew's rooster and the dogs nearly ate Kathryn's rabbit and we have regular tragedies with Will's goldfish. The house we live in is bigger than yours but we really don't live in it and it really doesn't belong to us, it belongs to you."

Later, walking, I was already thinking about business offers that were very attractive after ten years of not making so much money. On the other hand, when people asked, "What are you going to do next?" I really wanted to say, as Thoreau would have, "Nothing. I'm going to confront life."

Thurs., Dec. 18—Maggie Sherman had finished my plaster "death mask"—something I had agreed to do for the state museum—so after lunch I went to see it and the others. People who work with words had the simplest masks—Alex Haley, Andrew Lytle, newspaper editor. Mine was more complex. My face was covered with family, cabin, rail fence, a picture of the mountains, everything going on in all directions at once, kids' pictures off the side upside down, Honey's picture somewhere in the center. One hiking boot on top. Pieces of a red-and-black shirt, torn up. A little piano dangling on a string from the side. Tennessee Homecoming '86 rocking chair poster.

Maggie said, "It was your idea, you know, to cover yourself all up."

A black-and-white photo, taken the same day the mask was made, startled me: my face without features, a worn-down face of a used-up person. When I told Honey, she said, "You've been getting up at three A.M."

I said, "I feel like I'm just flinging around to get one last thing done, like a beached whale thrashing."

Kathryn had been listening and said, "The reason why Alex Haley's mask is so simple is because he works by himself so much he knows himself and so he can be simple."

Sat., Dec. 20—How long had I been sounding like a governor when I talked with my own children? "Easy, Dad," Drew would say. "We've gone over this before." Heavy, ponderous, officious, more like a referee than a father. Too many words. Too overbearing. No patient listening.

After reading to Will: "Turn off the light, Will."

"Dad. Could you please say please more often?"

And at supper, Leslee: "Dad, your tone of voice is sharp with me. You act like you're mad and it hurts my feelings."

No patient listening. I telephoned the Maplewood High School teacher who was shot by a student last week. He appreciated it so much I wished I had done that more.

Sun., Dec. 21—Will: "Why do I have to go to church?"

Me: "So you can learn how God made the world."

Will: "I've already told you how that happened."

Our last Christmas at The Mansion: My Christmas Eve job was to put Will to bed. I failed. Will: "Can I open the Santa Claus presents early in the morning, before the others wake up?" I thought, He knows his mother doesn't like to do that and that I'm a pushover.

Nine-thirty P.M. Leslee brought down presents she had wrapped. She was seven at our first Christmas here. In eight years the most visible sign of change has been the children growing up; everything else has gone by too fast to notice the change. Our first Christmas tree for the Mansion came from Roan Mountain; we went there together to cut it. Mother was here and Dad had always been here at Christmas until he died two years ago.

Our worst family arguments—except for posing for family photographs at church—have occurred while decorating the tree:

"You put that one on."

"Put it on yourself."

"I like it better on the right side."

"Hold the ladder."

"Say please."

That's how it would start.

Shipping anything extra to Australia by ocean would take thirty to forty-five days, if there were no strikes, which there usually were. Five hundred pounds would cost $645.00. My eyes felt red and heavy and tired. And I had completely forgotten about moving expenses. Where would I get *that* thousand dollars? Almost no days left, little rest, and then we'll slide right out of here.

Christmas Day—Will downstairs at six. Little piles of gifts for everyone around the tree. Stockings. Drew always has had two stockings. Honey always has had the smallest piles—she gets the least because she is busy giving the most. Will leaped on his new flying turtle with wheels. He and I sat on the polished black-and-white marble floor, flat, shining, and smooth, plenty of room for a flying turtle to hit top speed. On the floor with him I got a seven-year-old's perspective—down there the floor surface was blacker and whiter, shinier and flatter and longer and slicker and, to Will's great approval, I also had an impulse to try something: "Look, Mommy, look at Dad go! He's not too big for it!"

I had an overpowering urge for simplicity. To strip everything down to a few things. Made list for an address book. Leaving people out was like shredding relationships. Packed carefully my elephants, walking sticks, books, all go to storage. In two weeks my life would go on ice.

Christmas Day telephone call to Bryce Harlow, who was dying in Harper's Ferry. I had worked for him, learned from him in the Nixon White House. He had been counselor to five presidents.

"Australia wha-a-t-t . . . ?" he said. "What are you going to do? You won't have a job?"

Bryce's wonderful gift was that he was always willing to be interrupted. When you attracted his gaze or his attention or reached him on the phone, he made you feel as if he had been sitting there hoping you would call or, better, drop by—that he had been wondering about *your* life, wondering what *you* might be thinking and doing. When I worked for him I spent most of my time explaining to congressmen why he couldn't call them back. They were never very mad because they knew it was because he was taking so much time with someone who had gotten his attention, and so they would wait for their share of that special attention.

This availability sometimes made Bryce horribly ineffi-
cient. But, I thought, as his life is ending, what is more important? Efficiency or caring for others? I have never liked being
interrupted, although the people I have admired the most—
Bryce and good school principals, for example—have seemed to
thrive on interruptions.

When for eight years you have lived life by fifteen-minute
scheduled segments, an interruption takes you off course. And
if you're off course, you don't get your way, do you? So, if you
allow yourself to be interrupted, it suggests that getting your
way is not so important, although success is usually measured
by how much you get your way. Albert Schweitzer must always
have been interrupted in Africa. Perhaps that's why he went
there. His *move* to Africa interrupted the career of the world's
greatest Bach organist. *How* he lived his life was what counted.
Maybe the laid-back Australians can teach me something about
this.

Fri., Dec. 26—Morning at the Mansion.

Drew (with his rock music turned high): "Get up, Leslee.
This is my last day in Nashville."

"Forever?" Leslee said sleepily and too hopefully.

It *was* our last time together as a family in this house. Drew
would leave the next day for National Outdoors Leadership
School and for a month of kayaking on the Pacific coast. We
would see him next in Sydney one month later. He'll miss the
end, I thought, or he'll have his own end. Drew sat with friend
Patrick Keeble on moving boxes piled in front of our other
Christmas tree—the official one in the front hall—blasting
Grateful Dead music, drinking Coke, and consoling the dogs.
"It's going to be six months, old boy." And to Patrick: "I'm
going to get a last Coke. Who knows if they have Coke in Aus-
tralia?"

Sat., Dec. 27—Woke up at six in the dark, thinking of undone things: *Reader's Digest* article. Money. Americans Outdoors
report for President Reagan. Farewell address—why should I
still be so busy? Will's friend Reed, who spent the night, left to
go bowling with his dad. I had never taken Will bowling. Honey
back from doctor: She was fine, but she was the only one. Will's
rabbit was dying, and there was a suspicion that Corfe's friend,

Lady, might be three weeks pregnant. Molly, the cat, was throwing up, ate something in kitchen.

Jan Talley came by to take away the dogs. We all hugged Corfe and Lady and said good-bye and wondered if we would ever see them again. They would be living in the country for their six months off. Molly Weaver would be coming to get Molly the cat. Houston Goddard, seven, would take the goldfish. Leslee's horse would stay at Brownland Farms. The old tom cat would remain at the Mansion. He was here when we came. The rabbit looked like it might not even make it to inauguration day.

I was surprised how satisfying packing was, stripping away nonessentials. We had recently visited the house of a friend who had just died. His things were still everywhere. It made me think how unimportant *things* are—when you leave they just stay there. It is certainly no mark of your life that you owned things; it might be if you did something with them.

Will shouted. He was watching an evening network news story of "Tea and Coffee" train that travels across the red center of Australia delivering supplies in the bush; nostalgic, wonderful photography. Is that why Americans are hooked on Australia? Is it because Australia is a vision of America as it was—and perhaps still ought to be?

Next the news told of a North Carolina runner so driven that during a race she jumped thirty feet from a bridge, and was paralyzed from her waist down. Being your best is not all there is to life. 2 Timothy 2:15. Everyman is not Mozart. More of us are Salieri, the journeyman composer.

First week of January, in Miller's Cove—Everything now was laid bare. Even the oak leaves had fallen, and nothing interrupted the view through the tree branches from the tops of the ridges. Frost was in the valleys and snow outlined the high mountains and the fields were more brown than green. The creek that had been slow in October was now roaring and plunging over the rock dam we made in August. Chimneys fumed busily and front porch woodpiles were half-gone and cattle huddled by rolled-up hay. The sun's light slanted against the red barn's south side. The wasps—finally—slept in the log cabin walls.

These are the shortest days, when night arrives in midaf-

ternoon. It is wet and cold and cold has the advantage—it lasts
for days in a row. It bores in. It takes its toll. It is the killing cold
of the dead of winter. In our mountains the dead of winter
arrives in late December and stays until February. It is a time
for cleansing and relief, a time when nature quiets the suffering
of so many barnacle-ridden lives. It is the end of many things,
but it is also a refreshing prelude to many new beginnings.
There can be no renewal in spring without the killing cold of
the dead of winter. We accept winter with all of its consequences in the natural order of things. We even enjoy it. I love
the briskness in the mountains, the trails without tourists, the
open views from almost any ridge. Why, then, do we have so
much trouble with our personal winters and the winters of
others we know?

Last week in the Mansion—Honey sat in the kitchen, cheeks
streaked with tears, reading Jeanne Pearcy's letter—Jeanne who
had lived with us for eight years, part of the family, now was
going her own way: "I remember looking under beds and behind doors and everywhere for Kathryn's music; I will always
remember Leslee's love of animals, Drew's red, white, and blue
basketball in the yard," and Jeanne can hardly bear to mention
Will, who came to live with us after she did, "Please take good
care of William Houston."

The race was ending; the hard long race that I had wanted
so badly to start I now wanted as badly to end. Will used to say
at age five when he had finished practicing the piano, "I am
ready for an ending." Now I was ready for an ending. Sometimes it seemed that the only thing that had made this wonderful
race endurable was the certain knowledge that it would end. It
would end suddenly and absolutely in four days, and I was much
too busy even to think about doing anything more than collaps-
ing at the finish. I was racing anxiously to plunge into the
darkness with no time even to think about what darkness it was
or what might have been beyond it.

I worked with Leslee on her school application, then went
upstairs to bed early with Honey to watch *On the Beach*. Watching movies. That is one more make-up thing she and I had
resolved to do together in Australia. Kathryn peeked in the
packed-up room and said, "Your-all's room looks so sad, and

empty." While I fought sleep, Gregory Peck explained to Ava Gardner why the submarine *Scarfish* came to Melbourne: "*We stuck our nose up just outside Okinawa, then again in Manila. It was too hot. So we went down the coast of Australia and ended up here. There wasn't much of any other place to go.*"

CHAPTER 1 2

PEOPLE
REMEMBER
THE LAST
THING YOU DO

//

Good-by to the life I used to live,
And the world I used to Know;
And kiss the hills for me, just once;
Now I am ready to go!
—EMILY DICKINSON
"Farewell"

U nited Airlines Flight 22 rumbled and lurched into the air. The intercom voice said, "We're climbing to thirty-five thousand feet. We'll have some strong headwinds, but should land in Denver at four-twenty. It's twenty-one degrees there, with clear skies." It was inauguration day, Saturday, January 17, 1987, 2:36 in the afternoon and it was over.

I touched Honey's hand across the aisle.

"How do you feel?" I asked her.

She smiled. "Exhausted, but it's a happy tired."

I said, "These last few days have been a roller coaster. My blood was roaring. I thought I would explode."

Honey turned to her needlepoint, the children read, and I tried to reconstruct for my notebook our twenty-one-gun getaway.

There had been the service at the Downtown Presbyterian Church. The Reverend Pat McGeaghy had prayed, "Thank You for calling Lamar to be our governor and be with him until You call him again." When the service ended, a single state trooper drove me to the swearing-in ceremony.

There were unfamiliar voices on the trooper's car radio.

"Why don't you turn it to the governor's channel?" I asked.

The trooper replied, "It already is. Those voices are the new governor's troopers."

"Where do we go?" I asked.

"To tell you the truth, I'm not sure. You know we're not the ones running things anymore. But we'll find it."

When we got there I waited in a holding room until just before the ceremony was to begin. Three times the ceremony organizers summoned me to take my seat on the same scaffolding where I had been the center of attention twice before. Three times I strode out almost to center stage, and three times double rows of National Guardsmen came to attention and saluted. The first two tries were false alarms, mistakes of the organizers. The third time was the real thing, the last salute for this commander in chief.

At the moment of the oath-taking, at 10:31, the cameras' clicking sounded like cicadas swarming. But the salute cannons' booming drowned out the cicadas and the platform emptied quickly.

That ended it. We were on our own. One trooper confided to Honey that he was worried about whether I could take care of the family after all these years of people taking care of me, and that he was praying for her. Several troopers stayed near us to try to help. But I wasn't the governor anymore, and I was determined to do things for myself.

The troopers watched silently as we picked up our bags at

the home of our friends Carole and John Sergent, where we had spent the last three nights. It seemed to me as if the whole street was watching when I walked out the Sergents' front door carrying four heavy bags, and the screen door slammed in my face. People were still watching when, after loading the bags in the cars, I ran back into the house twice to get things I had forgotten. I was confirming everyone's worst fears.

When we arrived at the airport a swarm of television and print-news reporters had established a beachhead in the middle of the busiest corridor, the one we would have to walk down. The reporters watched while I put down the heavy suitcases and ran back to the parking lot for the video camera I had left in the car.

Draped again with cameras and books, and carrying one hanging bag and two briefcases, I struggled through airport security. My metal watch set off the alarm and my glasses got caught in the conveyor belt. The reporters smiled and the cameras whirred.

Then a strange procession came down the busy corridor. First there was a many-footed gaggle of newspaper reporters. Then came television reporters clutching the sweaters of their cameramen, leading them like seeing-eye dogs because the cameramen were walking backward, aiming their cameras at us— who, with a few loyal friends, staggered along next, struggling with the two bags apiece that we hoped contained enough to sustain us for six months.

When we reached the end of the corridor, where there were three ramps leading to airplanes, we stopped, and the reporters and our friends stopped, and all gathered round.

Someone asked, "Leslee, will you miss it?"

"I'll miss the people, but I'm ready to live in a regular house," Leslee said.

Somewhere I had lost my Stetson, the one with the special needlepoint band that told the story of my walk across the state, the one Memphis friends had made and given to me, and that I had worn for eight years.

Honey saw my distress. "I'll make you another hatband," she said softly. "It's time to go."

Christine, our Australian neighbor, hugged each of the children and exclaimed, "You're going to Australia at a great time." Her friends, Graham and Barbie Crawford in Sydney,

and her parents and brother in Melbourne were the only people
we knew in Australia, which was the way we had wanted it.
Christine had tears in her eyes. "You're going to have fun.
Americans have never been so popular there. Don't ruin it by
winning back the America's Cup. Have a great time in *my* country!"

I stepped toward our gate. Then I shouted above the hubbub to Christine, "Do they have typewriter ribbons in Australia?," suddenly realizing that I had forgotten to bring any.
"And do they have good bookstores?"

Will shouted after me, "And do they have McDonald's?
That's what I need to know."

Christine burst out laughing. "Of course they do. Where do
you think you're going?"

I reshouldered my cameras and briefcase and book bag, and
edged precariously toward the ramp that led to the gate for the
airplane. One persistent reporter followed, demanding to know,
"What has been your greatest accomplishment?"

I answered, "Landing in one piece. I guess that's it." And
I turned with as much authority as I could muster draped with
so many bags and things, and strode up Ramp 5 toward the
airplane. At the top, I turned for the last brave wave good-bye
to our friends and I saw the whirring television cameras, and my
stomach sank. I realized I had no idea whether Ramp 5 was the
right one. I had only been following the person in front of me,
as I'd done for eight years. I thought, Oh boy, what a fine
exit—briskly up the ramp to the wrong plane! Gloriously re-
corded on the evening news. Probably to the archives forever.
People remember the last thing you do.

It was my great good fortune that the person I had been
following was Honey.

Sensing my predicament, she whispered, "It's the right
ramp. Now why don't you let me have the tickets?"

I said, still waving and smiling, "I would like to handle
such things for a change."

"And I would like to get to Sydney," she said. "There will
be plenty of less crucial times for you to practice getting your
feet back on the ground."

CHAPTER 13

SPINNING

//

I went to the woods because I wished
to live deliberately, to front only the
essential facts of life, and see if I
could not learn what it had to teach,
and not, when I came to die, discover
that I had not lived.

—HENRY DAVID THOREAU
Walden

Will's kicking in bed woke me at 6:30 in our room at the San Francisco Airport Hilton. In these strange surroundings, my mind spun frantically like a computer searching for the right program. It spun past newspapers—which I didn't want to read—past great political thoughts—which I was tired of thinking—and finally it stopped, as bewildered as a long-distance runner on a short track. All that stretched before us was a big glob of time with nothing to do and I was not programmed to leave big globs of time empty. Honey said, "We'll see how long before you start making lists."

I dressed and helped the porter carry ten suitcases downstairs. There were still fifteen minutes to kill before I was to
meet the family in the hotel parking lot, where the BMW that
our friends Judy and Bob Waterman had bravely loaned to us
to tour San Francisco waited for us. On the lobby desk I found
a form for the "Hilton's Million Dollar a Day" promotion. I
began to fill it out until I came to question 8, which asked,
"Title"? and I stopped. I was not about to write "Former Governor." "Writer" didn't seem to fit, at least not yet. "Lawyer"? I
hadn't practiced law in ten years. There was really not any
comfortable professional title to put after the comma after my
name. Then when I got to question 10, "Office Address"? and
I remembered that I didn't have an office anymore, I tossed away
the form and walked to the parking lot.

Honey and Leslee and Kathryn and Will were already
loaded into the BMW. I maneuvered the car onto the highway,
and at the first intersection swerved into a gasoline station. I
then backed toward the pump marked SUPREME UNLEADED until
there was a crashing sound.

"You've knocked over something," Honey said.

"Quite obviously," I said. "I hope it's not the gas pump."
It was the water can and its demise brought the station attendant quickly out to see how he could help.

Honey said, "Maybe you will have a little time in Hawaii
to join George Ariyoshi for a driving lesson before you have to
drive in Australia." The attendant waited while I poked at but-
tons, seeking some way to unlock the gasoline tank.

The car jumped and so did the attendant, and Leslee yelled,
"Dad, you've got it in reverse and it should be in park." I shifted,
paid for the gas, found Highway 101, and headed toward San
Francisco.

After a few miles, Kathryn inquired from the right backseat corner, "Dad, how fast are you driving?"

"Not fast enough," Will said.

"This is worse than *European Vacation*," Kathryn groaned.

"We've got Chevy Chase for a driver all right, and a father," Leslee said.

Honey said, "At this rate we'll make our own movie."

"Chevy Chase had a better supporting cast," I said.

Will said, "Yeah, Mom, how about a TV series? We could

call it *Sitting for a Day* because that's what we're doing." Traffic on Highway 101 had indeed come to a complete stop.

Leslee reflected upon the congestion and noise, the number of billboards and crowded business places, and observed with Leslee logic, "California is crowded and ugly. Tennessee is greener. But I think I'd like to move to California."

In the morning mist we motored across the Golden Gate Bridge and stopped to photograph the city across the bay. We then drove back across the bridge to the Embarcadero, where we had lunch with the Watermans, then drove to the airport.

Trouble waited for us at the San Francisco airport that afternoon. Honey had not noticed that the United Airlines employee in Denver had pulled the wrong tickets. Now the Qantas employee in San Francisco told us to go to United to fix the problem, and the United official began giving Honey a lesson about how it was *her* responsibility to keep up with *her* tickets. This caused Honey to bristle and her voice to rise, and then of course I jumped in and in my most governor-like voice, and with appropriate exaggeration, said something like, "We've planned this for two years, to travel fifteen thousand miles around the world, *six of us,* and your people pull the wrong tickets and you say its *our* fault." Then I almost said, "And I'm the governor of Tennessee . . . ," but I really wasn't and I'd never liked governors who said things like that when I *was* one, so I sat down, frustrated, on the airport lobby floor and pretended to guard the ten suitcases while Kathryn read to Will and our lioness and the United supervisor worked things out.

Qantas landed us in Honolulu in the middle of the night. U.S. Navy Captain Dave Brown from Nashville was at the airport with a brown military van to drive us to our hotel. When we arrived it was 2:00 A.M. and Will woke up just long enough to say, "Mom, I can hear the ocean crashing against the rocks." We said good night to Captain Brown and found our beds, but I lay awake, my mind's computer purring. It had had nothing to do except focus on family or to rest, and it was not programmed for either. So it thought of unplanted white pine trees in Miller's Cove or of tax bills that might not have been paid. I wondered how long it would take to erase all those old programs or at least to store them. I fell asleep dreaming about possibly diving in Fiji. It would be my first time.

The next day Captain Brown took us to Pearl Harbor, where we boarded a navy yacht. The sun on the ocean hurt my eyes as we strained to see Kolekole Pass through which Japanese planes flew early Sunday, December 7, 1941. Captain Brown showed Leslee, Kathryn, and Will how the planes flew right over the place where a NEW AND USED CAR sign was now, and how they strafed the barracks and then flew across the harbor, spreading more death. We saw the battleship U.S.S. *Arizona* where it sank that morning. Captain Brown said, "There are more than a thousand American sailors still inside the *Arizona*. We lost more trying to get the bodies out. It was too dangerous to keep trying."

Wednesday vanished sometime between Honolulu and Fiji as we chased the night across the Pacific. My restless computer kept spinning and finding, then erasing and cleansing, worries about old bills, social obligations, job opportunities, acquaintances, people whose faces I should recognize, relatives, crutches like excuses, schedules, adversaries, old projects, new projects, the ruts of life, clothes, alarm clocks—all of those things now set the computer whirring a little less often. I wanted a nap when we landed in Fiji, even though it was midmorning.

Fiji was nearly freedom at last, a new time zone, below the equator, summer in January. At our hotel there was an invitation to visit the prime minister. I said no thank you; the old computer pitched a fit at such strange behavior and began spinning.

Fiji was sunshine and exercise and long meals together and no TV and talking on the beach and hearing parrots squawk and feeling the faint warm breeze floating through the coconut leaves and getting tired late in the afternoon because of the time change. The Fijians' loosely wrapped brown bodies and passive faces flowed by in the same gentle way their many syllabled language seemed to flow, in the same soft way the warm breezes stirred. When Will woke me from a nap and asked me to build a sand castle with him on the beach, which surprised me, I said yes and did, which must have surprised Will. It had been seven days exactly since our great twenty-one-gun getaway, but it seemed instead like *months*. Australia was still only a dream, a happy thought that someday soon might even become a real adventure.

The second day, I rented a Toyota Corona and organized a family drive around the island, thinking it would be good practice for driving on the wrong side of the road in Australia.

I explained, "In Fiji there are not as many cars to dodge." I then climbed into the left (and therefore wrong) side in the front. As I did this, Leslee got out of the backseat and ran back to her room to get a Walkman stereo. She returned in about five minutes and inquired, "Anything mellow on the radio?"

I heard some familiar guitar rhythms and turned it up and offered, "Beatles?"

"Stop," Honey said, although I had not yet started. "I need my travel book." She opened the door on her side and ran back to the hotel.

"Oh, I forgot *Huckleberry Finn*," said Kathryn, following Honey. And, of course, Will wanted a book, too, so he joined the procession. After ten minutes Honey returned for the key to the room, and then she went back and stayed until everybody had a full load of diversions that would help make more meaningful a family car tour.

Meanwhile, I had been experimenting. So when they all returned, the windshield wipers and the parking lights were on. Leslee was the first to be helpful, "Dad, the windshield wipers and the parking lights are on."

Kathryn was not far behind, "It's Chevy Chase again."

I inquired, of no one in particular, "Is the gearshift in this Japanese car backwards, too?," and finally backed the car out uneventfully and headed toward the town of Nadi.

Honey asked, "Why are you swerving off the road? I'd feel better if you didn't drive into the ditch."

But Will shouted encouragement from the backseat. "Faster, Dad. I checked this book out of the library called *How Not to Drive* and you're doing fine."

Honey interrupted. "Why are you now swerving over the center line?"

Kathryn supported her mother. "Watch the white line, Dad. That's what it's for. Mom, will you drive?"

I gained confidence along the highway toward Suva, catching one hill after another. I kept in mind that from the other direction another American father, in just my circumstances, might come at me, aiming his rented foreign car toward mine, more or less in the other lane. I avoided several purple buses on narrow bridges. The wipers came on several more times while I was adjusting various handles. I navigated several right turns and invented an important new Rule of Life, which was "Think Right, Right, Right," because when you are in a driving-on-the-wrong-side-of-the-road country most things that might kill you come from the right.

The next morning I drove by myself along the Coral Coast. Cane waved in the cool breezes, and bright-colored clothes swung on lines between trees outside thatched huts. At 8:30 I arrived at the Fijian Hotel, where Collin King met me. Collin was a twenty-year-old Fijian who appeared to have been sculpted rather than born. He was six feet two and finely muscled, and his frizzy hair was short. We walked into the warm sea, and Collin taught me how to blow water out of a mask and to talk with hand signals under water and to recover a lost air hose, and how to equalize ear pressure by holding my nose and blowing, and he finally delivered the ultimate instruction, "Never stop breathing. You can rupture your lungs."

At about 9:30 Collin and I emerged from our practice session onto the hot sand. I went to the bathroom twice, the way I used to do before college track meets, put on gloves and fins and mask and a thick wet suit. My suit, unlike Collin's, bulged embarrassingly. I suddenly felt too full, even poisoned, and like a garbage can which over time had accumulated so much unnecessary food and drink that it had begun to expand dangerously at the middle. We stepped again into the warm water, and I felt the air tank rub against my sunburn as together we swam to the motorboat that would take us to the Golden Reef ten minutes away.

The boat sped over the blue water.

Collin said, "I never take a beginner below thirty or thirty-five feet."

"Anything dangerous here?"

"No," he said.

The boat anchored and at 10:20 we fell backward into the sea. It was as warm as the air. We followed the rope down to the anchor and then Collin took my hand and we began to swim. I was so disoriented that I paid almost no attention to what I saw, but when my breathing slowed I became absorbed in an air-bubbling, blue-green fantasyland where every kind of oddly familiar-looking fish played. There was a formless old woman wearing bright yellow-and-white stripes—I learned later she was a blue-banded angel fish. Right after her came a prim English nanny, gray and venerable—a spotted sweetlip. Then two butterfish came cruising, flaunting yellow-and-black stripes, bunching together, creating swatches of yellow in the green-blue water. Some fish had long noses. Others had big eyes.

Several times water began to fill my mask, so I blew it out. Collin watched and gave me a questioning thumbs-up sign. When I gave one back he swam away deeper, looking under fan coral for yellow cowries, each piece worth five thousand dollars Fiji. I followed him and when he saw me he pointed out soft coral, which waved with the water. The only sound was my breathing, and I had completely forgotten about the old world of fresh air and sky and had almost forgotten where I was. The spinning computer had gone to sleep. I was on my own in a startling new world.

Suddenly I saw Collin's arm stretched out, pointing toward a large plate coral. He and I stood literally on our heads trying not to move, watching the biggest fish of the day emerge from hiding. The fish was five feet of gray with a flat, white mouth. When it swam away I found the anchor rope and climbed hand over hand, and when I splashed through into the warm air and saw the bright sky, I realized I was breathing very hard.

"Shark," Collin said.

"What kind?"

"White tip reef shark. Usually harmless."

"How long were we under?"

"Fifty minutes."

"How deep?"

"Fifty feet." The motorboat sped back toward the beach, and Collin said, "Last month we saw a hammerhead, fifteen foot."

"Where?"

"Where you were."

"What'd you do?"

"Hid in a hole."

"What'd he do?"

"Waited."

"How long?"

"Ten minutes. He swam away. Then we saw him the next day. So we canceled dives for a week."

B O O K   I I

SEARCHING

With God's help, let us endeavor to
live here . . . thankful that we were
not cast upon some bare and
inhospitable island.

—J. D. Wyss
The Swiss Family Robinson

CHAPTER 1 4

SKY BLOWN BLUE

//

Leaves and laughter
And legs hurl past
And I stride faster
Against the blast.
Where am I going?
What shall I care,
Buoyed by the blowing,
Living air?

—A. D. Hope
"A Windy Afternoon" (Australian)

The breeze began when the sun had warmed the hills
enough to pull the air from the sea, and it blew until
after midnight when the hills became cool again. It dried sweat
quickly on my first long afternoon walks and rearranged my

hair and I was surprised that it felt so strong before it felt cool. In the early evening the breeze would spill through the open glass doors and swirl under the dinner table. The cold made my bare legs uncomfortable.

Later at night I would be so sure that it was blowing up a storm that I would sometimes get out of bed and grope for the open window. But then even when the windows were closed tight, there still was a roaring outside, so I would sit up listening and become fascinated with how moonlight through the swaying trees made shadows dance on the walls. Beyond the trees I could see the black water of Mosman Bay and beyond that the outline of Sydney, buildings speckled with shining dots. If I kept the windows shut, the mugginess would soon make me wish that I had bought the desk fan at the little hardware store in Mosman Village. So I learned to leave the windows open, to pull up the covers, and be patient about the roar. The hills would cool and the breeze would die and the shadows would stop dancing.

By morning I would need the covers again. A new gentle breeze would be at work, pulling the cool this time from the hills to the sea. Through the open windows I could hear the crazy kookaburras laughing and the first raven crying and the cockatoos and the whole bird symphony. Sometimes I would walk outside to try to see which one sounded like the Australian telephone, *brrrng, brrrng,* and which one's pitch was as shrill as the smoke alarm, and which raven kept admiring itself in Kathryn's upstairs bedroom window and then crashing into it.

Many times, as the bird symphony quieted, I would wait on the upstairs porch listening to early construction noises and cars warming up, and watching the sea borrow the color of the sky and feeling the light sting my eyes and I would marvel at this land down under the sky blown blue. On some of our first mornings I went back to bed and under the covers because even the morning breeze had a bite. That was when I read *Huckleberry Finn* again (because Kathryn had laughed so reading it on our long plane trip) and *Robinson Crusoe* (it did not seem to be the same book I had read as a boy). One morning I let Thomas Merton's *New Seeds of Contemplation* pull me all the way through to its end and did not even feel guilty that I was still reading when Honey returned from running.

I put on shorts and a T-shirt and tennis shoes, and Honey and I walked the mile to Mosman Village. We left one white blouse at the 20-20 Good Looking Dry Cleaners and paused at the Cheese Shop ("I'm afraid the Gouda is nicer," the proprietor said when we asked for English applewood Cheddar). We admired chocolate inventions at the French Chef and stopped at the Australia Post to mail a puzzle to Will's friend John Austin Echols and to buy stamps. When we crossed Military Road, we met Mike Connell opening his Baronia Art Gallery, and spent fifteen minutes learning more about Fred Elliot's marine watercolors and hearing Mike explain what a hard time the first Europeans had painting Australia. "They couldn't get the light and they couldn't paint eucalyptus trees to look like eucalyptus trees. Australians couldn't paint better, but they could paint Australia better."

Back on the street, the smells from A. Lopez & Sons, Flowers and Fruit, were too much for Honey, so she stopped to select extra-choice yellow peaches and red plums and brilliant red raspberries and green and yellow mangoes and deep purple select cherries, and I crossed the street to the ANZ Night & Day Bank where the manager, Brian Loundar, saw me and came to the front.

I asked him, "Does it ever get really cold?"

He said, "Sometimes the dog's drinking dish freezes over. That's the coldest it gets. Even then, by ten o'clock, the dog will be drinking and by one it will be sixty-four. Everyone *thinks* it's cold in Sydney when the minimum is fifty-seven degrees. Forty-eight was the coldest maximum last year. We don't have the month-to-month cold like you do."

"It's hot today."

"Maybe ninety or ninety-one, but it was one hundred and thirteen yesterday out west. When you lose the breeze it's hot."

The breeze was just right for sitting directly in the sun at lunch. I ate yogurt and peanut butter on wheat crackers, and finished with a green apple, and wondered why in America I had automatically consumed so many sugared soft drinks and salted chips and chocolate desserts. It was almost as if those things had been sweet rewards for staying so busy and so unthinking for so long.

The postman whistled twice, and when I went to see what

he had left, I saw him jog away. Together Honey and I examined each postmark—eleven days from Washington, D.C., eight from Nashville, and we wondered which friend would be the first to forget to use an airmail stamp. The postman had already explained that surface mail to Australia meant it would come by ship, and from America that meant three months, more or less, depending on strikes in Sydney.

The house was clean and the children were in school. I sensed that Honey would enjoy being by herself, and I was therefore free to take a long walk—but not *really* free even after two weeks in Base Camp Sydney. Guilt hung on about something undone, although there was absolutely nothing to do. And there were occasional little desperate tugs of urgency, remnants of a discarded schedule-card life, although in my real new life there was nothing pressing, nothing urgent, nothing to worry about at all. I untied my shoes and pulled my socks up tighter and tied the shoes again and concentrated on a different dilemma, one that presented the sort of pleasant problems a feast presents—the dilemma of where shall I walk? Back through the village? Or up to Rawson Park for the view? But I resolved the issue as I usually did and turned down Coronation Avenue toward Plunkett Road.

Last Sunday cars had been parked on both sides of Plunkett Road all the way to the cricket fields, where Royal Australian Navy sailors played and mothers watched children under huge fig trees. The milk bars had been busy and the streets crowded. Barbecue smells and car exhaust and walkers and lookers were overwhelming the esplanade. Balmoral Beach looked like Coney Island in old photographs, and the only way I found Honey among the slick, smeared sunning backs was that she had all of her bathing suit on, one of the few who did.

On that Sunday afternoon the real esplanade had been Sydney Harbor itself which became like an Easter parade. Brightly colored racing spinnakers created occasional patterns of order, but on the whole the harbor was like a big-city intersection with all the lights green. Windsurfing hotshots cut close to double-furled white finery. Cruise boats meandered. The hydrofoil walked on water. Catamarans careened across, sometimes in pairs, seeking perfect balance on a blissful afternoon. The ferry boomed a stately hello, its diamond flag flying, everyone else giving way. A dark gray U.S. Navy submarine rested, the world's policeman ominously off his beat.

Now, four days later, what I saw on my walk at Balmoral Beach was not much different from what I had seen on Sunday, although school was still in session and work presumably was, too. There were swimmers in the sea even where there was no shark net, and a bare-chested girl was performing sit-ups. Everywhere on the beach there were slick backs glistening and feet bottoms sandy and real bottoms packed into many colored bikini pants and nothing else. Along the shore, anchored sailboats rocked, their single masts looking as lonely as sailors' widows waiting, and I wondered, Waiting for what?, because last Sunday afternoon, when Sydney Harbor had been shore-to-shore sails, the same masts were rocking and waiting then, too.

Along Balmoral Beach the sun burned and the sea breeze was strong and the splashing waves overpowered and subdued all the other noises: skateboards clattering on the esplanade, then gone, babies calling, car engines revving and slowing, footsteps and balls bouncing, cricket players shouting and the *thwock* of tennis balls, a motorboat's whine, rare for this harbor of sailors. Sea gulls glided against the wind, hanging and squawking above picnickers.

I headed back up Plunkett Road beneath a canopy of sweet-smelling gum trees. The road narrowed and flattened and emerged into the sunlight, and I picked up speed on sidewalks that had obviously been there a long time. The tight lanes, and close-packed federation-style houses with red-tiled roofs and yards with lemon and orange trees and dogs barking were becoming familiar. As I turned on to Middle Head Road, my thighs tightened and the new hardness in my legs felt good. My muscles reminded me how arms can get sore, too, from walking five to ten miles a day. My legs had begun to feel like newly useful weapons, good as fine wheels newly conditioned and now ready to take me places.

This morning when I had shaved, the lines beneath my eyes had been harder to see and the top of my head had been freckled brown and peeling, and at breakfast I had noticed a difference in Honey's face, too. The bathroom scales said that I had already lost eight pounds, which hardly seemed possible after just two weeks when the only thing that was different was

that I was walking more and eating less and going to bed when
I was sleepy and getting up only when I wanted no more sleep.
And it had been a long time since I had tasted the sourness that
came sometimes when I had been busy for too long.

I was striding by the time I reached the gusts of wind
coming off Rawson Park's hilltop. A company of 8th Brigade
army men jogged by, counting loud. On Bradley's Head Road
I slowed down to watch six lanes of white-outfitted players at
the Warringah Lawn Bowling Club. I detoured past the Uniting
Church, and smiled when I remembered what the Australian
children who had been called to the front of the church last
Sunday had been thankful for: beaches, holidays (it was the first
Sunday after summer vacation), sailing, playgrounds, and birds
and, yes, friends, too, and it had only been after some prompting
from the minister that one child had finally said, "For His good-
ness."

I began to notice that Australian men wear as many different colored shorts as American men do baseball caps. The
painter wears white, the mailman blue, the jogger green; a cou-
rier was in tan, students in uniform wore dark blue. I couldn't
help but notice, too, that not many women wore shorts and not
many women wore slips beneath their skirts, which made walking in Mosman Village nearly as disconcerting as walking on
Balmoral Beach. So quickly did I pass by the butcher and the
milk bar and the newsagent and the chiropractor and the sign
that announced where to find W. J. Nicolls, F.B.C.O., Optome-
trist, that I reached Cremorne before I realized it.

Young women in leotards danced and rock music blared
from the big second-story windows across Military Road, where
a sign read: THE RANCAN SISTERS WORKOUT CENTRE; LOW IMPACT
AND GRADED AEROBIC CLASSES. Below the sign and all that noise,
older women in print dresses sat on a bench waiting for the bus.
I was walking now almost without thinking, with no special
destination in mind and no appointed time to go home. Straight
across from me was the truly huge McDonald's Hamburger
Restaurant with its golden arches, waiters in blue uniforms and
white caps, quarter-pounders and even french fries instead of
the usual Australian "chips." We had investigated it on our first
night, and Will had proclaimed pretty much for all of us, "The
fries taste like fish. But I guess this place is going to be all right."

When I arrived home a little after five, Drew was on the patio gazing at the harbor and I stopped beside him.

He said, "Sometimes I look for twenty minutes."

What was special to see that evening was the beginning of the Thursday ballet of white sails, dipping, flowing one by one onto center stage, a parade from behind the cliffs hiding Manly Cove. We occupied a balcony seat higher than three gum trees—Drew and I—and we could see the whole stage. The rest of the audience was spread across the amphitheater to our right and left and below us. We just *supposed* they were there because all we could see were red-tiled roofs, nearly hidden by the perpetual green of the fragrant gum trees.

Below us, at the front of the stage, were lonely masts rocking and waiting, and beyond them Windsurfers darted faster as the wind picked up, and at center stage now the ferries joined the parade of dancing sails and the hydrofoil pranced high on the water and the backdrop curtains were the gray sloping hillsides of sandstone protecting the most beautiful harbor in the world.

God may not have been looking when he made Sydney Harbor. I have an idea what happened, though. Australia may have been God's first try on this earth, the first continent, and He tried nothing too fancy, just practiced with His cutting tool, fashioning a nearly oval huge crust, then rimming its edge with little harbors and jetties and coves, a nice backdrop for the beaches—when all of a sudden something roaring in His Tasman Sea, something in those choppy waves, diverted God's attention and He turned His head. It was just long enough for the cutting tool to run wild. It cut in and then abruptly out, and then went twisting deep into the sandstone, creating Watson's Bay, then Double Bay, then Shark's Bay, and bay after bay and bay, and then on toward the Blue Mountains and then back down again toward the Tasman Sea, and suddenly danced back again into the land for cuts and twists and turns, then back out quickly near where it had begun its wild run—leaving a deceptive mouth, an entry so small that the first English explorer, Captain James Cook, failed entirely to see it the first time he sailed by. Captain Cook saw only the steep three-hundred-foot-high sandstone heads and sailed on north up the coast of Australia. It was not until the first fleet of English convicts landed, two hundred years ago on January 26, 1788, that Europeans saw this piece of God's handiwork.

When Drew and I walked into the kitchen, where Leslee and her mother were preparing dinner and discussing the sunset, Leslee said, "Some people at home told me the sun set in the East here. They thought it was backwards like everything else."

I said, "The water in the toilet does go down the wrong way."

Kathryn and Will were in the den watching Australian network television news, offering occasional suggestions to Honey to hurry supper along so they would not miss *The Cosby Show* at 7:30. Some of the news was familiar: drugs in the schools, the crisis in Lebanon, car wrecks, and murders. Some was familiar, but with an Australian twist, such as the controversy over whether a Northern Territory mother had murdered her baby or, as she contended, a dingo (wild dog) had run off with the child.

A surprising amount of the news was American—of three hundred thousand American tourists a year coming to Australia, and of visa waits two weeks long. There was the daily report about "Irangate." And we all crowded round when we thought we heard familiar voices, and a news segment came on about a blizzard in Nashville, Tennessee, causing spectacular three- and four-car pileups. And there was some Tennessee citizen explaining what it was like to slide at thirty miles an hour on two inches of ice across the Jefferson Street Bridge. Except for the familiar Tennessee accent, it seemed like news from another planet.

For supper Honey had sautéed our tastiest fresh-fish discovery, John Dory fillets. We began eating on the porch overlooking the harbor, but within minutes we moved inside because the warm hills were pulling the cool air in so strongly from the sea. And the wind blew through the open glass doors shifting and spilling cold over the table across our faces and under the table around our legs. But it was welcome refreshment for the end of a muggy February day two weeks after we had established Base Camp Sydney.

C H A P T E R 1 5

P O T A T O
S A C K S , G R A Y
S O C K S , A N D
B L A C K S H O E S

//

I am singled out and separated, as it
were, from all the world to be
miserable.

—DANIEL DEFOE
Robinson Crusoe

L eslee has always believed that anything is possible and
not only has she been willing to try it, she has usually
been willing to organize it. But for once, Leslee seemed stymied.
She listened raptly to Mrs. Morley whose gaze in turn was
riveted on Leslee's watch, and who was saying: "The watch will
be fine." The gaze shifted to Leslee's dangling earrings. "No
earrings, or they will be confiscated until the term ends." Mrs.

Morley was the British assistant to the American headmistress at the Queenwood School for Girls, and she seemed unaware that long funky earrings were a crucial part of fourteen-year-old Leslee's presentation.

Mrs. Morley introduced us to the American headmistress, Judith Wheeldon, who had met her husband, John, at the University of Wisconsin in the early 1970s when she was a student and he was a visiting Australian Labor party senator crusading against American involvement in the Vietnam War. Now John was an editor of *The Australian* newspaper, and Judith was brand-new headmistress, but she seemed to have things well under control. After a forty-five minute interview, she placed Leslee in tenth grade and Kathryn in eighth, and she told us, "The girls will be taking English, maths, science, modern history, ancient history, geography, Australian history, Latin, commerce and music, arts and crafts, physical education, and Scripture. My impression is we're ahead of America in maths and sciences and behind in English and the language arts. I'll be interested to see what you think."

After about twenty minutes Mrs. Morley had politely begun to interrupt. ("I'm worried about your time . . .) Any prime minister in a long conference would have been grateful for her skill. ("I'm so sorry to break in but I'm afraid . . .") Mrs. Wheeldon excused herself and rushed to a board meeting. Mrs. Morley ordered the clothing pool opened for an extra day to accommodate our girls, and as we left she said cheerfully, "Remember now. Black shoes. No *dancing* shoes."

Walking home, Leslee said, "It's silly to have so many rules about what to wear when you can walk across the street to a topless beach."

Her mother corrected her. "*One* might walk across the street to a topless beach."

"Well, I didn't mean me, Mom!" Leslee said.

Kathryn said, "I don't think I'm going to like it."

"Why not?" Honey asked.

"I just have this feeling."

"It's the black shoes," Leslee said.

Kathryn said, "I have to wear black shoes and gray socks."

"And the potato sack, and don't forget the hat," Leslee said. "Really nasty uniforms. Gray polyester potato sacks and awful caps and I already know that they yell at you and you get in trouble if you don't wear the caps. The shoes are clunkers but not too bad. And the blazers won't be so bad."

"Everybody else will be wearing the same thing," I said.

Kathryn said, "But I know how bad *I'll* look and I won't know what *they'll* look like until they get there."

For dinner everyone wanted something different, and to eat at different times, until finally the exasperated lioness declared that we would have hamburgers. Then the gas stove wouldn't work, so we had tacos.

Leslee said, between tacos, "Mom, did you know you had us believing there were kangaroos and wallabies and kookaburras everywhere in Australia before we came and I haven't seen one."

"You could have asked me," Drew said.

"I've seen a lot," Will said.

"Where?" Kathryn demanded to know.

"At the zoo, but they weren't all in the best shape," Will said.

Honey said, "I saw more deer in Nashville when I was running than I've seen kangaroo in our first two weeks in Sydney."

The end of dinner was a relief. Especially with the tension of the girls' first day of school tomorrow I could see a nuclear-family explosion coming. It began to dawn on me why parents invented school. After two weeks of such thick living together in Australia, we were all ready for some organized relief from just sitting around with nothing to do but focus on each other. School would provide that. Even Leslee and Kathryn looked forward to it, despite potato sacks and black shoes and gray socks.

After dinner everyone became busy. Drew cleaned up after the tacos. I tried to fix the gas grill. Leslee and Kathryn washed dishes, and Honey explained to Will why he had gotten in trouble earlier in the day when she had ordered him to clean up his room and he had demanded to stay outside under the lemon tree playing with his trucks.

"It was for not respecting your parents," Honey was saying.

"Where does that idea come from anyway?" Will asked.

Kathryn said, "It's in the Ten Commandments."

So when the kitchen was clean, Kathryn and Will got out the Bible and Honey read the Ten Commandments out loud. When Will came upstairs for bed, he let me know that "the part about the mountain and the fire and the smoke was really cool."

The next morning I stationed myself in the breakfast area.

"Don't say a word," warned Leslee, who was the first to appear. She was uniformed: gray dress, red ribbon around her ponytail, tie, gray socks, black shoes.

I said nothing.

"I know you're going to say something."

"I have resolved not to say anything."

"See, you said something."

Fifteen minutes later Kathryn stumbled in, her wet hair straight and stringy and an oversized potato sack pathetically draped over her slight frame.

All she could say was, "Girls don't wear ties."

I tried to help, but I couldn't figure out how to tie a tie that was not around my neck, so Leslee tied Kathryn's.

"Just feel this bag, Dad," Kathryn said as she staggered up the outside steps with her satchel filled with books and lunch. I felt so sorry for the girls that this once I agreed to drive them the half-mile to school, but first Leslee took off her black shoes and laid one under each back wheel of the car.

"Drive over my shoes, please," Leslee said.

The request was so shocking I did it.

"Didn't do much. Do it again, please," she said. I did it again and she seemed satisfied to have properly run-over black shoes.

Driving down Plunkett Road, we saw other girls in uniforms and hats, and boys in uniforms and straw hats.

Leslee pouted. "You even have to wear the hat walking to school."

"And *from* school," Kathryn sadly reminded her.

At dinner after that first day of school I asked, as gently as I could, "How was it?"

Kathryn slumped in her chair. Leslee, who had been snapping at any provocation, gave this report: "Well, I walked in in my funky uniform and I didn't know where to go and there was Tara who was my showing-around-person who was very nice and she took me to class and I had no idea what was going on and every one spoke different than I did. When I said I was from America they would ask me if I knew so-and-so from Colorado or from California and of course I didn't. People would ask, 'When did you get here?' And 'Will you talk for us?' And did we date? All the maths and sciences are different and combined in one course. There're cliques but I'll meet nice people, but I won't meet any boys. Tell me again why I can't go to the government high school, like Drew."

I tried to reassure her. "Leslee, you're going to fit in fine."

Leslee exploded. "Dad, you don't realize how hard this is for us, to be *accepted.*"

While Leslee was letting off steam, Kathryn was practicing an easy Bach fugue on the dining room table. She had started tapping her fingers on the airplane tray table during the long flight to Sydney, and now did it so regularly that I had rented a piano, which had not yet arrived.

Honey interrupted Kathryn's fingerwork. "How was *your* day?"

"Could have been better," Kathryn answered.

"Well, tomorrow will be better, certainly," her mother said.

"I'd like to go home tonight," Kathryn said and continued the Bach fugue until everyone was permitted to leave the table.

N E W F I R S T
T H I N G S

//

Living is the constant adjustment of
thought to life and life to thought in
such a way that we are always
growing, always experiencing new
things in the old and old things in the
new. Thus life is always new.
— THOMAS MERTON
Thoughts in Solitude

"I don't need transport. I'm self-sufficient." Drew walked
out at 7:40, almost without saying good-bye. He was on
his way to be one of sixty new students getting acquainted the
first day of Mosman High School's new year.

A week earlier Mrs. Pitts, the principal, had told us, "We
expect seven hundred sixty-one altogether, grades seven through

twelve, but class size still ought to be twenty-five in Andrew's eleventh grade. We require uniforms through the tenth and after that most of the boys wear gray pants and a white shirt."

That afternoon after school Drew was not happy. "They could tell right away I was an American. It was something about my clothes."

"Maybe it was those shoes," I said.

"Probably was. They said only *tourists* wear flip-flops [sandals with thongs]. They thought my accent was funny and that *theirs* was normal English. They try to be American, but it's the America they know from TV. They talk about America all the time, but they don't want you to think they do. I hear them doing it. They talk more about President Reagan than we do at home."

Drew had been on top of the world when he had left America for Australia. He had spent a month kayaking off the Pacific coast of Baja California at a National Outdoors Leadership School. He was very proud of it when he arrived in Sydney: "It was one hundred in the day and it stormed a lot and sometimes we couldn't get off the water in time. Kayaks don't handle waves so well. Once we flipped and had to swim through six-foot breakers, maybe a hundred yards to the beach. We damaged four kayaks and it was five days before we could leave. We were low on water and low on food and at night we had to look out for tarantulas and scorpions in our sleeping bags."

Before this kayaking experience Drew had finished a strong school semester in Nashville and before that, he had spent two weeks at guitar camp and then worked hard outdoors in the mountains. But before these successes, he had had such a truly miserable sophomore year at school in New Hampshire that the rector had suggested that it might be better if Drew did not return. This crushed Drew who lived so much to attend that school. So he proposed to the rector a program of work and study and outdoors adventure, and succeeded so well at it that the rector had welcomed him back. Drew had just learned about this in December, so he was feeling great when after kayaking he flew from California to Sydney.

"But when I got to Sydney I felt worse than I have ever felt in my life," he said to me after that first day at Mosman High. "To start with, I flew all night and I was tired, and then I was in this alien world ten thousand miles from anything and everybody I knew. All I had was my guitar. The first day Leslee and I walked down the beach and I thought, 'Those are all the people who will be in school. How am I ever going to meet them all?' I knew it was going to be hard. It's not so easy to meet the people you really want to meet."

Will was quick to point out to us each new "first thing" he accomplished in Australia, but it was not going to be an easy adjustment for him, either. When we visited Balmoral Infants School, we learned that he would be the twenty-fourth second-grade student and the only American. His teacher, Mrs. Locke, who was also the principal, showed us around. "This was a postwar baby-boom school. It opened in 1952 when the babies were all seven. The metal buildings were sent from London, very inappropriate for our climate in the summer. Please excuse the mess. We've been away on summer vacation since December 17."

Balmoral Infants School had one kindergarten class, one first-grade class, and Mrs. Locke's own second-grade class—a total of sixty-nine students. "We have a very strong parents' group," Mrs. Locke said. "The children learn to read according to their ability. Uniforms aren't compulsory. You need to bring lunch because we have no canteen at all. We begin at nine and leave at three twenty-five. It's small but I hope they don't close it. It's just perfect. Everybody knows everybody. Anyone can come who wants to."

I walked with Will to his first full school day. "I won't even know where to put my lunch," he said sadly. The day before, on our visit, Mrs. Locke had assigned a student greeter to Will. But today there was no greeter. Five little Australian boys stood talking in the playground, their tanned arms and legs sticking out of blue pants and light blue shirts. I said good-bye and walked almost around the corner and waited and watched. Will hesitated, then approached the boys. The Australians ran away to play on a tower. Will walked after them. They ignored him. Will played by himself in the sand. He looked hurt and, watching, I was sure I hurt even more. I wanted to go comfort him, to help him with his new life. After four or five minutes, which seemed like forever, the other boys climbed down from the tower and began playing and Will joined the game. Then the bell rang and the Australian boys ran to their classrooms, leaving Will to walk by himself.

"Why are you leaving so early?" Honey had asked on *my* first day of school. I had signed up for two all-day lessons to learn how to use a personal computer.

I said, "I want to have plenty of time when I get there to size things up, and get settled." In fact, I was nervous. I returned to the house to get a sweater in case the classroom was air-conditioned. Although I double-checked the route and the address, when I reached the city I missed the Grosvenor Street exit from the expressway.

Honey joined me for the second day of classes, and I discovered that for a husband and wife to take computer lessons together can be worse than teaching each other to play tennis. Honey and I sat side by side. The same teacher gave us the same instructions at the same time. But Honey's printer always started a little ahead of mine, and her hands were folded in her lap, her lesson finished, while I was still struggling. As we drove home, I told her, "I know now just what it would have been like sitting next to you in Texas in the ninth grade. You would have driven me crazy, being so cute and smarter, too."

When we reached home in Mosman, half-filled Coke glasses cluttered the TV room, crumbled potato chips littered the floor, and Will's trucks sat on the dining room table. Honey's eyes got that look and she said, "When we get our own computer, I'm going to use it to allocate chores. I'm getting tired of being the maid and the dishwasher and the grocery-store shopper as well as the cook. This family eats all the time."

"Other families eat all the time, too," said Kathryn, who had begun helping to pick up.

Honey said, "But most families eat at the *same* time. Most families haven't lived for eight years in a house with a short-order cook."

My most memorable "new first thing" was learning again how to drive. My training car was affectionately named "the Tank," a Ford Falcon wagon that I rented from an airport entrepreneur who offered the best rate.

Honey and I went to pick up the car, I paid for it, and climbed into the driver's seat.

I put my camera into the glove compartment, and the glove compartment dropped to the floorboard.

"I'll get that," said the entrepreneur. And when he had reinserted it, he added, "One thing to show you—the gear indicator is broken, but you can feel the gears change nicely. Just take care not to confuse reverse and drive."

He sounded so reasonable that I thanked him and felt reassured until my right foot pushed against a metal stub in the place where the gas pedal should have been.

"There's no gas pedal," I remarked.

"Right. You'll find it quite operable," the entrepreneur said confidently.

I buckled my seat belt, which nearly ripped it from its moorings. I was embarrassed suddenly to realize that Honey was still waiting outside because the door on her side would not open. "It opens nicely from the inside," I said, getting into the spirit of things, but when I leaned across to open the door, my seat belt ripped out completely.

The Tank had no power steering—but I had not thought to ask about that before I paid. I *was* able to open the windows, which was fortunate since the air conditioner did not work.

Honey held on grimly to the shotgun seat, while I maneuvered the Tank into a fast-moving expressway flow of smaller American and Japanese cars. Motoring along in our newly acquired Tank, I felt like an aging sousaphone player marching with the high-school drum and bugle corps.

I accepted much abuse during that week of learning how to drive again—and learning to do it on the wrong side of the road. One of the things I also learned was that I could often drive best by watching Honey instead of the road. For example, Honey's fingers drumming on her right knee meant that the Tank was veering to the right. Honey gripping her right knee meant the car was off the road. Honey suddenly sitting erect and slapping both hands to her forehead meant we were about to hit something. Tapping the dashboard meant, go a little faster now. Occasionally Honey would issue helpful screams about things coming from the right.

After seven days I turned in the Tank and began looking for an Australian car that would fit a family of six. It took a month. Finally Holden dealer Barry Smith put an extra seat in the back of a new Commodore Wagon and sold it to us. Five months later, when we left Australia, he cheerfully bought it back at a stated price even though changes in the value of the dollar must have cost him most of his profit.

During that month, we all missed the Tank, but having no car meant we walked more and learned the bus routes and discovered that riding the ferry to the city was cheaper and nearly as fast as driving. But occasionally we all felt a terrible locked-up sensation of being in unfamiliar territory, not able to go where we wanted to go when we wanted to go.

Learning to drive and how to operate a computer were not my only adjustments. One evening, as Drew and I sat back to watch a tape of a championship basketball game an American friend had sent, I discovered that American VCR tapes didn't work on an Australian VCR. Another time I had to pay two hundred dollars for a step-down transformer for my new Macintosh computer because Australian voltage is 220 instead of 110. I was making all my own appointments and answering my own mail—which began to consume more than an hour a day. I was trying to be assistant mother and learned that my schedule sometimes had to fit into Honey's and that occasionally I needed to be a part of the whole family. On some days I yearned for my old ruts. So much new learning made me feel like a rusty bolt twisting and not fitting.

We all did so many "new first things" that gradually we began to create new patterns and sink into new ruts. I vividly remember one Friday night five weeks after we had arrived in Sydney. We had attended a reading of Australian poet Mary Gilmore's work. Afterward I drove home the way I used to in America, confidently and almost without thinking. I walked upstairs easily without lights so as not to disturb the children, and went to sleep wound down instead of wound up, thinking of our base camp now as a familiar place. I was becoming comfortable in a routine of learning new habits rather than struggling hard to unlearn bad ones. I was planning less, and opening myself up to more. I was thinking of Sydney now as a familiar place, thinking for the first time that I was settled.

That calm almost exploded the next morning when the Reagan White House staff turned upside down because of the Iran-contra affair, and the telephone rang at odd hours with invitations and suggestions about returning sooner to America. But when it became clear that I would not go back to help out the White House, and that nothing in the presidential campaigns was going to pull me away from my family, either, I felt serene and happy and rooted in our new home.

Neighbors invited Honey to play tennis and those matches led to luncheons and more friends. At the Graham Crawfords' first-week "welcome to Sydney" party, Drew met Billy King, who lived only four blocks away and also liked the guitar. Soon our basement became a favorite place for jam sessions. From almost the first day, Leslee, as well as Drew, brought friends home from school. Kathryn spent the night with Sharon Hacker, a classmate who had lived for a year in Los Angeles. Will began to insist on going to school at least thirty minutes early to play with his new friends.

We knew Will was growing more independent when he made his first long-distance telephone call. It was to his best friend, John Austin Echols, in Nashville. Will told John about school and then was doing some explaining:

"While we're talking, there's this big telephone line that goes right under the ocean. That's how we talk. It only costs a dollar a minute to have this phone call going through it. This is the longest phone call in my life. . . ."

There was a long silence at our end. John Austin must have been saying something.

Then Will said, "Well, I have one or two. But you're my *best* friend—*in the whole world.*"

CHAPTER 1 7

THIS IS AUSTRALIA!

//

"The only thing that makes Australia
what it is is the landscape. What else
is there?"

—Ross Terrill
quoting Arthur Boyd,
The Australians

Seven of us were crowded into the Aero Commander.
"We'll swoop to drive the kangaroos off the runway,"
the Pig Man said. "It's bloody dangerous to land without swoop-
ing in first. Brumbies [wild horses] are the worst. They'll turn
and run when they hear the plane and they may run at you
instead of away from you."

The Pig Man was Jack Giles, assistant director of the New
South Wales Park Service. He had lived for eight years, two
weeks at a time, by himself in the harshest environment of the

Australian bush, trying to get rid of wild pigs there and to control the problems they caused. Another passenger on the plane was John Whitehouse, a lawyer and archaeologist who now headed the park service, along with two of his employees. And their overall boss and my host was Bob Carr, a Labor party member of the state parliament, whose title was Minister of Heritage and the Environment. Minister Carr's sprawling territory, the state of New South Wales, is larger than one tenth of the continental United States, although it has less population—four million— than Tennessee or Washington State. Three of those four million live in one coastal city, Sydney.

Flying west from Sydney we had watched the landscape change. "During the glacial period Sydney's harbor was a sunken valley that filled when the sea rose," John Whitehouse, the park director, explained. He added that Sydney itself spread from the ocean to a rim of distant mountains, the Blue Mountains.

"How high are they?"

"Some, seven thousand feet, but most, no more than five thousand."

"About as high as the Smokies, the largest ones in the eastern U.S."

John said, "There are a million hectares of national park around Sydney."

"Someone was thinking ahead," I said.

"Australia's Royal National Park was begun in 1879. It's the second oldest in the world after your Yellowstone."

We passed over the mountains quickly, then the land was flat and a dull dry green, not the rich wet green of western North Carolina or the Pacific Northwest. There were trees every three or four meters and neatly sectioned wheatfields.

"It's the best wheat land in Australia, although there's only twenty inches of rainfall a year." As we flew on, the color of the land slipped to brown with a tinge of red. "Maybe fourteen inches here, one wheat crop every five to seven years."

"How can you make a living on one wheat crop every five to seven years?" I asked.

"Barely can," said the government minister, Bob Carr. "The average-sized property in western New South Wales might be thirty thousand acres with one person working it.

There's almost no unemployed labor in the western territory anymore. A farmer might have $250,000 [Australian] dollars' worth of land with a half-million dollars' worth of machinery and rely on one wheat crop every five to seven years."

John Whitehouse said, "From here on west to Perth—about twenty-five hundred miles—it looks the same except for a few outcroppings. Old, old, old land—oldest in the world. Mountains once as tall as the Himalayas have been weathered and ground down to six hundred feet, until now nothing geologically ever happens. It's just sediment on sediment on sediment."

After we had been flying nearly two hours, the runway we had been watching for appeared. The land around it was red tinged with green, like northern Arizona after a rain.

The pilot circled and landed, the airplane stirring up red dust.

It was ten minutes before five when the plane door opened downward. The pilot motioned for me to be the first one out. I uncrouched, then emerged from the coolness of the plane and felt as if I were leading a procession into some dreadful outdoor furnace. The afternoon heat was so strong that I had to stand up straight to clear my head. The ground smelled rotten, as though it had been burning for centuries. I saw that the bush looked more blue than I had thought it would and the sky was an even more wondrous blue. I began to sense the vast emptiness of this land. Most startling were the big black buzzing flies that descended upon us immediately, biting wherever they landed. They swarmed so thick that I instinctively lifted my camera and photographed the layer of flies that coated the white-shirted back of the minister of the environment and natural resources, for I had never seen anything like it.

The park director was the last to emerge from the plane. He stepped onto the runway, then onto the red baked earth, proclaimed, "THIS is Australia!" and stood looking for a while without saying anything else.

We said good-bye to one passenger, a conservation worker named Judy. We left her sitting alone on a bench at the empty airport, waiting for someone to come pick her up. The rest of us got into a park service helicopter, which had been waiting to fly us north.

The late sun was still hot through the many-windowed helicopter. "The first settlers said the ground looked like picnic grasses," said John, "but now the woody weeds have taken over because of the sheep grazing and the rabbit and the fox." I thoroughly understood him when he said that most Australians are tourists in their own country, visitors to their own dreamland. Ten million of the sixteen million Australians live in just seven coastal cities. This pioneering rowdy bushland—the lair of Crocodile Dundee—is the most urbanized nation in the world. Most Sydney children have never crossed the Blue Mountains to see the *real* Australia. Indeed, this was the minister's first time this far out. And the park director? "I'm here twice a year if I'm lucky," said John Whitehouse.

The endless landscape below the helicopter looked like a giant child's paint playground. It was as if some huge child, on hands and knees, had first smeared red and brown all over a boundless floor, and then stood back and thrown handfuls of green at it, and then smeared on some more brown and red this time lightly so that the green seeped through in lots of unexpected places—this was the green tinge that had lasted after the rain. Then the giant child had had some real fun, using fingers to spread all around in waves and designs: patches, spots, splotches, tentacles of green, in a vast moonscape, conjuring up images in the way that clouds do—images of a bird's claw, a scarecrow walking, a man thinking, like Rodin's sculpture.

Below us, swamps looked like meteor craters filled with gray mud. "It's an odd river system," said John. "Rivers flow to the center of our continent, creating gray lakes that turn green. The birds start to breed within six weeks after it rains and the rivers are cultivated until they dry up. The Paroo River, where we are going, starts in the north in Queensland and spreads down into New South Wales as lakes. There are no real river channels.

"Starting now as far as you can see this was one man's land," he said. Two trucks on a long, thin brown road stirred up clouds of red dust that trailed for a mile. A voice on the radio crackled a welcome to us. It sounded especially friendly as I realized there were not many voices in this vastness. I saw a pair of emus running.

The horizon was whitish gray, merging with darkening

blue. Then I saw a metal roof gleaming, and a barn and sheds. It was a homestead on what had been the Nocoleche sheep station. The helicopter circled and fluttered to land on what was now a new state park.

When I stepped out of the helicopter, something bit me that was not a fly.

"It's the mozzies. The wet brings them out," said John. "Mozzies" meant mosquitoes. (Australians abbreviate everything. Youngsters will say, "How's your Chrisie?," meaning "How has your Christmas vacation been?"; or "my olds," meaning "my parents.")

"Doesn't take the rain to bring mozzies out," said the park ranger who met us and drove us to our quarters. He and his family lived on the Nocoleche station.

A rain barrel of drinking water stood outside the abandoned sheepshearers' cottage with corrugated metal walls and wood floors where we were to spend the night. Inside aluminum cots held mattresses with torn covers. Ants crawled everywhere on the mattresses. The kitchen had a pie safe that would keep out the mice and flies, and the only other room featured an old brick fireplace. A generator rumbled in the background, furnishing electricity for the light bulbs that already were burning brightly in every room. The front screen doors were left open, a tacit admission that trying to repel the mozzies would be futile. Clearly, for them this cottage was an oasis and we represented an unexpected feast. After a while no one even bothered to swat them—or the flies, either. I could readily understand why frantic swatting motions are called the "Australian Salute."

"My God!" exclaimed the minister. "How did the settlers find this hospitable?"

"They weren't looking for hospitality when they came, I believe, just for a place to graze sheep," John Whitehouse said.

Before this visit I had done some reading about the first Europeans who penetrated the northwestern area of New South Wales about 1830. They had come up the Darling River from Adelaide in southern Australia. The sheep loved and fattened on the grass, which grew then to their shoulder blades. The settlers would mark the boundaries, shoot the resident aborigines, and control the waters. "They would just sit on it," John explained.

"The size of their holding was measured by the area you could fill with sheep. This one had a million acres. It was harsh, but even the surveyors dressed for dinner each night, in tails."

"Tails?"

"Some of the homesteads even had tennis courts."

We walked out into the backyard to watch the red sunset, and presented ourselves to a new and eager army of flies and mozzies.

John continued. "Today it's so overgrazed that maybe six sheep an acre is all you can put on it, or maybe a wheat crop every three to seven years. It's not such good cattle country. The land is priced above its value as production land. No labor plus high cost fuel plus an uncertain world market plus only a few good seasons makes it a hard living, almost an impossible one. That's why the park service gets the properties. The smaller properties now are sixteen thousand to thirty thousand acres. Anything less is not economical."

The next time I looked up the sky was black and filled with stars, their brightness threatened only by the blazing round moon, edging up over the horizon behind the coolabah trees. Emily, the seven-year-old daughter of the ranger who lived on the sheep station, looked through my binoculars. "They're round!" she shouted as if she had never seen stars like that before.

I said to the group, "I've never seen the Southern Cross."

Jack Giles, the Pig Man, took from his shirt pocket a package of Tally-Ho cigarette paper and from his jeans a pouch of Port Royal tobacco. Patiently he shook the tobacco into his right hand and put away the pouch as, with his left hand, he bent the paper in half. He pressed the tobacco into the paper and rolled it slowly, leaving a clean edge. He licked the edge, tamped down one end of the cigarette with his mouth, and lit the other end.

Then Jack said, "The Southern Cross. It's a good south. I've used it many times. Look." He pointed to a place two thirds of the way high in the sky. "It's lying on its side. Look for five stars, that's the cross, and then look for two more below it—they're the pointers."

For the first time, I recognized the cross. It was obvious. Then Jack showed me how to use the stars to draw two lines in the sky—one that crossed "the pointers," perpendicularly, and one that ran through the whole length of the cross. "Imagine those two lines and then run them out until they cross, down low in the sky. That will be south. You can count on it," he said.

Now the moon was over the coolabah trees and everyone was stargazing.

Emily's father, the Nocoleche station ranger, spoke in a tone that was absolutely serious. "When Armstrong put his foot on the moon he knocked things off balance. You stop and think about it. We had twenty-five inches of rain not too long after he landed. There were sunspots after that. Hasn't rained twenty-five inches since. He knocked things a bit off."

John Whitehouse said, "There is Mars, low in the west."

And there was the outer edge of our own galaxy, the Milky Way, strewn across the sky. As our eyes adjusted to the darkness, we saw more stars, and then with the binoculars, more and more, and even other galaxies.

Emily's father spoke again. "Nothing like that sort of rain since Armstrong put his foot on the moon." He paused and looked straight at me. "We're a long way from civilization, so we think of these things."

Some of the park officials slept outside the cottage. I slept inside in a corner on one of the aluminum cots, hoping the fresh supply of park officials outside would satisfy the mozzies. For protection, I kept my clothes on and tucked my long pants inside my wool socks, wrapped an extra shirt around my hands, draped my pajama tops over my face, and pulled the pajama bottoms over my head. I must have looked strange, sweating inside my sleeping bag, but it must have confused the mozzies, for they left me alone and I slept well.

At dawn the next morning before breakfast we took a walk, which became a lesson in paying close attention to things I would never have noticed. "What looks like arrows pointing in the mud are emu tracks," said Jack, the Pig Man. "And those over there are snake marks." The muddy road by the river was filled with different types of marks and tracks. For instance, beneath a large bush at one side were two scooped places in the red dirt. "Kangaroo slept there last night," Jack said. "See, the tracks are in one place, four claws and the tail, resting. A nice hieroglyphic." He pointed to another trail. "Those are pig. Pigs drag their feet."

During the next hour's walk, we saw a whistling kite's nest, an eagle's nest, a fox skull. "Foxes can even climb trees," Jack said. By seven A.M. the sun was already strong and hot. He commented, "Could be forty-two today, that's about one hundred ten Fahrenheit. Gets up to forty-five sometimes." We passed a hill of ferocious-looking ants scurrying about their morning chores, and Jack picked something up carefully. "Cat's-head burr. The most vicious burr. You can hear it crunching under your feet." I wondered how the aborigines walked on those, as well as on the burning hot sand, barefooted.

I asked Jack how long he had lived out here in these conditions where we were.

"About eight and a half years. I'd come out about two weeks at a time by myself and then go back to Sydney and then return here." He pointed. "See the old abo campsite?"

I saw nothing.

"The rocks. This river has no rocks of any kind, so the aborigines must have brought these in. Maybe ten thousand years ago and the rocks are still here because nothing has happened here in the last ten thousand years."

"I'm highly skeptical," said Jack's boss, the government minister.

Jack picked up a small, sharp stone. "It's silcrete. Doesn't exist here. Comes from the hills. They carried it here to use as a cutting blade. And they brought in corestones from twenty or thirty kilometers to fracture tools." He stopped and pointed. "This is a grinding stone."

The minister picked it up and examined it and said, "That's credible."

"An abo tribe might have had twenty to fifty people. They'd camp by the river in family groups. They fished by the river, caught shellfish, birds, game. They camped on the edge of these depressions. The river fed them, and everything that fed off the river fed them. They might kill a kangaroo and just throw it on the fire. They would stay until the food became a bit harder to get, then they'd move on and years later might come back again to these same sites."

Jack pointed to a plant. "Nadi," he said. "That's what the explorers Burke and Wills lived on when they were lost."

Although there was some breeze, the band of my Stetson

was wet with sweat. (I had been surveying each ranger's hat and had concluded that an Akubra, Snowy River model, size 58, was what I would buy when I got back to Sydney so I would have a real Australian hat to at least temporarily replace my American Stetson.)

"Where else did the aborigines live?" I couldn't forget what Jack had said about the aboriginal people once having been wantonly shot, and I told him. Jack said, "Some places, it was worse than that. Once a band of Europeans rode through an abo camp here, swinging stirrup irons, killing them, and some others put strychnine in flour and left it on a convenient post for the abos to find. And they would put big-jawed bear traps around that would trap them.

"The abos go back at least forty thousand years. We're pretty sure of that now. Then, the kangaroos were twelve feet tall and the wombats six feet. The abos lived all over Australia. Europeans live only on the edge of Australia. After two hundred years here, Europeans still don't adapt very well. Burke and Wills died along Cooper's Creek, which is full of fish they apparently didn't know how to catch. The abos would have caught the fish. The *Sirius,* one of the ships in the first fleet, wrecked on Norfolk Island with fish all round, but the English ate maggoty meat instead, and the first settlers never ate much kangaroo because it wasn't considered proper food. The abos eat anything—plants, moth larvae. They discovered gallons of drinking water in the roots of the mallie plants. They love freshwater crayfish. In the north, where the crocs are, the abo women stand in the water on the edge of the billabong and catch snakes with their toes and crack their necks with their teeth and then throw them on the fire and cook and eat them. The abos have learned to live all over Australia."

I told Jack I certainly couldn't envy his being alone in that country.

"Wasn't entirely by myself. I had dogs. Learned to work with dogs. I was like the dominant dog. The others followed me. They were bloody smart. Anytime I put my fingers to my lips—the way you do when you want quiet—they would react. I didn't always realize I was doing it. I was unaware what my body was doing instinctively. But they understood, even if I didn't.

"You notice things. I learned to smell things that usually only the dogs could smell, to be hyperalert as they were. For instance, if something moved quickly, I'd spin down and crouch. Then when I'd go back to Sydney and walk along Kent Street, I'd hear a noise, I'd start to spin and crouch. The city desensitizes you until your instincts don't react. Try it sometime. Just keep track of all the noises in the city which in the bush would make you spin and crouch."

"I imagine you'd see some pretty hyper instincts come alive again if you brought some city folks out here," I said.

Jack smiled. "Yeh. But in the bush, the pace is so much slower, like I said, you notice things. About dusk is when things come alive. Most of the animals wake up, and then in the early night they are busy feeding, drinking, breeding. Then the middle of the night is dead, hardly any activity. They're sleeping again. Then at dawn you can see them get up again, scratching, feeding, breeding awhile, then back to sleep for the day."

"What about the pigs?"

"They're not native, they tear everything up. I've learned a lot about pigs. They'll eat other pigs for example, if they're out of food. But still they have feelings. Once I trapped and shot a sow and killed her four little piglets and threw one at the sow. She savaged it, then put her head on it and cried.

"I've seen animals forgoing food for other animals. I saw a kangaroo standing on the trail transfixed where her mate was shot, wouldn't leave the other hurt animal."

The Pig Man stopped walking. "They have a language among themselves, the animals, and, if we pay attention, a language to humans, too. Watch a kangaroo as you walk toward him. . . ."

Even I could respond to that. "They run, then they stop and turn those horsey faces around," I said.

"They're looking to see if they can trust you, or if you're something they should worry about, something not supposed to be there, something about to put their environment out of order."

We had walked back to a long sheep-shearing shed with heavy wood floors, metal sides, and a galvanized metal top.

"Australia's wealth was accumulated in sheds like these," said the minister, Bob Carr.

John Whitehouse added, "It was hard, hot work. See the roof is raised on each side so the breeze can draft in. The only occupant now is that boobook owl, just there."

The owl's cold stare reminded me of the North Korean guards' stare at Panmunjom—imperious eyes never leaving mine, from a distance, narrowing that distance. The owl's brown-and-white feathers framed him against the galvanized metal top of the shearing shed.

"Wool from sheds like these started us off as 'The Lucky Country,'" said Minister Carr. "Then came the gold discoveries in Victoria in the 1880s, and by the end of the nineteenth century, we had the highest per-capita income in the world. After the war, we sold our coal, and then when synthetics started hurting wool, our wheat helped. We've boomed on minerals, on the great iron ore in Western Australia, on Queensland's open-cut low sulfur coal to Japan and Europe. We found energy offshore in the Bass Strait, which made us nearly as oil-sufficient as you in the U.S., and we sell our offshore gas from Western Australia to Japan.

"From 1900 to World War Two we used tariffs to build a protected manufacturing base—for example, steel and cars. Our electricity was cheap because of coal.

"But it's hard to keep a string of luck like that going forever. Nobody wants our iron ore now. Europe protects its farmers, growing wheat, cane, sugar. Our beef can't get into Japan because the Japanese legislators elected from farm districts block it out. The U.S. has tariffs on our minerals and uses subsidies to undercut our wheat prices even though you have a trade surplus with us. There's a somewhat popular book out about Australia entitled *The Worst Is Yet to Come*. The author says we're on a downhill slide because we won't change and we can't be lucky forever. He has a following."

We had arrived back at the cottage and sat on the front porch in the shade while the temperature climbed. When I walked into the sun I could actually feel my skin shrink from the irradiation.

I got out my notebook and said, laughing, "Help me. I can't remember all the things that make this place so inhospitable."

"Start with the heat," said John Whitehouse. "Up to forty-six or forty-eight degrees centigrade. That's one hundred twenty Fahrenheit. Heat so bad you can't walk, can't do anything, can't even lie down and be comfortable through the night."

"No water," said Jack, the Pig Man. "Even the rivers dry up here. This place and one other place about fifty kilometers away are the only permanent water sources in all of western New South Wales.

"Flies," said Minister Carr. "You're fortunate that these aren't the kind that bite and suck your blood until they're gorged. Some say that's why we Aussies talk with our mouths closed, to keep out the flies."

There began an intense competition to complete my list.

"Mozzies, even bigger than in your Minnesota."

"Sandflies."

"The soil. Red sandy soil. Gray black stuff near the water. When it's wet it sticks to you until you can't move. When it's dry dust storms choke you and ruin your engines' motors."

"No transport. No way to get anywhere. Once when the Darling River dried up there was no transport for two years. You just got stuck in the mud and cane grass three feet high."

"Don't forget the abos."

"I didn't think they were dangerous," I said.

"Not like your Indians. They didn't use guns. But sometimes they were dangerous because they feared for their lives."

"Appendicitis. There was nothing to do for you if your appendix burst in the bush."

"Snakes," said Jack. "That's the one good thing about wild pigs. They eat snakes. Nearly all the snakes are poisonous. The Western Brown is very venomous and aggressive. Step on 'im and he'll rise up to your shoulder height, his head as big as your wrist. And the death adder—he wiggles his tail to attract birds—has the most deadly venom in the world. King Brown, too. Hope you never step on one barefoot."

"They are all around here?" I asked, writing furiously.

"Sure are."

"Well, at least there aren't any dangerous *animals*," I suggested.

"Well, we've got the saltwater croc in the north. He'll take you quick. And the Tasmanian devil down south. He'll bite you. But not here, you're right."

"Don't forget scorpions."

"Or hornets. Oh, we've got world-class hornets. And ants that can bite into bones," said Jack. "And our dry lightning storms. No rain, just awful thunderbolts."

"And the remoteness," one of the park officials said. "Only sixty-six employees lived on this sheep station in 1964. No telephone. And the mail rider came every month or two. Until the motor cars came in about 1945–50, you relied on each other for entertainment. Before the cars came, the towns were nine miles apart, day's drive for a bullock team bringing in supplies or hauling out wood. Then, with the cars, towns went to twenty miles apart . . . now they are fifty."

"And in all of that, they dressed in tails for dinner?"

"The men wore tails, the ladies put on high lace collars in one-hundred-twenty-degree heat and their Irish housekeeper served the meals."

When a plane arrived to take us to the Yathong Nature Park, two hundred miles south, just sitting out on the field awaiting takeoff was like being in a sauna turned up full-bore. Then finally the plane wove down the bumpy, dusty runway and bounced into the air.

Honey had flown to meet us at the next site, which was even dustier and windier. White clouds streaked across the sky. There had been five inches of rain within the last month, and the land was greener than usual. Herds of emus bounced across the bushland, flouncing and prancing, something like a gaggle of British ladies running home from afternoon bridge.

Honey said, "It's like South Texas." And I felt more at home, too, almost seasoned to the new environment. After only two days in the bush I had acquired a sense of what could kill me, and knowing that made me more at ease.

With the Pig Man and John Whitehouse, we set out looking for kangaroos to photograph, but we stopped and sat by a tank (pond) to watch the daily sunset gathering of the galahs, common Australian parrots. The sun was to our back and when we sat down at 5:45, no galahs were to be seen. Then two appeared on the tree across the tank, then three more. These five were all sentries who flew excitedly over the tank looking all around; whereupon four more galahs, seeing the first five had made it safely, moved in to join them. They all sported white heads, red necks, gray coats, and red vests that shone in the setting sun. Then another pair came, and another, until a thick group of galahs walked slowly about, squawking and conferring, then they suddenly all flew to the tank to get a drink.

The sun was setting fast behind the clouds as we turned away. Two kangaroos, a young male, red, and a young female, gray, hopped a safe distance away, then stopped and stared at us with their horsey faces, then hopped away again, racing along, their strange paunchy bodies almost parallel to the ground, looking as if they were *really* going somewhere.

We returned home to Sydney the next day, flying low in a park service helicopter. As we left the moonscape of the western territory of New South Wales, the fields grew greener, the tanks for trapping water grew more numerous, and the Blue Mountains looked as refreshing as the Green Mountains of Vermont. Lightning streaked from dark clouds on our left, but there was a rainbow ahead over the mountains. Like a roller coaster we whirred over the mountains. It was startling to see the Sydney basin again, the swimming pools, sometimes ten in a row, in the western suburbs, some alongside orchards and row crops, but especially the red-tiled roofs and the tower of downtown Sydney. We landed in a drizzling rain at about 5:00 P.M. and John Whitehouse offered us a ride home to Mosman.

As we crossed the harbor bridge, Honey said, "We've been here for nearly two months and this is the first time I really feel as though I've seen Australia."

John said, "Cities are the same anymore, aren't they? At least at first. Live in Sydney a long time and you might find its subtleties. But to learn a country flat out, you have to go to where it came from. It's only out in the bush that you can see what Australia's really like."

"The oldest daughter knows what to do, but the rest of us will
need help."

Drew, before discovering
Donkeyhead: "It's just a
family picnic."

Drew: "I'm riding
Donkeyhead!"

Honey and Will: "He can
talk to me better when he
touches me."

Honey and I found
ourselves holding on to each
other more.

"Why don't you put your camera away and let's just look."

One of my greatest new joys was that Will and I were becoming
better acquainted.

You could walk right up to
the emus at the
Melbourne Zoo.

"Dad, I've done some new
first things in Australia."

"Did the United States invent McDonald's too?"

With the Tabuchis: Good friends, so much like us, yet so different in such a distant part of the world.

Their eyes never seemed to leave Drew's curly hair.

We were relieved they let us wear bathrobes when we tried the
healing hot sands of Beppu.

C H A P T E R   1   8

THIRTY RELATIONSHIPS

//

Whether he is part of a hunting tribe,
an industrial city, or a late twentieth
century corporation, man thus seems
to function best in groups of less than
a thousand persons and to find it
difficult to deal personally with much
more than a dozen.

—RENÉ DUBOS
A God Within

Within our family of six there are thirty relationships,
always changing. I began to discover this in Australia
when I volunteered to be the assistant mother, and it did not go
so well.

"Why are you carrying the toilet paper and paper towels, which are light, and I am carrying the three-liter bottles of Coke and mineral water, which are heavy?" Honey asked as we walked homeward after an hour of navigating our way through the narrow aisles of Franklin's Grocery.

I kept trying. That evening, I elected to help with the dishes.

"Why did you start the dishwasher?" Honey asked.

"The dishes were dirty."

"But the dishwasher wasn't full. If you wait until it's full you don't have to do it so often."

"I don't mind doing it often. I was only trying to help."

"If you want to help please take out the garbage, or the trash." And Honey went upstairs to persuade Will to take a bath.

Kathryn, who had been listening, saw her opportunity. "Assistant mommy, would you please hand me some milk?"

I said, "You are right next to the refrigerator. Can't you help yourself?"

"The real mommy would have gotten it," Kathryn said.

I took out the garbage and the trash and for good measure emptied the dishwasher now that it had stopped, and I had begun to put the dishes away when Honey walked back into the kitchen.

"Mom, he didn't let the dishes dry before he put them up," said Leslee, who'd been watching.

"I'll do it," said Honey, firmly moving between me and the dishwasher.

"I'll be glad to."

"It's easier if I do," she said.

When my career as assistant mother had stumbled so miserably, I developed a new strategy for becoming part of the family: just being there. I sat in the kitchen or in the dining room before and after meals. I sat there conspicuously, not saying anything, figuring someone would come and say something to me. I would get to know my family again by letting them get to know me.

Just being there worked sometimes, mostly in unexpected ways. For example, Drew's frustration with his broken stereo might begin a conversation that would turn into a financial analysis of how much more it would cost to pay for a new stereo by the month. Or Leslee might bring up what she was planning for the weekend, so we could talk about it without my bringing it up which would have meant that I lacked confidence in her judgment. Without being there I might never have noticed how much Kathryn and Will had drawn together in the first weeks of absence from their friends in America, or witnessed the musical dueling between Will's "Old Macdonald Had a Farm" and Kathryn's Bach fugue when the rented piano arrived. My new station in the kitchen even gave me a chance to sense Honey's feelings better: Her sternness one rainy Sydney day about who turned the dishwasher on before it was full, properly interpreted, meant: "A person who grows up in South Texas is usually a lot happier when the sun is shining." Already, I thought, in two months I have spent more time just being there than I have during the last eight years.

As time went on, I became braver and decided that family living required my more active participation. One evening, I was waiting for just the right opening, ready to say something wonderful, but just as I started, Honey turned on the garbage disposal and when the clattering was gone, so was that opportunity to insert myself into the fast-moving family saga. I settled back again to just being there, watching and waiting until somebody said something to me.

Studying family living this way, I began to see that it was not just a barrier of five family members interfering with my advances, but instead a carefully structured web of many different relationships, because in fact each member of a family has a specific relationship with each of the other members. It was so obvious that the more I considered it, the more I wondered why I had never thought about it that way before. I supposed I had been *too busy* to notice. I also began to think about the devotion each of us—especially me—had to pursuing relationships *outside* the family. Reaching for these outside relationships—friends and business and social contacts—sometimes seemed to be life's great preoccupation. It was also one of life's great frustrations because these outside relationships were seldom as satisfying as we had hoped. Still, we chased them at the expense of relationships *inside* our family, which were much more important and satisfying.

What was different about living in Australia was that our preoccupation with outside relationships had been left behind, half a world away. All the possessions of our old life were packed into two suitcases apiece. So in Sydney, we were left only with each other. There we sat facing one another—the six of us—around the dinner table, then at the breakfast table, or in the car, or watching the TV, or talking, or just sitting. To put it another way, in Australia we experienced the closest kind of family living.

I realized that back home in America, each of us had been in orbit, a planet in a family solar system, each now and then passing by another family member close enough to have some sort of relationship, but usually glad to speed on past at a safe distance and avoid the entanglements, conflicts, responsibilities, and anguish that also can accompany the joy of close relationships. Now, in Australia, that frenzied orbiting and insatiable reaching-out beyond the family was suspended—at least for a while. Now there were only six of us, or rather the thirty relationships that the six of us had with the five others.

Things became even more complex when I realized that these thirty relationships inside the family *were always changing.* I thought of our lives together as something like the changing bright-colored patterns in a slowly turning kaleidoscope. Each family life pattern is like each pattern of the kaleidoscope: such a fragile, precious long moment that you do not want to miss sharing one because you are likely never to see that pattern again. Suddenly I had a staggering thought, "How many of these intimate family experiences have I missed in being *busy?* How many of them are gone forever, never to be seen again?"

Thinking of thirty always-shifting family relationships helped answer Honey's occasional question on Saturday nights, "How could it seem so much quieter when only Drew and Leslee are gone?" It was quieter because when two of our children were away for a while, ten relationships disappeared— theirs with each of the rest of us, not to mention all the outside relationships that teenagers haul along with them. This must be why when finally all the children are gone, they leave behind exhaustion, a perplexing emptiness, and life in some sense shrivels. I thought, when Drew and Leslee and Kathryn and Will all go away to college, or to work, or to the military, or to married life, it will not be a matter of losing four children, it will mean losing twenty-eight of the thirty most intimately important relationships in our lives.

Oh, yes, relationships continue with children who are gone, as they do with brothers and sisters who have flown from the nest, but they cannot be the same. Thick living within a growing-up family can make good memories, but they are only memories. Our children will develop their own new very important relationships, most likely within *their* new families, and Honey and I will be left at the dinner table, and at the breakfast table, facing only each other as when we began.

I remember the long lunch hours on the new green grass in the cherry-blossom Washington springtime when Honey and I could not find enough time to be alone with each other; I remember my hurried phone calls to her from work in the midmornings and in the midafternoons and any other time there was any slightest excuse. I remember a stolen weekend in Williamsburg and, on Honey's first visit to Tennessee, hiking amid the autumn colors in the Great Smoky Mountains. She was the first to get to the top of Mount LeConte, not even short of breath; I remember lying together on the heavy rug, half watching Saturday television with nothing to do, and then that night being in no hurry to leave after eating manicotti in Georgetown, and turning the earth in our damp little garden in Wesley Heights, and planting "ruberous tooted" begonias and yellow Dirksen marigolds on lazy Sunday afternoons. I remember all those things we used to do when it was only the two of us at the beginning of our lives together, and I wonder what it will be like when twenty-eight of the thirty most important relationships in our life disappear and two are left to become one again.

C H A P T E R   1 9

HUNTING
BROWN TROUT

//

Water colour country. Here the hills
rot like rugs beneath enormous skies
and all day long the shadows of the
clouds stain the paddocks with their
running dyes.

—Vivian Smith
Tasmania

"Have you been there?" I asked the taxi driver.
"Once," he said. "I was knee-deep in mud. It
was snowing there and it was one hundred four in Sydney. But
it's a nice place, Tasmania. Someone once said it has the cleanest
air in the world."

At the airport a television set above our heads blared a
newscaster's alarm: "If there were a nuclear attack on Sydney,
what would happen? A UCLA professor is here to be inter-

viewed about it! And quite hair-raising it should be," exulted the newscaster. A newspaper headline speculated: GENERAL STRIKE IF LIBERALS ELECTED.

How much news is shoved at us that is designed to produce shellshock and to leave us in a semi-permanent state of cardiac arrest. It uses up almost all our concern, absorbing these distant disasters and speculating about all the terrible things that might happen everywhere. There is not much of us left over for people down the street—for neighbors whom we really might help.

The TV set blared again: This time, it was an apartment fire in New York City. There was a picture of a body on the ground after a thirty-six-story jump to escape the flames. Then the fire chief was interviewed. Finally, more pictures of smoke pouring from the thirty-sixth-story window. Tasmania seemed like a good place to go to avoid all this.

Australian Airlines Flight 6 flew above the clouds south toward Melbourne. The sun was hot through the window. Drew read my copy of *Einstein in America,* but gave it up for a Stephen King book he had purchased at the airport. After a quick stop at Melbourne, we flew south another hour to Hobart, the capital of Tasmania, an island south of the Australian continent and its oft-forgotten seventh state. As we approached the Hobart airport, the ground below looked like East Tennessee or New Hampshire. It was cloudy, fifty degrees Fahrenheit. Yesterday's high had been sixty-three. This was the land of King Island Cheddar, the finest Australian cheese; of Port Arthur, the finest relic of early Australian prisons for English convicts; and of the central highlands of Tasmania, the land of three thousand lakes and (as so many had said) "the finest brown trout fishing in the world."

The park ranger who drove us to Port Arthur talked as fast as he drove. "When I traveled in the U.S. I would say I was from Tasmania and people would say, 'Where's that?' Those that could guess usually confused it with Tanzania in Africa. In 1978 our seventeen-year-old daughter was an American Field Service student in Erie, Pennsylvania. So we took a leave to see her and made it a round-the-world trip."

I said, "That's a lot of vacation."

The ranger explained. "It was my long service leave. Most Australians get three months leave after ten years at full pay, or six months at half pay if we want it. I took fifty-one days of mine then, in 1978, added on twenty days of annual leave, then nine to ten days of accrued leave, so I had eighty-one days of vacation to use."

At Eagle Hawk Neck, a narrow stretch of land led to a peninsula and Port Arthur. The sea on either side of the neck was blue-green where the bottom was sandy. Where the bottom was rock, the sea was darker. The ranger said, "There was a dog fence across the neck to contain the convicts and savage dogs inside the fence. Swimming was pretty hard, too, because of the sharks. A bloke named Billy Hunt dressed as a kangaroo and hopped across the neck but all he got for his trouble was caught and one hundred lashes."

It began to rain, and then, ten minutes later, the sky cleared. Port Arthur was selected for a prison because it had a deep-water harbor, timber on the hill, and the isolation of a peninsula. When we arrived at the prison site, the only sounds were of waves and sea gulls and tourists. Two hundred yards ahead of us offshore was the tiny island of Point Puer.

"They kept the boys there, boys from ages seven to seventeen. The boys of Point Puer."

Drew left his book in the car and began to listen.

The ranger continued. "I suppose the seven-year-old boys were six when they left England. It took them eleven months to get here. Usually they had stolen something. 'Sentenced to transportation,' they called it. Sounds unbelievable today, doesn't it?"

It was so unbelievable that the Australians sought to erase the memory. Port Arthur's name was changed. For a long time Australia seemed embarrassed to recall the landing two hundred years ago of the convicts and their guards, the first white settlers. But now Australia was preparing to celebrate its bicentennial, and the archives in Sydney buzzed with "first fleet families" searching for evidence of their largely convict ancestors—and Port Arthur had become Port Arthur again. Australia was coming to terms with itself.

Huge old oaks and ashes and poplars provided Port Arthur with a friendly, almost warm English quality. The English soldiers had planted these hardwoods 150 years ago to remind themselves of home and to offer some relief from the 500 varieties of Australian gum trees. But Port Arthur had remained essentially a cold and hard place. There had been one hundred rules. When a convict broke one, he was locked in the dark for three days. This isolation broke so many men that it became necessary to build a lunatic asylum. I stood in the cells. The chill of each ran through me, although it was still late summer. I tried to imagine how those men, and those boys, kept from freezing in the winter.

We stopped for lunch at Bush Mill Inn. The canned background music was Nashville-style—Floyd Cramer playing "Please Release Me, Let Me Go." The ranger, who had visited America, said, "I was amazed at the amount of food Americans put on their plates. Couldn't get over it. I asked them, 'Who do you expect to eat all that?' And one of the first things I noticed was water on the table in all the American restaurants. And I was surprised not to find any footpaths. I asked somebody about that. 'We don't walk here,' they told me. I told them, 'In Australia, everybody walks.' Americans don't know much about Australia. They think they do, but they don't. *Crocodile Dundee* is giving everybody the wrong impression about Australia. Kangaroos running through the houses—that's what Americans think of Australians. That would be like us thinking that all the American girls look like Dolly Parton."

"They all do," I said.

We found a train that we agreed Will would like to ride, a zoo with deceptively tame-looking Tasmanian devils, and we even discovered a Tasmanian *tiger* exhibit.

"Aren't the tigers extinct?" Drew asked.

"Depends on who you ask," said the ranger.

At six that evening we met Honey's father and mother from Victoria, Texas, who would be traveling with us. At the airport we all stopped for a snack, and Bette Jo, Honey's mother, immediately noticed the slight upward lilt at the end of the children's sentences—the Australian way of ending a sentence that makes everything easier to hear, sounds innocent and inviting, and makes you seem interested in other people. And when Drew asked the waiter for the "toe-mah-to" ketchup for his "chips," his grandmother asked, "Do *all* the children say 'toe-mah-to' when they order ketchup?"

"Only if we want to get it," Drew said, dumping ketchup on his hamburger.

We said good-bye to our ranger friend, then hired a taxi and began a two-hour climb fifty-five hundred feet to Tasmania's fishing lakes.

We arrived after dark at the fishing camp called London Lakes, driving slowly the last hour to avoid "skittling" wombats or wallabies or possums in the road. It was too dark to see trout. We would save that for early the next day.

At six-thirty the next morning we were standing sock-footed in heavy rubber boots, sloshing in mud at the lakeside. Our squishing walking noises and the kookaburras laughing and the usual symphony of wattlebirds and butcher-birds were all that interrupted the silence. Black swans watched us, but we watched for fish midging.

This was no ordinary sort of fishing. We were fly-fishing, and only for brown trout, and if Jason Garrett had his way, only *dry* fly-fishing. In truth, it was not even fishing. It was hunting. The idea was first to hunt and see the trout, then to present him a tasty-looking fly for breakfast.

So we practiced. The first object was to serve breakfast close to the trout. That meant getting the fly *beyond* where the line to which the fly is attached falls on the water. Jason Garrett, the entrepreneur-fishing enthusiast who owned and operated London Lakes, showed me how to do it: "Lift the line out of the water high and behind you, take it off the water correctly, watching the tightness of the curve behind you. Lift. Flick. Steady weight on the rod. Stop at twelve o'clock." I needed my metronome.

The water reflected the clouds as faithfully as a child imitates his parent. There! There was the head of a trout. Then the tail! "Old ones will bump the young ones for territory," said Jason. We were standing just out from the gum trees in the tall grass at the edge of a manmade lake. At 7:45 a little wind came up. "Just the kind that sometimes spoils this kind of fishing," Jason said. The wind blew my line into the same spot where the fly fell and when I pulled back, the line tangled. My cold fingers bent slowly untangling it. It was eight A.M. before the sun rose over the trees and the reflections of the clouds in the water disappeared and the gray water became blue like the sky.

By 8:10 there was a new freshness to the air, the clouds were gone, and wind rippled the water. Too much wind. There would be no more fishing here this morning. As we stomped through the reeds and bushes along the muddy lake edge back to the vehicles, Jason explained that in April 1864, on the fourth attempt, small pine boxes of tiny eggs arrived. The boxes were covered with moss and packed under nine feet of ice for the long voyage. From these eggs, a month later, the first brown trout were hatched in Tasmania—and, Drew and Frank and I said quietly to each other, so far as we were able to tell, not one had been caught since.

"This is snake time," Jason warned, but he did not seem much concerned. "Watch for the four-foot tiger snake; not much venom, but the most poisonous snake in the world."

"We watch out for bears at home in country like this," I said.

Jason stopped. "I'd rather walk through this marsh knowing there were five hundred snakes here than know there was one bear."

At noon the wind changed again. We were back squishing pleasantly in the mud, feeling the water lapping at our rubber-booted ankles. Drew is a good fisherman, I reminded myself. Father-in-law Frank is too. I am not and this is a chance to learn.

Jason pointed into the lake. "Can you see the fly? That is the first thing. You must be able actually to see it." I put on my new Polaroid sunglasses, which were supposed to help. In the white bubbles and ripples, the fly was still hard to see. There is a little bit of panic in this, I thought, the panic that always comes with trying something new, as when I looked for the first time in the western sky for the supernova. All the newspapers had had stories about how this supernova appeared only once in four hundred years and how everybody was seeing it. So one night I tried to see it, too. "There it is," experienced viewers would say. "Don't *you* see it?" Well, the truth was, I didn't see it. That was the little panic. It was something I should have easily been able to do. It was so frustrating, this thing I was trying to see, that I thought it might be better just to pretend that I was seeing it. Then—I saw it!

"I see the fly," I said to Jason.

Jason said, "Now the difficulty is to make sure you *keep* seeing it. Don't lose sight of the fly."

Another little panic. Then I saw it again . . . and then again.

Good practice. I am becoming a fisherman, I thought. I see the fly, but where is the fish? The wind changed and we had to leave.

Driving back in early afternoon on a road high above still another lake, we saw three huge rainbow trout, swimming quietly at least forty feet below us. Rainbow trout are not brown trout but they are fish, so we stopped.

Jason offered instructions. "Cast from the middle of the road, or he'll see you. And leave it there. A second cast is more splashing, more line in the sun." For two hours we stood in the sun casting to fish. It occurred to me that I hadn't made a speech in two months.

It was dark when we pulled off our muddy rubber boots and crowded into Jason's Jackaroo for a bumpy ride back to his fishing lodge. It was cold, and I was hoping that Jason would use the big clean fireplace I had seen in the lodge. I constructed a mental scorecard: After one day of hunting brown trout, I could cast, I could see the fly, I could even see the fish. I had had two strikes (I thought). But I had caught nothing. Drew had been the only one to catch a brown trout, "a little one, six or seven inches, creek size." He threw it back to grow up. But my face was sunburned and I was pleasantly tired and happy because I had spent the whole day outdoors in the magnificent central Tasmanian highlands. I calculated that I must be as far away from home in America as I could ever be and still be on earth. As we drove to the lodge, we counted thirty wallabies—little kangaroos—including one ambling creature of obvious age whom Drew immediately named "Uncle George."

It was 9:30, after dinner at Jason's homestead, and the night was black when I walked by myself into the bush. It took only seconds for my eyes to adjust to the darkness but in that unfamiliar stillness it seemed like minutes. The Milky Way spread broad and wild across the sky, becoming dimmer as it reached toward earth. I am in that Milky Way, I thought. And I am riding along the earth just on the edge of this galaxy. There was a rustling in the tree. I remembered Jason's warning, "Don't get under the possums in the tree. They'll pee on you." I moved away quickly. The rustling stopped. The night was clear. There was an occasional thumping sound. Wallabies. I listened for a special slow ambling thump, for "Uncle George," who might also be out for an evening stroll.

* * *

We got dressed at five-thirty in the morning on Wednesday, our second day at the lodge. It was still dark, but it was time to hunt trout. Jason's wife, Barbara, was preparing eggs and bacon. Her television was on loud, and it was faithfully delivering that day's horrors. Baby Victoria had been stolen from her mother. There was a schoolbus wreck, killing children. Terrorism continued in Lebanon. It was a harsh reminder that any concern from any remote corner of the world could be transmitted immediately, even to four sleepy fishermen in the central highlands of Tasmania.

The door opened and slammed, and a white-bearded man with a creased pink face came in. He wore a lumberjack coat and boots. He was fuming and talking fast. "Bloke came up from the States. High up in timber. Figures Japan is laughing up its sleeves at us. Didn't have to win the war. We've gone from ninety percent to forty percent in timber. The Japs are taking it all. Clearing and felling everything. Even down to the edge of the lake which is shocking. Pretty soon there'll be nothing left. You could go into any lunatic asylum and pick out a better government than ours. They're doing it. The blokes are crazy."

The man interrupted his tirade long enough to say hello to Barbara—"owl-oh" was how he said it—sat down to drink a cup of coffee with us, and continued talking.

"I'm Lonsdale Smith. Was a dairy farmer. Came from the rich, red chocolate soil in the northwest dairying country. Now they grow a lot of vegetables there. Was there thirty-five years. But it was only a means to an end and the end was getting here. I'm afraid now I only go fishing when it's worth going. Sometimes I only look at 'em."

It was time to go fishing. We split up. Drew and I rode with Lonsdale, and Frank with Jason. On the way a logging truck passed and that set Lonsdale off again. "That's those fellows going to clean up our forests with undue haste. Pretty soon there'll be nothing left. It takes all kinds of people. Some people bring boats and bottles up to these lakes and throw the bottles over the side and go home thinking they've had a good day."

Our vehicles stopped at several lakes. The wind was too high, the fishing no good. Drew picked up an insect. Lonsdale congratulated him. "A High Dun Mayfield fly. That's what we're looking for all right, because that's what the brown are looking for."

My line got tangled. Lonsdale inspected it and advised, "Best thing to do with a tangled line is to stop and deal with it. Keep going and it gets worse. Your President Reagan might be in better shape on the Iran stuff right now if he remembered that, huh?"

We climbed back in the Jackaroo and drove toward another lake. A red kangaroo scooted across the road. Lonsdale said, "Good eating, you know. I had a bloke once from the States who was a very keen shooter, shot all sorts of game from all over the world. Made a thing out of shooting and eating different game. I took him out and he shot three roos. Said they were the best eating in the world. A bit like something between venison and wild duck. It's best to get a small one. Big ones have a rank and gamy taste." Drew and I thought simultaneously of "Uncle George" Wallaby, and winced. Lonsdale went on. "I used to be a very keen shooter. But I'm afraid I've gone a bit soft. I saw a beautiful twelve-point deer just last week and couldn't pull the trigger."

We met Jason and Frank at a large lake, which Jason had fished as a boy. This was to be our best hope for finding brown trout. Jason led us around a dusty logging truck trail; then we stopped and we listened—to the southerly wind rippling across the water, to the birds and the buzz of insects, but we listened mainly for the click of trout snapping flies on the surface of the water.

"Fishing with your ears. We do a lot of that here," said Jason.

At water level it was especially hard to see fish. A duck squawked. We tried to silence the slushy sound of our boots walking. Jason said softly to Drew, "You found the only mayfly. There are caddis flies everywhere, too, but they're of no value."

We took off our sweaters and tried casting. When my rod was up, the wind blew by, making the roaring sound you hear when you hold a big conch shell to your ear. I was standing in short, cropped highland grass in clear water that was blue as the sky. The grass under water was a carpet, and at the water's edge the grass grew so evenly that it looked freshly mowed. The bullrushes were thick and straight, like straws inviting you to drink. Midday fishing conditions were near perfect, but no one had told the fish.

We stopped and climbed on rocks and sat in the sun, and ate apples and sandwiches and drank mineral water that Barbara Garrett had packed, and then we wandered from lake to lake. This was a remote land of three thousand lakes, almost no roads, a great many sheep, a few very determined graziers, dozens of fishing huts—but so far as we could tell, not so many brown trout.

In the late afternoon I stood again, squishing in the water, wiggling my toes inside my loose rubber boots. An orchestra of black swans accompanied me. Their wings thwacked, announcing a beginning. High notes came next, oboes piping. The warming-up sounds creaked and spread, as with the first notes played on dry clarinet reeds. Then the rest of the oboes joined in. Deep bassoons answered. All the warmed-up reeds piped and honked together, and wings thwacked like kettle drums, when suddenly the instrumentalists finished and rewarded themselves by plunging their necks into shallow water for a feast of weeds. I listened and watched the changing light make shadows on the lake, and once in a while I remembered to look for a fish midging.

In the fading light we rode peacefully back toward the lodge, passing old fences, twisted gum trees, olive bushes, and settlers' century-old log houses, driving more cautiously as darkness thickened to avoid skittling animals. When we turned into London Lakes, Drew spotted our friend, "Uncle George" Wallaby, whose ambling and turning around to see and casual hops away were distinctly slower than the others. We were glad that "Uncle George" was too old and tough to be much of a tasty target for Lonsdale Smith's shooting friends.

C H A P T E R 2 0

F A M I L Y
V A C A T I O N

//

And down by Kosciusko, where the
pine-clad ridges raise
Their torn and rugged battlements on
high,
Where the air is clear as crystal, and
the white stars fairly blaze
At midnight in the cold and frosty sky,
And where around The Overflow the
reed beds sweep and sway
To the breezes, and the rolling plains
are wide,
The man from Snowy River is a
household word today,
And the stockmen tell the story of his
ride.

—BANJO PATERSON
"The Man from Snowy River,"
from *Collected Poems*

❙ read about it in the "Holiday" section of Sydney's February 22 Sunday *Herald:*

> One of the most refreshing holiday experiences on offer this time of year is a week-long, 100-mile horse trek in the Snowy Mountains region of Koskiusko National Park. Riding five hours a day on fit, well-fed mountain horses able to carry riders into the high country. Lunch by clear creeks, freshly cooked trout for dinner, fascinating campfire stories of brumbies and the bush. TO FIND OUT MORE: Contact John and Rosalyn Rudd at Reynella, Adaminaby, New South Wales; phone 42386.

I telephoned immediately. Rosalyn Rudd answered and I asked, "Can you take six the second week in April, including four children, and one of them's a seven-year-old?"

She said, "I'll book you. And John will teach the seven-year-old. And the others? How do they ride?"

I said, "Well, the oldest daughter has a horse at home in America and the mother grew up in Texas and knows what to do but the rest of us need help."

"Four beginners. No worries. Neville will be along with John and he'll help, too. I'll put aside oilskins and sleeping bags and boots and fishing gear for you. Bring warm clothing. It's our last trip before winter and it could snow. You can never tell. The weather in the Snowy Mountains can change several times a day."

I could barely contain my excitement. I walked to the postbox that afternoon and mailed my check for a week for the six of us—and the next day I bought plane tickets for the flight that would take us five hundred miles south to Cooma at the edge of the Kosciusko National Park, the northern reaches of the fabled Snowy Mountains of Australia.

No image of Australia stirred me more than that of the "Man from Snowy River," the famous story of what happened when the expensive colt from old Regret ran away and joined the wild bush horses, how a "slight and weedy boy" was allowed to join the chase because "Clancy of The Overflow" promised he could ride like a Snowy Mountain man. I had rented the film for two dollars and watched the mysterious images again—the prancing horses topping the high ridge, the riders' Akubra hat brims low, their dark oilskins flowing, sky and space spreading everywhere. "Bushmen love hard riding where the wild bush horses are." This was the stuff of legends, about a hero in the everyday affairs of life, a kind of Australian David and Goliath story. This was the Australia I wanted to see and to know. But Honey and I were the only ones interested enough to watch the film.

"I've seen it," Kathryn said at supper.

I said, "Well, Les, *you* should like a Snowy Mountain horseback trip as much as you like horses."

Leslee said, "My horse jumps, Dad. I don't really like trail rides. And everybody on the trip will probably be old. You know Mom doesn't like to sleep out, either."

"I'll be fine if I have my feather pillow," said the lioness, who ran five miles a day and who in a pinch could outsurvive us all, but who had wanted her feather pillow every night on our trip through the Grand Canyon, and who had taken it on an Outward Bound course in the North Carolina mountains.

Kathryn looked at me. "You'll probably want to ride a camel across the desert next."

"In fact, I have already called to see about that," I said.

"Camels smell," said Kathryn.

Will said, "I'd be glad to take a train across the desert."

"And camels spit on you," said Drew, who added, "I'm never taking another family vacation. They're too embarrassing."

At supper the next night I opened a book of Banjo Paterson's bush poems and said to my captive audience, "Listen to this."

"Dad!" said Kathryn.

I began to read:

So he waited sad and wistful—only Clancy stood his
    friend—
"I think we ought to let him come," he said.
"I warrant he'll be with us when he's wanted at the end,

"For both his horse and he are mountain bred."
He hails from Snowy River, up by Kosciusko's . . .

"Koz-ee-os-coe," corrected Drew.

. . . up by Koz-ee-os-coe's side,
Where the hills are twice as steep and twice as rough,
Where a horse's hoofs strike firelight from the flint stones
   every stride,
The man that holds his own is good enough.

Leslee got up to leave. "That's nice. Bec's waiting on me to study."

Kathryn saw her opportunity, too. "Can I go now?"

I protested. "But we haven't even come to the part where the wild horses—they call them brumbies here . . ."

"Dad, Mrs. Locke told us about brumbies in the first week of second grade," said Will.

I continued. ". . . 'when the wild brumbies plunge over the mountain summit and the tried and noted riders all hold back . . .' "

" '. . . all except the man from Snowy River.' We've got it, Dad," said Drew.

"But you don't really know a poem until you've read it out loud and since none of you seem likely to read it at all, you may just sit still and I will read it out loud to you."

There were groans of deep discomfort:

But the man from Snowy River let the pony have his head,
And he swung his stockwhip round and gave a cheer.
And he raced him down the mountain like a torrent down
   its bed,
While the others stood and watched in very fear . . .

The familiar background music began, the shuffling of chairs and feet that forms a prelude for the nightly dash from the dinner table by the four.

I put down the book. "Just one minute. This is Australia's best-known poem, written by a man who sat in Sydney in his cramped law offices and imagined that he was in the *real* Australia, the bushland, alone in the never-ending outback high in those beautiful Snowy Mountains, lying on his back and looking at the stars . . ."

Kathryn broke in, "Then why didn't he just move out there and live and lie on his back and look at stars instead of writing poems that we have to listen to at the dinner table? Dad, you do some weird things—singing and humming in front of my friends in the car while the radio is on is bad enough—but reading poetry at dinner! I'm glad nobody else is here."

Leslee then said, "I'm waiting for the clincher, when he says . . . ," and she paused in a practiced way. The others understood her signal perfectly, and so, in chorus, all four said in surprisingly good rhythm, "THIS MAY BE THE ONLY CHANCE IN YOUR LIFE THAT YOU EVER HAVE TO GO HORSEBACK RIDING IN THE SNOWY MOUNTAINS."

Undaunted, I read on, to the last line.

"There," I said, leaning back in my chair and closing the book. And there was an exit from the table faster than a fire drill.

CHAPTER 21

ACROSS THE SNOWY MOUNTAINS

//

A crow cries: and the world unrolls
like a blanket; like a worn bush
blanket, charred at the horizons. But
the butcherbird draws all in; that
voice is a builder of roofless
cathedrals and claustrophobic
forests—and one need not notice
walls, so huge is the sky.

—RANDOLPH STOW
Landscapes (Australian)

The Australian Airlines plane approached the Cooma airport, Honey looked out and said, "It looks like Wyoming, just before winter." And except for the gum trees, and the cockatoos spread like Kleenex on the brown grass, it did look like Wyoming. A van met and took us to Reynella Lodge in Adaminaby at the northern edge of the Snowy Mountains. There we met our hosts, Rosalyn and John Rudd, and sixteen others from Australia and England and the United States who had signed up for the week's adventure.

After a good night's sleep, the van took us to a grove where the horses waited. The morning had begun clear and chilly, then turned cloudy and rainy. Now it was clearing again and it was not yet noon. Neville, who helped John Rudd with the horses, walked a horse over to Will and handed him the reins and said, "William, this is Harry." Neville was wiry and wore a rough face; one eye looked as if it had been hit a long time ago and never repaired. On his head was a battered Snowy Mountain Akubra hat and when he walked, he dragged his left leg. He would limp among the horses, slapping their rumps and cursing, clearly in charge. No one ever said how Neville had hurt his left leg, but I suspected it was a brave horse who did it when Neville wasn't looking. Now it was the second week in April, the end of the summer riding season, and both the horses and Neville appeared well ridden. Within a few minutes, Neville returned with another horse and handed its reins to Will, too, saying, "Here, William, hold both horses."

And then to Drew, Neville said, "Use the small brush on this one."

I had mounted my horse, but without being introduced. Neville said, "This is Soldier."

I said, "Hello, Soldier," and patted the horse's neck.

Neville asked, "How's your stirrups?" and he yanked one. "All right are they? Bring 'em up just here. Hang on to your reins anytime you're doing anything." He yanked the other one, and asked, "What do you do?"

"Lawyer," I said, so quickly that it surprised me.

He grunted and looked up and said, "The rider makes the horse."

"I'm sorry to hear that," I said to Honey, who was sitting nicely on her horse, Duncan, while Neville worked his way through the crowd helping others mount.

For the horses it was hard walking up the first steep ridges. Stones were loose and there were burned logs to step over and bushgrass grew as high as the horses. At the top of the ridge, at about one-thirty, we stopped and dismounted and let the horses drink. I put on my sweater, lay down, and enjoyed the warm sun and tried to guess which way the winds would blow the gray-white clouds. There were American-style peanut-butter-and-jam sandwiches and canteen water, and, to finish, billy tea had been boiled black as the charcoal in the fire.

As we mounted, the sun hid again behind the clouds. Soldier and I always seemed to find ourselves at the end of the procession. Neville would ride back and encourage us, but it was not easy to catch up because when Soldier did anything but walk, I bounced, and bouncing, I discovered, had a cumulative effect on the muscles and other padding that covered my sitting bones.

Once when Neville was checking the back of the line, I asked, "What if Soldier decides he wants to go a different way?"

"He won't. Any track you put 'im on he'll follow. They're stupid things, these horses," which was more reassuring than what he had told me earlier about the rider making the horse. Soldier and I, I thought, would be better off if the horse made the rider.

We arrived at the first night's campsite as the clouds covered the sun's last burst of light. We turned the horses loose and staked our tents and fried trout in skillets and boiled potatoes and stood around the fire gossiping about wild horses.

"They're still here?" John, the distinguished-looking pilot from London, asked.

John Rudd said, "Oh, yes, I saw tracks today. You see evidence of them. The park service was going to kill them, like the burros in the Grand Canyon, but there was an outcry in Canberra. Brumbies in these mountains are a bit of a tradition. Bushmen ride all day trying to catch them."

Neville said, "Finding 'em's the hard part, not catching them."

The sky had cleared, so we walked away from the fire, looked at the stars, and found the Magellan cloud where the supernova was supposed to be. I gazed for a while, then I said good night and crawled into our tent and found Honey and Will there, too, and slept until about midnight when I heard rain on the tent. The wind was sweeping down our ravine, sometimes sweeping under the tent cover, threatening to lift it into the valley. After making sure Honey and Will and my feet were not wet, and seeing Drew's tent and the girls' tent were still in place, I congratulated myself privately for apparently getting the tents up right, and then slept again until about dawn when I heard the kookaburra and the "telephone bird" and the "smoke alarm" bird in chorus at once.

When I emerged from the tent, John Rudd was standing close over a new fire, hands in his pockets, drinking coffee. He said, "The big blower [storm] was to our west, just to the left of those round hills with the short grass where we saw the Magellan cloud last night."

We rounded up the horses, and that day rode twenty miles to about five thousand feet, where we camped and turned in early. Sleep at higher altitudes was easier and longer.

On Wednesday morning the wind was gusty and my breath frosty but the sky was clear. We rode west onto Blanket Plains, where there was nothing but us in the way of the wind. From my vantage point at the rear, the long line of horses created a stunning scene—riders with Snowy River hats leaning into the wind, Dri-za-bone oilskin coats flapping. It was as if we had dressed up for parts in a fairy tale. It was a vision of the Australian past—and of the kind of dreams the American past is made of also.

At Witses Hut we stopped for lunch and let the horses go free. In the 1840s, settlers had sawed gray ash boards to make the hut. In the high winds its roof rattled and the insides shook and shifted and gave easily in a way that suggested the hut had learned deliberately how to survive. I lay down in the tall grass in front of the hut to escape the wind.

On Thursday morning the wind roared around the tent, sounding cold, and our feet *were* cold, despite Honey, Will, and I being bundled together. When we opened the flap, the tent outside was covered with melting frost. I felt better knowing that tonight we would stay in the same campsite. The clouds were as dark and gray as the gum trees, and the wind swept around the corner of the tenthole and back into it. I joined John Rudd, who was encouraging the morning cooking fire. My fingers took a very long time to warm up. He said, "Weather changed three times last night. Snow's forecast for today. If we lose the clouds we'll get frost tonight for sure."

Before breakfast Honey went running on a dirt road that wound from the campsite around a hill. When she returned an hour later, she told the group gossiping at the campfire, "I saw two wallabies and twelve kangaroos just off the road, up on the hill, and I thought I saw a dingo way across in the fields chasing something."

"Probably was. Chasing pigs," Neville said.

Drew had been fishing in the side creeks for trout.

Neville asked him, "What were you using?"

Drew said, "Just grasshoppers, and I caught a little one." And then he said loud enough for both Neville and me to hear, "This is no adventure. It's just a family picnic. Who ever heard of not breaking camp on an adventure?" We were in the presence, after all, of the young man who, just two months earlier, had kayaked in the Pacific Ocean, thwarted black widow spiders on the beach, wrestled with scorpions in his sleeping bag, and craftily escaped from waves smashing against cliffs.

Neville left for a minute and came back and walked over to Drew and said, "Here's an adventure. Ride this," and offered him the reins of the brown mule that had been serving as a pack animal. "I'll take it," said Drew, delighted, and he turned and shouted, "I'm riding Donkeyhead! At least he'll go where we want to go instead of just following along all the others." It was amazing to see how the promise of one mule and some maneuvering room transformed the attitude of this seventeen-year-old adventurer.

My calves hurt from moving around in the saddle, so I swapped Soldier for Honey's horse, Duncan. I thought Duncan might make me a better horseman for the ride to six thousand feet, but Duncan and I, too, wound up at the end of the procession. "The rider makes the horse," said Honey when she rode Soldier back down the line in the late morning to say hello.

At noon we rested at the Murrumbidgee River. The water was clear enough to drink, and the river big enough to contain mountain trout, and the wind was strong enough to make little waves on the water's gurgling surface. John, the pilot, gave Will lessons in the English way of skipping rocks across the river. I gave each child a ration of M & M's that I had bought in Sydney and saved for the right moment. We seemed so far away from everything, but in fact we were only fifty miles from the Pacific coast, and we could hear and see the 727 jets taking off and landing at the Australian national capital, Canberra, to the northwest.

John Rudd gave lessons in galloping on the plains, and he quickly realized the calamity that would occur if Drew, Leslee, and Kathryn learned to gallop and Will did not, so he worked with Will until he was galloping, too. Will was immensely proud of this, and talked at length about it later in the afternoon as he rode between Kathryn and Honey's horses. The three of them held hands. "He can talk to me better when he touches me," Honey explained.

When we returned to camp that evening, Honey and I walked along the road where she had seen the wallabies and kangaroos. Suddenly in the middle of the road there was a medium-sized cuddly brown bearlike creature. Honey put her fingers to her lips and whispered, "Wombat." Mr. Wombat was feeding and heading downhill and the wind was blowing toward us, so we stood still. I took seven or eight shots with a 210mm telephoto lens, hoping this would work in the near darkness, and finally got so close and made so much noise that the wombat scurried on down the road. We got back to camp as the sun was going down and clouds were building up in the west. Neville observed, "Tomorrow it'll be beyond nicely," which, in Australian, meant bad weather coming.

On Friday morning, our last day, Will was the first to stick his head out of the tent. He scrambled back inside, shook his mother, and then shook me. "Oh, wow. I looked out. It's all white. It looks like snow."

Honey crawled outside, and in a few minutes reported: "It is white everywhere and spider webs are frozen on the fence posts. But it's not snow. It's a hard frost."

I said, "The ground felt so hard last night I couldn't sleep."

Honey said, "Every time I rolled over and touched the tent the ice outside crinkled."

I said, "Let's go see some kangaroos." I packed two cameras, my tripod and one extra roll of film, a telephoto lens, some lens cleaner, and a small pouch, and we all bundled up and stepped outside the tent. Will ran to stand with the others at the campfire, while Honey and I walked down the road where she had seen the wallabies and kangaroos during her run. I became such a busy photographer that I didn't even notice that soon she and I were walking our separate ways.

The sun, rising on the right, bathed the horses in the valley in shadows, and the sun felt hot even at six-forty in the morning. Honey walked toward me and said, "The frost'll be gone quick."

We walked up together through the bush. "The snakes will be in their holes this morning," I reassured her. Within fifteen minutes we had seen three kangaroos. I took several photographs, changing lenses twice.

Honey said, "The kangaroos will like the hills today instead of the cold valley," so we followed the road to higher ground. We reached a plateau and I stopped to reset apertures and got out a tripod. Experimenting with different f-stops, then with different lenses, I tried desperately to record the fragile scene before it melted.

Honey said, "We can go on up the hill if we hurry. It was near here when I saw them last night, on the left. I thought I saw my old friend from a couple of days ago." I stopped long enough to take twelve or fourteen shots and changed rolls of film.

"Look. They're everywhere." Honey was excited. Above us to the right, about fifty yards away, dotting the slope were at least a dozen kangaroos. They were all turned in our direction, looking at us in that quizzical kangaroo sizing-up way, seeing just how much we intended to disturb their lives.

Honey said, "I could hear them thumping as you took pictures."

I hurried to the top of the hill and used my 35mm widest-angle lens trying to capture the panorama of fog and frost on the plains. I composed each shot carefully, hoping to highlight the frost. The camera eyepiece frosted over, confusing me, and I worried whether I had done anything else wrong to ruin the pictures; then I reached in my pack and realized I had no more rolls of film.

"Only two shots. I've only got two left," I said, disgusted.

"Save them for the top," Honey said. "Those should be the best views."

We were on one of those endlessly rising ridges, so we stopped climbing before we found the top. I asked her, "Should we go on? They must be cooking breakfast. I'll take my last shots here." And I got out my tripod.

Honey looked amused, and then walked around and looked up at me and said with her eyes as much as with her words, "Why don't you put your camera away and let's just look?"

I stopped being so busy and packed my cameras and all the accessories. For a while we said nothing, did nothing but look. There was everything to see—frost on the gum branches, spider webs frozen white, fog spreading low in the valley, the sun rising red over the ridge. We walked slowly in step down the road and tried to hold hands and then laughed about how clumsy that was wearing such thick mittens. I tasted the cold air and listened to the bird symphony. Honey listened for the thumping of her kangaroo friends. I thought, I almost missed it. I was so busy picture-taking that I almost forgot to look, forgot why I am here, and the sun is about to melt it away.

C H A P T E R 2 2

C H A N G I N G

//

"It'll be no use putting their heads
down and saying, 'Come up again,
dear!' I shall only look up and say
Who am I, then? Tell me that first,
and then, if I like being that person,
I'll come up: if not, I'll stay down
here till I'm somebody else—but, oh
dear!" cried Alice, with a sudden
burst of tears. "I do wish they would
put their heads down! I am so very
tired of being all alone here!"
—LEWIS CARROLL
Alice's Adventures in Wonderland

Before we moved to Australia, Will had never lived anywhere else but in the governor's Mansion in Nashville.
For his first seven years there had been a long, slick black-and-

white marble floor downstairs for racing big wheels and shocking tourists. There had been helpful troopers for driving to school and a kitchen full of friendly cooks and Justin Minor to "help" plant onions and carrots and beans each spring and Jeanne Pearcy always available to read when Mom or Dad were busy. Sometimes there were even visitors inspecting Will's bedroom and future presidents of the United States or Elizabeth Taylor sleeping in the next room and even Captain Kangaroo dropping by for lunch—for a growing-up boy it must have seemed like living in a museum, a wonderful museum, but still a museum.

However, it must also have been confusing. Every night in the Mansion, Will would find his way from his corner room through the big dark second-floor hall to our bed, and burrow between us and snuggle as we protested. While he slept, we would carry him back to his room, but sometimes he would come back and we let him stay because it was evident that staying gave Will so much security.

Then, when Drew became sixteen, old enough to drive, he and Will rode back and forth to school each weekday. They became friends and big brother Drew became Will's idol. He tried to talk like his older brother, and wear Grateful Dead purple and green and yellow T-shirts like Drew did sometimes, and to act like him and he yearned for Drew's ultimate stamp of approval, a high-five handslap and an "OK BILL!," which was what Drew called Will when he did what his older brother wanted him to do.

In Australia Drew became a sort of third parent, trying to "toughen Will up" after his soft life in the Mansion, promulgating various older-brother Rules of Life: "You're part of the group, bub." "Help pick up the corn flakes from the floor—even if you didn't spill them." "Don't be negative." Drew enjoyed these new responsibilities so much he broadened them, helping us diagnose twelve-year-old Kathryn's growing rebelliousness.

"She's just a teenager."

"I am not, yet."

"You're acting like one."

Having a third parent around sometimes crowded the house, but it turned out to be as good for Drew as it was for Will. It became a part of Drew's surprising and generally welcome emergence from the Period of the Perpetual Frown, which had begun when he was about thirteen, and which was interrupted only by long periods of isolation in his room with the door closed. After our first few weeks in Australia, Drew surprisingly began to linger after dinner, and he would actually join conversations and even express faint hints of approval or at least acceptance of having parents around. This was a wonderful and unexpected and thoroughly pleasant, resounding event that arrived in spurts and stages, but nonetheless clearly arrived. It was as if suddenly the family contained five new relationships, because for four or five years Drew's contact with us had been mostly from behind that closed door of his room smothered by thundering rock music. Big brother Drew out in the open was such a nice change that none of us dared to comment.

Leslee's fifteenth birthday was during her seventh week in Australia, on Saint Patrick's Day. She was becoming more than ever like her mother who, in remembering how *she* had felt at fifteen, and what *she* had done—or at least what she *might* have done—became sterner than ever with her daughter. Leslee seemed to spend much of her time practicing to be twenty-one, if not twenty-five, and seemed to be imagining she was somewhere else instead of at home with her family. To Leslee, Kathryn had become even more of a little sister, and Will a seven-year-old brother who attracted a disproportionate amount of parental attention, while big brother Drew was a fast-moving panther to be admired and competed with and even caught up with. And Dad? Well, Dad had become bossy and occasionally in need of correction. For Dad this was a very hard change in Leslee to accept, even though he hoped he understood that this was the way things had to be. It was an especially hard change because one of the nicest things about our family had always been the old, warm, and cuddly relationship Leslee and I had.

Kathryn was changing, too. She would be thirteen in June, and she kept so much to herself and was growing up so nicely that she became a subject of fascination to her mother and to me. Kathryn was like neither of us, yet like both of us. She was slim and built like her mother, but she had the cantankerousness and reserve of my railroad engineer grandfather, Reu R. Rankin, who felt a lot but showed it only on his own terms. As Kathryn and I approached our respective birthdays, numbers 13 and 47, there occurred something of a collision of transitions. An example was the time when, at a traffic intersection on Military Road near where we lived, she and I simultaneously grasped the other's arm, seeking to help each other cross the street.

"Careful, Kath."

"Car, Dad."

I wasn't old enough yet to need that kind of help, nor was she still young enough to need it, but we had arrived at a delicate point of equilibrium, where it wasn't clear who was the custodian of whom. Who was more likely to need a warning about crossing the street, about leaning too far over the cliff, about swimming in too deep surf? Was it the daughter or the father? Things are about even, I thought, and, with each other, we are almost equally awkward.

Honey had been feeling like a circuit expander with five outlets, with the current increasing all the time until the fuse was about to blow. There was too much mothering and other things to do: "All of you assume I've replaced a kitchen staff of three." But Honey was also like a sugar cube, with five of us each so hungry for some of her that by the end of each day she came close to being used up. The situation kept Honey on the defensive and in a giving position so much of the time that it was hard to see how she was changing, but she was. She was desperately hoping to go on the offensive, to do the things that her own need for change cried out for her to do. Honey urgently needed *her* six months off, too, but something inside her told our lioness that unless she held things together, then nobody would; so she had opted to continue to be the circuit expander and the sugar cube.

It had to be a shock to the rest of the family as I increasingly intruded upon all of this. "The egret," as Leslee's school application had described me, standing on one leg, pondering the world, suddenly decided to join the family. It was an unsettling event. I had been gone for a long time—eight years of swiveling in the governor's chair. My return created five new relationships in the same way that Drew's emergence from the Period of the Perpetual Frown had also created five new ones. Drew and I arrived at this point at about the same time, both self-consciously—charting unfamiliar waters, uncertain of just what we were doing or why we were doing it—but the end result was that we joined the family and added new complications to the web of relationships for everyone to deal with.

One of my greatest new joys was that Will and I were becoming better acquainted. Some days I walked him to school or met him. On Saturday mornings we would drive to Australia's "Lay-go Cen-tah" (Lego Centre) where there was a space ship with so many pieces that it took 599 hours to build. On Saturday afternoons we might try Luna Park for ferris wheel rides and to my delight—and especially to Honey's—on more nights Will would announce, "Dad, let's read some Swiss," and we would wade through another chapter of *The Swiss Family Robinson*, with Will chortling at each one of the Swiss father's "capital ideas" while the grateful off-duty lioness desperately grasped for the rare chance to read a page in *her* book, *The Fatal Shore*.

During all of this change and confusion, each of us tried hard to hold on. Rock music was still Drew's anchor, although now it was rock music thundering out in the open, in our basement, in daily jam sessions with new friend Billy King and other assorted Australian high-school musical wizards.

"I'll walk to school by myself," Will announced one morning, and he did that day, but that afternoon when the bell rang and Balmoral Infants School emptied, he seemed to hold my hand more tightly than usual as we walked from the schoolyard to Peter Rose's milk bar for a vanilla shake.

Leslee surprisingly invited Kathryn to join some of the older girls for Saturday shopping in Sydney, and Kathryn had a hard time concealing her delight. They both had fun, but when they came home tired that afternoon, Leslee went directly to her room and wrote long letters home, and I heard the familiar Bach fugue coming from the living room where Kathryn and the rented piano were.

Family dinners became imperceptibly longer but more relaxed, and everyone pitched in to help plan our train trip through Japan and even talked about how much fun it would be.

And Honey and I found ourselves holding on more to each other—as on Will's birthday when Honey was busy making prizes and a cake. It was already eleven o'clock when I said, "How about a picnic?" (Honey loves picnics.) So she started packing oranges, grapes, crackers, some leftover barbecued chicken, and English Hutsman cheese, and I got a watermelon and a blanket and some peanut butter and made a jar of iced tea, and forty-five minutes after the idea sprouted we were standing on the giant sandstone North Head, our hair blowing, looking out across the white-capped Tasman Sea. It was a blue, bright day, and we counted the ships waiting in the harbor and two big ones waiting far out, too. We ate all we wanted and then slept on the rocks in the sun until it was time to go, and on our way to pick up Will and his birthday-party friends, we plotted our next time together.

B U L L E T
T R A I N

//

"What's Japan like?"

"Very, very different from this."

"Oh, I'd just love to see Japan!"

All at once there was a great rushing of wind and she felt herself speeding skywards and she gasped. . . .

"We're in Japan," she cried out excitedly. "How did you do that, O?"

—JAMES CLAVELL
Thrump-O-Moto

Honey had cautioned me when I first started talking about the train trip through Japan.

"But it's not so far and there's only a two-hour time difference," I said.

"It's a ten-hour flight and the Japanese Air Line seats seem smaller," Honey said.

I was eager to make the trip. Australia's end-of-the-summer briskness had something to do with it. The chill had caught me by surprise. In January there had been more humidity than we expected, and in February there was too much rain; and now this almost all-day cold.

Honey particularly looked forward to traveling north across the equator to springtime in Japan. "The cherry blossoms will make me think of our dogwoods, and the azaleas and the tulips will be blooming in Hibiya Park. It'll be beautiful running around the emperor's palace. I didn't want to miss spring."

This was the first trip that I could remember where I had made all the arrangements, had plenty of time to pack and plan, and nothing else to do but go. It would be fun seeing old friends in Tokyo and trying to accomplish something at the conference on U.S.-Japan affairs I would attend before the rest of the family arrived. Everything was neatly packed: passport, yen, traveler's checks, glasses, ticket, books.

The sun outside Narita Airport in Tokyo was pleasantly warm even at 6:30 in the morning. "Taxi to cost two thousand yen," the driver said carefully. Then he wrote it out: It was *20,000* yen. Nearly one hundred twenty-five U.S. dollars to go from the airport to the Imperial Hotel in downtown Tokyo. The driver reached 145 kilometers per hour even before we had left the airport. Careening like Darrell Waltrip on Saturday night at Darlington Speedway, this Japanese speed merchant dodged noise barricades and outraced a turquoise commuter train. His short stops at toll stations would have made Waltrip's pit crews jealous. Suddenly it was seven and we were stuck in a jam of traffic for the last creeping twenty minutes into Tokyo. I had plenty of time to play one of my favorite Tokyo games, counting the different English names on Japanese cars. (There are no Japanese names on cars, even in Japan.)

At the Imperial Hotel I ordered one hundred calling cards. These *meishi* are indispensable in Japan. They are the central prop of self-introduction. A Japanese without a *meishi* runs the risk of being forgotten. But I felt unsure about what to have printed after the comma after my name. I settled on "Lamar

Alexander, former Governor of Tennessee." I had always vowed *never* to be a "former governor," a harmless relic hauled to events to be applauded by people who could not remember why they were applauding. But I had to be *something*. I could think of no precedent for printing "In Transition" after the comma after my name. I relented, only once, and had one hundred new *meishi* printed that read: "Lamar Alexander, Governor of Tennessee (1979–1987)." Better to be a tombstone governor than a former governor, I thought. Only slightly better, but better.

No other Americans rode the train to Oiso, only Japanese, almost all of them dozing—dozing standing, dozing leaning, dozing sitting, hanging from straps and dozing, leaning against steps or sitting or slumping and dozing. Every strap had someone hanging on it riding, sleeping, leaning, reading. Some read newspapers or little books with Japanese characters carefully arranged up and down the pages. These riders rode and dozed and waited patiently while the trains moved too many people in too little space exactly on time. If the Japanese were half as rowdy as we Americans are, their islands would explode, I thought. At the stations seven-year-old schoolgirls in uniforms changed trains by themselves and there were long rows of bicycles neatly parked—not dozens but hundreds. As we moved farther out of the city, youngsters were playing baseball in parks and the first onions were sticking up in gardens.

Modern Japanese cities are ugly. It is sad to say, but it is true. In general it is congestion and clutter that create the ugliness. Vending machines protrude into sidewalks. Cars are parked on the *front porches* of the nicest-looking homes. Oversized gray expressways and concrete noise barriers seem to be everywhere. Huge steel utility poles stand in front yards. Brash neon signs and big wire safety fences decorate train tracks. Even in Oiso, a fabulous seaside resort, concrete and fumes and traffic overwhelm the natural beauty with grayness and stench and noise. And there seems to be a power line in the way of every good view in Japan.

Japan is *naturally* beautiful. There are moments when you feel this especially, such as in Oiso on a warm spring morning, when the sea breezes spread fragile blossoms and you can smell the early onions being pulled and stacked. Japanese families employ hoes and spades almost desperately to uncover and to create new spots of beauty. Tiny gardens. Tulips in the windows. Fences to keep out clutter. A few marigolds here. An azalea there.

At the conference in Oiso I was invited to talk about whether the United States would elect a protectionist president. I said, "People expect congressmen to vote that way but Americans know the difference between voting for a congressman who looks out after local interests and a president whose job is to look out for the whole country, and so while that may be confusing to the world the answer to your question is, no, America won't elect a protectionist president," but afterward all anybody wanted to ask me was about my six months off.

"I almost did it," said a forty-nine-year-old businessman from Dallas whose company had been sold, leaving him with plenty of money and nothing to do. He was attending the conference with his wife. "I almost did what you did but I choked. I was afraid that after two weeks of doing nothing I would feel there was a collar around my neck tightening. Then I found myself getting involved in other things and all of a sudden I was as busy as I had been before."

A young labor leader from America sought me out before a meal.

"I'd like to take a break. I'm forty."

"How old are your children?"

"Five and seven. I'd like to spend more time with them." I felt a little guilty for making him feel guilty about not being with them. I began to feel like the patient turned counselor.

The chief executive officer of one of America's major insurance companies, a man I had known before, stopped me as the conference ended.

"As you describe it, I wish I'd done it."

"Well, do it now."

"I'm too old. Sixty-five this year. I'm retiring."

"Age has nothing to do with it."

He hesitated. "I'm going to become chief executive officer of another insurance company, in the Midwest."

"It would be a perfect time to take some real time off."

"I know. But my wife says I wouldn't be happy because I'd have nothing to do and she's probably right."

The first day our family was together in Tokyo, we went to the top of the Tokyo Tower. Japanese schoolchildren in uniforms giggled at Will and stroked his blond hair, and asked to have their photographs taken with Leslee and Kathryn, and shook hands and practiced speaking English with Drew.

When we left the tower, we walked by rows of flowering dogwood and maple trees with new leaves. The children took photographs of gardens lined with baby Buddhas topped with bright red caps and guarded by paper windmills whining in the breeze.

There was a familiar squawk.

"A normal-sounding crow," I said.

"I think a Japanese accent," Honey said.

"Why are so many things in English?" Will asked.

"It's more American here," explained Drew, who had been to Japan once before.

Walking to the Ginza shopping district, Will discovered something quite as spectacular as the two-hundred-fifty-meter red-and-white Tokyo Tower from which you could see Tokyo Bay and a city of fifteen million. He saw: *an honest-to-goodness American-looking Wendy's hamburger place.* Will rushed inside and, with the money that he was not saving for a model of the bullet train, bought a plain hamburger and french fries and a milkshake and a medium-sized Coke.

"I feel like I'm home. I'm really happy. These are the best chips I've had in months. Wendy's has the best chips." he said.

Kathryn corrected Will, "Chips are french fries here."

Will turned to me. "Dad, did the United States invent Coke?"

"Yes."

"Wendy's and McDonald's, too?"

"Yes."

"That's pretty good for us, isn't it?" Will said.

After lunch I asked, "Who wants to try a Japanese harpsichord?"

"I do," said Kathryn, who was the one I'd hoped would want to try it. So while Honey and Leslee shopped, the rest of us disappeared into a mammoth four-story Yamaha music store. At one cacophonous moment Kathryn experimented with Bach on a harpsichord, while Will attempted "The Three Pigs" on the clavichord, and I practiced Czerny exercises on a nine-foot Yamaha grand piano. Drew became oblivious to the rest of us because he was happily earphoned in a plastic cage, picking intently on a new Yamaha electric guitar.

"Oh, look, Dad!" Will had stopped playing the clavichord and was tugging my shirt and pointing across the street. The sign said in the most unmistakably plain English: THE LARGEST TOY PARK IN THE WORLD.

Will exclaimed, "It will have exactly what I've been looking for"—and so he and I rushed across the street and wound through floor after floor, department after department, until we reached the train department, and Will discovered exactly what he had been looking for.

"How do you know it's a bullet train?" I asked.

Will looked disgusted. "The way you tell a bullet train is by the engine, sort of a half-circle in the front and the cars have a blue or green line running straight through all the cars to the end. But you can be sure by the way the front of the engine looks."

The next day we sped along at 170 kph on the real bullet train.

"You can't tell me this is as fast as these things go," said Will.

Will and Kathryn and I sat in the dining car, watching out the large windows for Mount Fuji to appear. We ate rice with chopsticks and drank hot Japanese tea, while the Japanese around us ate rice with forks and drank American coffee. The train sped in and out of tunnels, up and over three-story bridges as it rushed through one of the world's most congested corridors of population.

"How do you like it?" I asked Will.

"I love bridges but I don't like subways. The train stays underground too long."

"What about Tokyo?"

"The best thing about Tokyo was when I went to the toy park and was playing with the bullet train I got. Tokyo is really like America. It has some really fun things, like my train I got. I would have had to look really hard in Australia to get what I got. There's Fuji!" Will pointed to a looming sloping, snow-capped peak hiding in the clouds.

"It's bigger than I thought," said Kathryn.

Kyoto Station was full of children in uniform. Their eyes seemed never to leave Drew's curly hair, which was now long enough for a ponytail or, I was about to comment (but thought better of it), a floor mop. In the old temples, we clapped our hands to get the giant stone Buddha's attention and walked on the floor that squeaked like a nightingale, took pictures of lions that looked like shaggy dogs because ancient Japanese painters had never seen real lions and they did have real shaggy dogs.

"Who wants to go to paradise?" Honey asked as she dropped some coins in a bowl and crawled through a hole in a temple wall.

"I do," cried Will and ran to follow his mother.

Kyoto is the ancient capital of Japan. It seems to have the perspective of an old traveler, one who has been sitting for centuries on the ancient Silk Road. Kyoto enjoys the mellowness that comes with age and with understanding and with being comfortable with its own long history and traditions. Australia and America, which are younger, possess a kind of sharpness. In Kyoto the sharper edges are now all rounded, all except for the modern raw edges of cluttered postwar Japan— gray buildings, power poles, impossible traffic jams, delivery trucks, motorcycles, vehicles of every shape, progress slowing to a creep. But the cars all seemed new and were so clean and nicely proportioned and the object of so much affection that in an ironic way they served as a substitute for the fragile natural beauty of Japan they have helped to obliterate.

"It's a good thing we brought sweaters," said Honey. In the mist and the rain in Kyoto there was still the feel of winter. Yellow wildflowers had begun to spread in the fields and the first rows of cabbages were growing in gardens, but there were frost coverings on the outside plantings. Young tomato plants grew in protective greenhouses and green tea leaves were covered by black plastic. The pruned and cut vineyards were not yet showing leaves.

Honey said, "The azaleas are blooming here and in Sydney, too. What confusion." We sat around a table laden with Japanese food—*shabu shabu*, fish, turtle soup, and chopsticks.

"Wait till you get to China," Drew warned those who were turning up their noses.

We stayed overnight in a *ryokan*, a traditional Japanese inn.
"The room is short," said Will.

"It doesn't have to be so tall when you begin from the
floor," explained Honey.

"Hey, there's nothing to sit on."

"Or to sleep on," said Kathryn.

"There are *tatami* to sleep on—the mats on the floor," said
their mother.

"It's soft," Leslee said, lying down, "and I want to take a
hot bath."

I said, "Everybody uses the same bath."

"At the same time?" Leslee's eyes widened.

"Not at this hotel," her mother said.

A powerful odor filled the room.

I said, "Can we put the shoes outside somewhere?" I had
forgotten until this instant what it's like when everybody takes
off their shoes at the same time in an locker room.

"I'm going out for a walk," said Drew.

His mother asked, "Did you see the curfew? It says, 'If you
don't come back by eleven-thirty P.M. you can't come in until
seven A.M. Don't call us, please.' I don't want to have to try to
find any of you at midnight somewhere under a pagoda."

Drew said, "The shogun probably wrote the curfew."

"And enforces it," Leslee said.

Kathryn looked at me. "Dad, are you still taking notes?"

Leslee said, "It's the way he deals with not being in charge
of anything anymore.

"What's the book going to be about, Dad?" she inquired,
doing some fast footwork to maintain my goodwill after such a
comment.

"I'm not sure it's going to be a book. It gets more like a
television comedy every day," I said.

CHAPTER 24

TABUCHI *SAN*

//

Our desire was the rainbow over the
Pacific.

—GWEN TERASAKI
Bridge to the Sun

We first met the Tabuchis in 1979 when we invited the
families of all the Japanese businessmen living in
Tennessee to come for a country dinner on the grounds of the
Mansion, and then to visit the Grand Ole Opry. The Tabuchis
had moved that year from Ashiya, near Osaka, to Jackson,
Tennessee, where the family's company had built a plant. Katsuko and Teruhisa Tabuchi and Honey and I discovered that we
had been married in the same month of the same year, January
1969. We enjoyed watching the three Tabuchi children play
with Drew, Leslee, and Kathryn because they were about the
same ages.

We were excited when our old friend, Tabuchi *san,* met us at the hotel in Osaka. (In Japanese, the word *san* is the closest thing to "Mr." but it is a friendly sort of "Mr.," and friends use it when addressing one another.) Tabuchi *san* said, "Yoko is now in twelfth grade, Choko is in ninth, and Atiko is in eighth." Driving through the crowded streets, he explained that "seventy-five percent of ladies in Japan have name that ends with 'ko.' Like Katsuko, my wife." The Tabuchi girls took Leslee and Kathryn to a dance show, and Drew and a boyfriend of Yoko's—who also had lived in Jackson, Tennessee, for a while—went to a baseball game between the Osaka Tigers and the Tokyo Giants.

It took forty-five minutes to drive with Tabuchi *san* from our hotel to Ashiya, where the family lived.

"Ashiya is a village of seventy thousand, between Big Osaka and Big Kobe, which have millions. First I want to show you my father's home."

The elder Tabuchis were waiting for us in the rain at the end of the sidewalk holding brightly colored umbrellas. They wore kimonos. We walked between twisted pines and red maples to the porch of their traditional Japanese home, left our shoes at the door, and entered. The interior furnishings were of wood and paper, uncluttered, each item having a simple reason for being in its place. A single pine tree grew outside in front of a large window. The window framed the pine, making it a part of the house instead of the landscape.

"There is only one western room in the house, the bedroom," said the younger Tabuchi. "Six *tatami* rooms and one western room. Most younger Japanese have six western rooms and no *tatami* rooms." He laughed the little laugh that seems always to punctuate conversations between Americans and Japanese who are working to be friendly. "Still, everyone takes shoes off. I have only one friend who lets people wear shoes in his house. Now we will show you a typical Japanese western house."

"It's beautiful," said Honey when we entered the home of the younger Tabuchis. They had obviously been heavily influenced by their three years and three months in Jackson. The house was American ranch style.

"It is a humble house, by U.S. standards. When we lived in Jackson we lived in a mansion." Tabuchi *san* spread his arms wide to show the size of the place. "It had more than two acres. There is not so much land here."

That evening while Katsuko and Honey visited, and before the older children had returned, Tabuchi *san* and I talked about his worldwide business.

"Tabuchi is not big business. Not small, but not too big."

"How big?"

"Two hundred fifty million dollars, U.S., of sales last year. We have six plants in Japan, eighteen hundred employees. We have a new plant in Britain, near Newcastle. Would you like to see the video of when Prince Charles visited our grand opening?"

"I'm sure the children would like to see it, too. Maybe later, after dinner," I suggested.

"Two hundred sixty people work there now. There will be another one hundred soon."

"What do you make there?"

"What we make everywhere—transformers for VCRs and TV and electric typewriters and microwave ovens and radios."

"You have a plant in Korea?"

"One in Korea, with about five hundred employees. There soon will be four in Mexico, and of course the one in Tennessee. It has about two hundred twenty employees."

"Where do you do most of your selling?"

"U.S.-Canada and Europe and Japan—this is the market. Number one is U.S.-Canada. About two hundred sixty million people in U.S.-Canada buy consumer products. Europe is number two, although there are more consumers there, about three hundred thirty million. Japan is number three because it is smaller. We only have about one hundred twenty million consumers. In those three markets, that is seven hundred ten million people buying consumer products."

"But the rest of the world is much bigger than that."

"There are another four billion more people in the world, but only about five percent of those have an active mind to buy consumer products. So that is only about two hundred million more potential customers among all those four billion other persons and many of them are in New Zealand, Australia, and Scandinavia."

"What about China?"

"In five to ten years China will become good. We would
like to do it, to sell there, but it is very hard now."

"I have just been to a conference in Oiso where there was
a lot of discussion and worry about the relations between Japan
and the United States."

"Some people in Japan are afraid the United States will
elect a protectionist president."

"That won't happen, but the Congress is very upset about
trade."

"Do you know what the biggest problem is on your side
between the United States and Japan?" Tabuchi *san* asked. "It
is the meaning of the word 'unfair.' It is totally different for you
and for us. You have a sixty-billion-dollar trade deficit with us.
You in the U.S. say that is unfair. That is very confusing to
Japanese. We still think of U.S. as an elder brother who has been
saying since the war, 'Work hard and succeed and be like us.' So
we have worked hard and succeeded and become more like you.
Now, why is that unfair? We are low price and high quality, and
have learned to sell to the whole world. What is our fault?"

"So it's *our* fault, in the U.S.?"

"That is what I used to think, that it is mostly your fault."

"You've changed your mind?"

"Yes, some. When I first started thinking about this, I
thought that the attitude of America toward Japan—resentment—is very strange. America is the most popular country in
Japan. So why should America resent us? Then I notice that the
attitude of other countries toward Japan—resentment—is the
same as American attitude. And so I thought maybe they are not
strange. Maybe it is *Japan* who is strange. I thought about America. If we continue to export to America at our present rate, in
fifty years we earn enough money to buy up all the value of
American land. We buy up the value of America in fifty years.
That is why America is so upset. We in Japan don't understand
the big meaning."

I asked, "What can you do about it? You have to trade to
buy food and energy. All the experts at the conference in Oiso
knew a lot, but no one seemed to know exactly what Japan could
do or even what America should expect Japan to do. I think it
would help for Japan to open its markets."

Tabuchi *san* said, "Open markets is not a solution. You are twice as big as we are, richer than us. Americans like the things we make. And since you don't save money, you have to borrow from someone to keep your living standard. We take all the barriers down, you will still have a big trade deficit with us. There will not be much difference and you will still be unhappy with us."

I said, "It will not change the trade deficit much, I agree, but here is where *our* definition of 'unfair' comes in—most Americans believe that if both countries will just play by the same rules that deficits will be easier for us to swallow. But I've been thinking about what to do and I think I have the answer."

"Please let me have your plan," said Tabuchi *san*.

"Merge Australia and Japan. That's it. In the new merged nation, the Japanese could teach the Australians how to work harder and how to export more, and the Australians could give the Japanese a lesson or two in how to enjoy life. Think of what that would do for Australia. Productivity would rise. Vacations would become shorter. Exports would go up. Government debt would go down. The Aussies would have more money and less time to spend it, so savings would rise. They would be richer and would have to move fast when they traveled, and so people from other countries would begin to resent them and whisper about them the way they do now about Americans and Japanese tourists. That would be healthy, it would spread the resentment around."

"I am afraid to ask what your plan might do for Japan," Tabuchi *san* said, smiling.

"It would slow Japan down. The first thing to do would be cut out the monopolies that Qantas and Japan Air Lines have on flights between Sydney and Tokyo. Let in Singapore Airlines and American and United Airlines. That would cut the fares by seventy-five percent, and the Japanese would pour into the Australian beaches. They would have so much fun they would want longer vacations. Some might even insist on six-month Australian-style vacations. Japanese productivity would drop. Exports would drop—think of all the goodwill Japan could earn around the world!"

"And think of all the laid-off workers in Osaka and

bankrupt owners in Tokyo," said Tabuchi *san,* making a face.

I went on. "It would be worth it. Japanese savings accounts would disappear in wild spending sprees on the beaches of Australia. Personal debt would rise. Japan's national debt would grow out of control. Interest rates would rise. Japan would even develop huge trade deficits with some countries. Japan would become even more like America, a model nation!"

"And for the rest of the world, what would they have to say about this new nation?"

I was wound up now. "Why, the free world would especially welcome such a new superpower—one with the hedonism of Spain, the institutions of Great Britain, the bargaining skills and history and tenacity and family structures of Asia, the exporting and production skills of modern Japan, and the pioneering spirit and international popularity and wide-open spaces of Australia. What a country! This new power would be friendly to the West and rich enough to buy from poor countries. It would give the Communists and the terrorists someone else to have to deal with."

"It is a good thing it is almost time for dinner," Tabuchi *san* said. "But just supposing, just supposing for a moment that your plan does not work, I think I have a small suggestion that would help our friendship with the United States and it is something we can do from the Japanese side."

"I'm ready to listen."

"We need a more internationalist policy," he said.

"What does that mean?"

"It means that our businessmen have gone around the world better than our politicians. The businessmen have learned to sell everywhere, but the politicians have not learned to prepare the way everywhere. And so we are in trouble with almost everybody. To ease that problem, we businessmen must start making overseas what we sell overseas. Today, in our small company, seventy percent of our production is in Japan, but sixty percent of the sales is overseas. We will turn that upside down. We will shift thirty percent of the production overseas, and then we will produce overseas almost all of what we sell overseas. We can do that in just a few years."

"And produce at home what you sell at home?"

"Yes."

"Will you send overseas the high-tech part of the business?"

"No. We will leave the high-tech part in Japan. It does not work to move sophisticated operations overseas where you cannot be sure you can hire the right employees and supervise very carefully."

"Your plan makes a lot more sense now that the yen's value has risen so much compared to the dollar."

Tabuchi *san* winced visibly. "This exchange rate is crazy, terrible, very hard for us. Japanese wages are now higher than American. Korean wages are one seventh the wages in Japan. Our most expensive plant anywhere in the world is here in Osaka. But so life goes."

"But Japan is rich."

"Not so rich. The American life-style is richer than Japan's. Most Australians live better than most of us. The standard Japanese house is a humble kind of house. No one has much land. A businessman doesn't feel so rich in a country on a fifty- or seventy-thousand dollar-a-year salary when it costs one hundred fifty to five hundred thousand dollars to join a country club—only to play golf!"

All at once from all directions the children returned from their excursions.

Tabuchi *san* asked, "How was baseball?"

"Just like home, only smaller players," said Drew.

I remarked to Tabuchi *san*, "The children say Japan is more like America than Britain, even more like America than Australia."

He said, "In business, Japan and America *are* very close. After the war the American manner of service was imported from the United States to Japan. We learned how to sell and provide services even before Japan was very commercial, before we learned how to produce. In that way we are closer to America than to Britain. It is easier for me to do business in America than Britain. And there is a very American surface here—our western clothes, our houses, our fast foods. We are all getting bigger and fatter on bad American fast-food diets. We are even getting more lawyers."

I said, "That is our secret weapon, exporting lawyers to Japan. It will grind you to a halt."

He said, "We only have ten thousand lawyers in our whole country. You have six hundred forty thousand in a nation of only twice as many people."

I countered, "You can find ten thousand American lawyers in just thirty or so American mega-law firms."

Tabuchi *san* said, "Be very careful in thinking Japan and America are really alike. Japan is a country of many layers, and the American layer is only the most recent. The other layers are still there, too. All those layers is one reason we have such trouble changing in Japan. What I told you about making overseas what we sell overseas—that way of thinking is my way of thinking, but it is not the old way of thinking and there are still more in Japan who think the old way. Redefining our orientation and purpose is very hard. There are many bureaucracies that have built up since the Meiji period, and there are many people who have been protecting their ground for a long time. We have special problems with trade around the world because we have no oil—you have oil—and no place to grow much food—you can grow all your food. Unlike you, we must trade to survive. But I believe we have even harder problems at home to solve first. We have attitudes to change."

I said, "But so do we. America is in transition, on a sort of uncharted course in terms of its policies and maybe even in terms of its values. That's one reason I think Americans are so fascinated with Australia. We see in Crocodile Dundee and the red desert and the sheep stations and the free-spirited life the same sort of pioneering values that made us strong and that still make us most comfortable when we think about ourselves."

Tabuchi *san* seemed concerned. "Sometimes in its criticism of us, America looks as if it does not know itself. What will this mean for Japan?" he asked.

"It means that your biggest customer for a while will be going through a process of searching, spending more time being deeply concerned about conditions close to home. Americans will care more about what goes on up and down the streets where we live and less about what happens in every place in the world. In an odd sort of way it may make us more, rather than less, internationally minded. But there will probably be a movement away from high-risk, high-cost foreign policies."

"That sounds like what China and even the Soviets are likely to be doing, too," said Tabuchi.

"You cannot be sure about the Soviets."

"We know. Their mainland is closer to us than Cuba is to Florida. And in case they don't stay home, that is one more change we need to make."

"What is that?"

"Self-defense. Russian ships stick their noses into our waters four or five times a day and all we can say to them, under our constitution, is, 'Please don't come. Please don't come.' We should be able to say more to the Soviets than, 'Please don't come.' "

The senior Tabuchis arrived, and we stood up and walked to the den for a Japanese-style western dinner, after which we watched a video of Prince Charles making small talk with Tabuchi plant employees in Newcastle, England. Mrs. Tabuchi senior had brought her *koto*, the long-necked, thirteen-stringed traditional Japanese guitar that she had learned to play as a girl.

Our children took turns trying to play it. "My mother says she has not had it out of the case for ten years," laughed Tabuchi *san*, interpreting for her.

When we drove back to the hotel in the rain, everyone felt warm and good. It was a special feeling to have friends who were so much like us, and yet so different, in such a distant part of the world.

C H A P T E R 2 5

H I R O S H I M A

//

There was no grass, no trees and no
houses left in Hiroshima.

—TOSHI MARUKI
The Hiroshima Story

The speedometer in the dining car reached 250 as the
bullet train sped through the gray mist.

"This is more like it," Will said, ripping open a hard roll.

After a week of living so close together in Japan, each of us
was feeling the need for space. The car was not full, so we had
spread out—Drew in one seat reading another Stephen King
(How many books has Stephen King written!?), and Leslee in
another, writing. Kathryn folded origami dolls with the young
Japanese woman who was our guide. Honey needlepointed, and
Will and I disappeared into the big windowed dining car, where
we ate rolls and drank tea and watched Japan go by. It would
be a good long bullet train ride, three hours to Mihara, and then
a ship would take us across the Inland Sea to Hiroshima before
suppertime.

At 250 kilometers per hour, the raindrops became tiny pellets that rolled across the outside of the windows. Gaily colored umbrellas brightened the gray streets and the train stations. There were puddles in the brown gravel in the small playgrounds—no baseball players today—and puddles on the roofs of the freight cars that rushed under us when the bullet train rose on its own tracks above the din. The morning wore on, and the mist settled lower in the hills as it does in the Tennessee mountains when rain sets in. The rain was no surprise. The forecasters had said it was coming today, from the west. The weather in Japan comes as the culture came, from the west, from China.

Japan has carved in its landscape a place for the bullet train. The train rides its own route on tracks built high over the shops and city streets—built even higher over the big gray concrete expressways—tracks that reach the height of a five-story building in downtown Okayama where we arrived at 10:30. We left Okayama at 10:32. Sometimes the stops were even shorter than two minutes, and they occurred every ten or fifteen minutes or so, but so gradually that after a while I didn't notice. As the train raced through the countryside, it went on tracks that were three stories high, and it took longer to travel at 200 kilometers per hour through the long, dark special bullet-train tunnels cut into rock than it did to stop in Okayama.

By 10:45 there were no more rain streaks on the windows. In the playgrounds now there were parents with closed umbrellas ready, watching little-league baseball games. We saw more neatly cultivated rows of brown dirt, vines, and trees. At last we seemed to be escaping the clutter of the people corridor from Tokyo to Kyoto and Osaka, but there did not seem to be one inch of unused land. There were large fields, which in the United States we would call farms, but here every farm looked like a garden. The train paused in Kurashiki. After forty seconds, the bell rang. After sixty seconds, the train left. One minute, on and off. I barely noticed.

At Mihara, before we boarded the ship to cross the Inland Sea, there was just enough time for lunch.

"We have to eat Japanese," said Drew, amid murmurings from the fast-food addicts, who were desperately glancing around but who had despaired of finding a McDonald's in the time that we had in Mihara. "When you're in a country you have to eat the country's food," insisted Drew. In we trooped to a clearly authentic Japanese restaurant, surrounded a small table in the corner, and sat down.

I said, "This looks like a Japanese White Cottage," recalling an out-of-the-way eating place in Nashville, locally popular for its devotion to home-style southern cooking.

In real Japanese restaurants, like this one, the menu is presented in a special way. Stiff-looking but remarkably accurate plastic replicas of what there is to eat that day are displayed behind the restaurant's front plate-glass windows. We trooped back outside to select lunch from a menu of displays that included dried octopus, seaweed, purple and green baby fish, and fried squid packed with rice. Some of us stayed at the window a long time before making a selection. When we sat down again, most of us ate a lot of rice.

Kathryn said incredulously, "It's worse than *this* in China?"

"Just you wait," replied Drew, the China authority who had never once been to China and who without a squirm finished his squid.

As the boat sailed in the rain on the Inland Sea toward Hiroshima, the children sat and read *Newsweek, Life,* and any other American magazine they could get their hands on. Japan had provided their first good supply of American magazines in three months. I had given up urging them to look out the windows and had almost stopped worrying about my giving up. Honey reminded me of the Australian friend whose family had visited Athens and who said her fifteen-year-old son had wanted to stay in the car listening to rock music instead of visiting the Acropolis. I thought, How *much* of this the children absorb may not be so important. What is most important is that these six months off will open new windows for them and they will never be able to escape from growing up in the whole world.

We stood on the deck as the ship approached Hiroshima Harbor. The rain had stopped and the clouds were breaking, but the cold wind nearly blew us down. Rocky hills, covered with evergreens and new spring green and too steep to cultivate, nearly surrounded the flat gray sea. Houses were crammed together at the base of the hills. I thought, eight hundred thousand people live in Hiroshima today, but from the clouds it would still be hard for an airplane to find among the dark hills and water and mist. The ship docked at 5:00 P.M. We went to our hotel and ate an American-style supper, after which we purchased several books about what happened in Hiroshima on August 6, 1945. After dinner, the older children read quietly and then exchanged books and read some more and said little. I read to Will from *The Hiroshima Story*, a book that Drew had bought for him, the story of a seven-year-old girl named Mi-Chow.

When I finished reading, Will said, "Without that bomb we might not have had what we had to eat today. We might not have had money to buy it."

Kathryn said, "Or we might be Japanese, or there might not even be a United States."

"Or there might not be a world," Leslee said.

"Dad," Will asked, "how do wars start? How did World War One start?"

Kathryn said, "There was one guy who killed somebody. We read about it."

"Just over that?" said Will.

I said, "That's not far wrong."

Will asked, "How could that happen?"

Monday morning was bright and clear. The streets were decorated with yellow and purple tulips and pink dogwood blossoms.

"Were there any streetcars then?" Kathryn asked our Japanese guide.

"Yes, but they are gone. The streetcars today are second-hand, gifts from Kyoto and Tokyo and Kobe, and from West Germany."

Monday, August 6, 1945, had been a beautiful and clear day, too, and it had been hot early. An air-raid warning had sounded at 7:30 A.M. and then, for reasons never explained, was lifted. Forty-five minutes later a single United States Air Force plane drifted over the mountains to a place above the center of the city, dropped one bomb, and flew away toward the ocean. Statistics cannot convey what happened then. It is too much to absorb, even when you are standing where children were playing beneath the place in the sky where the bomb exploded high in the air. Their skin melted. So did the tile roofs of their schools. Black rain for two hours. Fire everywhere all day raging into the sky. Human bones melting and fusing with trash. Burned-out intestines. No houses left. No streets left. Two hundred thousand victims. Cries for mothers and for children and for water—and then silence. Wounds that would not heal. Insects breeding in those wounds. Twenty-nine years later, glass fragments in a survivor's cheek. Today, a shadow burned into stone still looking for its owner. Today, the knowledge that a modern nuclear bomb is twenty-five hundred times the power of the one that was dropped that morning.

Each of us wandered alone through the exhibits at Peace Memorial Park, which was built at the epicenter of the bomb's blast. We did not talk much. At the exit there was a book in which visitors had written down their feelings and their nationality, and I copied in my notebook what some had written:

> *Woeful:* Irish
> *What can I say but we're sorry:* USA
> *Never again.*
> *Live and let live:* Indian
> *Unreal:* New Zealand
> *O God:* Swiss
> *No comment:* Swiss
> *Let us remember, never again:* USA
> *Never again is our prayer:* USA
> *No more:* Germany
> *Very sad. The lesson is there:* Australian
> *Hope the warmongers of the West realize their deed:* Indian
> *Imagine all the people:* USA
> *I saw scenes from railway station in 1945 about October that I pray I never see again:* California

How will the children absorb the enormity of this? I had wondered about this from the time I first thought of coming here, months ago. I felt that coming to Hiroshima had been the main reason for our visit to Japan, an attempt to make real for them somehow what it means to live in a nuclear world. But should we go to Dachau or another concentration camp on our way home so they can know the other side of how cruel humans can be to other humans, can think about what might have happened if we had lost the war?

At least, I could give Leslee and Drew Elie Wiesel's *Night*. But that book had burned in my mind for weeks when I read it and I was forty, and they have so much happiness left in their young lives—at least after visiting Hiroshima, reading *Night* would be too much for one week or even for one trip. When we are home I will take them to meet Austin Shofner in Shelbyville. He will tell them about escaping from a Japanese prison and about his death march through the swamps of China and how the next ones who tried were beheaded. The children have seen Pearl Harbor. They will remember standing above the U.S.S. *Arizona* sunk in Pearl Harbor, a thousand U.S. sailors' bodies still in it. And in July we will be going home through China and the Soviet Union, and maybe even riding a train across the Berlin Wall. Then they can begin to decide for themselves what freedom is and what it is worth.

We hired a taxi to an observation tower at the top of one of the high rocky hills overlooking Hiroshima. We saw what one plane would see if again it were suddenly to drift over the mountains from the east—mountains rising steeply on the three sides of the blue sea, the busy harbor, the crowded narrow streets, the hills green and dark on such a sunny day, and blue tile roofs gleaming.

Drew interrupted the silence. "Well, Dad, are you going to turn into a radical peace politician now that you've seen Hiroshima?"

After that comment, I stopped worrying about opening enough windows so that the children could discover the truth, and so inquired cautiously of Drew what he had figured out for himself.

He said, "I've thought about it before. We discussed it in class. We voted on it and voted the U.S. was right. I guess it might have gone the other way if we'd been in school here."

At 2:00 p.m. we caught a local train for Beppu, which is on Kyushu, the southernmost island of Japan. The tile roofs and the river gleamed in the afternoon sun. Purple clover was spreading through green fields, and there were deep furrows in rich soil ready for planting. We saw the real rural Japan, forests and fields and countryside. And the orange and white power-lines.

When our train passed other trains filled with men and women going home from work, there were more and more smiles and waves and people saying hello. Whenever we stopped, there were still more smiles and requests for auto-graphs and children anxious to practice speaking English, and many offers to help us with directions.

There was more and more of everything but Americans, or, for that matter, *any* foreigners. Drew and I became aware of this at about the same time—that as we rolled deeper and deeper into the part of Japan destroyed by the two American atomic bombs, we were the only Americans on the train. Despite the smiles, we both began to feel uncomfortable, and when we got off the train in Beppu, Drew said, "It is hard for me to under-stand how, after all we've seen today, that they can be so nice to us, that America can still be their favorite country."

At breakfast the next morning at a resort hotel in Beppu, Will said, loud enough for several tables to hear, "Drew looks weird."

Drew was the only one to wear a *yukata*, a Japanese robe. "I'm not sure this is the family thing to do," he said, glancing around to see if any of the Japanese at breakfast were wearing *yukatas*. (None of them were.)

"We could sort of hide ourselves," said Will.

"I'm sure everybody wears them," said Drew in a great display of self-confidence.

After breakfast Honey, Kathryn, Will, and I walked up the hill behind the modern hotel, and suddenly found ourselves in a lazy rural Japanese country scene. The sun was hot. Spring flowers bloomed in yards, and among more small Buddhas in their brightly colored caps. We watched a farmer on the other side of the old stone walls who had interrupted his planting to throw rocks at crows. As one crow would leave, another would arrive.

Honey said, "I'm about ready to go home, back to Sydney, but do you know what I've liked most about this trip? Spring. I was really missing spring."

On Wednesday we toured the Hells of Beppu, photographing the boiling, bubbling, sucking mud. Part of it was the color of milk, part the color of blood, part the color of mud. We found a geyser and waited for it to spout. (As soon as it started, Will proclaimed, "Compared to Old Faithful, this one is nothing," and got up to leave.) As the sun set, we exchanged our clothes for robes (which we were relieved to be allowed to wear) and lay on our backs in a row on a beach by the Inland Sea while heavily muscled Japanese women covered us from neck to toe with the healing hot sands of Beppu.

Riding in the jumbo taxi to the airport, Will and Honey were talking. "You told me you like spring, Mommy. Is it for the same reason I figured out?"

She said, "Because things come alive is a very good reason to like spring and it is exactly the reason I like spring."

"You know, Mom."

"Yes, Leslee."

"This is too short. We should have stayed in Australia a year or two. Just as we get into everything, it's going to be time to go."

Kathryn said, "I'm ready to go now."

I asked Will, "Now that you've seen more than Tokyo, what has been the best thing about Japan?"

He thought for a moment. "The bullet train. And there were other things I found out, too."

"Like?"

"Like the memorial stuff for the bomb. I knew it was big. I knew how many people died. But I thought it just blew up a building. I didn't know how bad it was.

"The other thing I liked was the toy park in Tokyo. There were things there I've never seen before, like an electric bullet train."

"Mom?"

"Yes, Leslee."

"Have you noticed how everything centers around Will?"

We flew back to Tokyo, and after a day of walking through a city celebrating Emperor Hirohito's eighty-sixth birthday, we drove to Yokohama to see old friends Mitsuya Goto and his wife and two daughters.

I said, "Goto *san*, I hope you won't mind one more time telling the children your story, about how you came to America."

He said, "I was about your age, Kathryn, thirteen or so, living in Nagoya. It was 1945, during the last few months of the war. Carrier-based fighter planes like Grummans and Corsairs came strafing our cities. I was fascinated with them. I would go out of the air raid shelter into the streets and watch them. Sometimes the planes came so low I could see the faces of the pilots."

"You could *see* them?" Kathryn was paying close attention.

"I wanted to see the faces of people from a country with the power and determination to do such a thing. I remember one May day standing in the smoldering ruins of my home in Nagoya after a wave of American bombers—B-29's, some three hundred strong—had dropped incendiary bombs. I said to myself, "Oh, God, what have we done?" That made me wonder why we were fighting a losing war against America. That made me wonder why America was so strong. That day I set out to find out what made America tick, you might say."

"How much bombing like that was there?"

"Days and days, for months and months, there was bombing. Nagoya, my hometown, is one thousand years old and none of its trees now are older than forty years. After the firebombings, not one was left. Then our homes were paper and wood, and Tokyo was almost like a tinderbox. The American pilots were very good. They would bomb very carefully in squares. That way the flames would rush toward each other trapping everything. When the air raid sirens stopped, I would go back to my home or the shelter and I would carve small wooden airplanes, miniature copies of the Grummans and the Corsairs that I had seen and some of the Japanese warplanes, too."

Leslee was now also paying attention. "But how did you get to America?"

"After the war an American serviceman from Ladoga, Indiana, befriended me, and then suddenly he became violently sick and died here. I sent his photograph and a letter of condolence to his parents and told them someday I would like to come to their country to go to college. They arranged a full scholarship for me at Wabash College in Indiana. When I graduated I came back to Japan and went to work for Nissan, which is how I met your father. We were searching to locate the big truck plant, which eventually went to Tennessee. Excuse me for just a moment."

Goto *san* ran upstairs and returned with a small box, which he handed to me. I knew what it was before I opened it, a miniature Corsair, carved forty years earlier.

Goto *san* said, "I believe it is my last one. I want you to have it."

We rode from Goto's home in Yokohama back to Narita Airport, not looking forward one bit to the ten-hour flight to Sydney. Not an extra one of the undersized seats on our Japan Air Lines flight was empty. Will slipped up to the front of the crowded plane, and when he came back he reported, "The bigger the plane, the better the first class. JAL has plenty of room between the first-class seats. You can see it all the way back where we are, in *last* class."

After we all were crammed in and the plane had lifted off, I read the JAL magazine, which reported that small-parcel quick-delivery services in Tokyo were thinking of closing on Saturdays. The magazine quoted Tahashi Otsuki, a motorcycle driver and delivery man, as saying, "Japan is becoming like America—more and more companies are taking Saturdays off."

If the taxi driver in Sydney hadn't been so talkative the following morning, he would have had sound-asleep passengers by the time he reached our home in Mosman. The driver talked a blue streak. "I find I can work it out so I can take three or four months off a year. Always go up to Queensland. It's the best state. Excellent fishing and good swimming weather in the winter, just like the nice summer days in Sydney. Lots of Japanese coming into Queensland now. They travel around in packs, buying everything and always taking pictures of each other. They've got the money now. But they don't stay long, three or four days is all. I'm up in Queensland three or four months. They're there three or four *days*. Why would they come all the way down here and just stay three or four days?"

CHAPTER 2 6

THE BASQUE

//

We always require an outside point to
stand on, in order to apply the lever
of criticism.

—C. G. JUNG
Memories, Dreams, Reflections

"*That's* where they catch twelve-foot barramundi."
"Barramundi?"
"The best-eating fish in the north," the general declared.
"You feel a good bite, you'd better snatch quick before the
crocodile gets it from the other end. Fellow caught a twelve-
footer the other day—one foot of fish and eleven feet of crocodile. Fellow got the head. Croc got the rest."

We were on the porch of the officers' quarters at George's
Heights, above Sydney Harbor, relaxing after lunch and savor-
ing the sea breezes and the sweet-smelling bush. The Australian
army general telling the fish story was just back from visiting

military installations in northwestern Australia, including highly secret U.S. communications centers. "It's bad," he said. "It's the wet [season]. Flies are thick. Heat's oppressive. Every poisonous snake you can think of. Crocs twenty feet long that will jump out of the water and run across the land faster than you can and take you before you know it."

(Australians have such a civilized way of discussing persons eaten by their crocodiles. You may hear them speak politely of one who has "unfortunately been taken," as if it were something that happened at afternoon tea amid deliberations about lemon or sugar. Or they may mention one who is "ripening," which is a polite term for the crocodile's habit of storing the "taken" victim in the mud under water for a few days before finishing him or her off. This teatime conversation most often focuses upon some unwary American tourist, some poor soul who has been "taken"—discovered and attacked and snatched and chewed and dragged to the bottom of a billabong or marsh and stuck in the mud and "ripened" and then consumed and eventually digested by a monstrous twenty-foot saltwater crocodile. At least this was the way I was thinking about it on the day before we left for a week in the Northern Territory of Australia.)

The next day, as our plane took off over Botany Bay, I imagined Captain Cook's ships sailing north along those sandstone cliffs two hundred years ago when he discovered Botany Bay—but failed to see Sydney Harbor. The opening at Botany Bay did seem bigger, more inviting. The opening at Sydney Harbor was a narrower gap that one easily could miss. Our airplane turned northwest, toward the desert center of Australia. Honey found Will's Crayolas and held them up, trying to match them with the earth's changing colors. "It's mahogany, rust, and red," she said. It looked desolate.

After landing for a two-hour stop in Alice Springs—a town mostly of taxis, tourists, buses, arts-and-crafts shops, and signs advertising FOTO CENTA and 20 PER CENT BIGGER PRINTS—we flew to Yulara. All the passengers were going into the cockpit to take photographs—except for Leslee, who slept with her windowshade down and with music pounding in her Walkman earphones. A fifteen-year-old female body with changing hormones will tolerate only so much "broadening" travel. Our airplane made a sudden right turn and landed as if the pilot were galloping on a brumbie and had suddenly seen the corral.

John Edwards, from the Northern Territory Department of Education, met us. He had a neat beard, a slight build, an American accent, but an Australian easiness and a teacher's penchant for delivering facts. "We have twelve of the most dangerous snakes in Australia, six of which are the most dangerous in the world. It'll be one hundred fifteen to a hundred twenty-five degrees for two to three weeks at a time. In the winters, at night, five below. Yulara is arid, almost a desert. Once it went ten years without rain."

John drove us to the new Sheraton Hotel, a series of rust-brown buildings constructed like low-slung sails. He warned, "You've only got about thirty minutes before we leave for our barbecue under the stars."

On our way to the barbecue, the bus stopped at the Olgas, where we walked among the spines and mounds of rock hundreds of feet high, thrusting out of bare flat desert. As we drove away, a soft blue and yellow and pink horizon was ahead, while behind us the Olgas created a black sharp outline against the setting sun, which was like a bush fire.

At the barbecue, we cooked steaks and chops. The sky turned black and the stars turned on, and some of them were as big and five-pointed as the star in the Christmas story. The Southern Cross sat up high, instead of lying on its side, the way it did above Sydney. And the Milky Way spread from the top of the sky right on down to the ground. "There're no city lights," John explained. "*Everything* is a thousand miles away in *every* direction—Sydney, Perth, Melbourne, even Darwin where we go tomorrow."

The next morning we were on the tour bus by seven. As we approached Ayers Rock, its imposing bulk still slept against the bluing sky. Everything else was flat. The bus circled and drove closer, and the rock's features woke up, became angry gaping rusting holes. Climbing up the rock, I began breathing hard and was grateful for a cable to hold on to. The sun's glare bursting over the top seemed to incinerate hikers walking the ridge above me.

At the top the wind blew cold and the view across the desert was a fantasy of color. I imagined going back to America and having to dress again in suit and tie and to report to an office everyday, and for a desperate moment I felt I had lost my freedom.

Back at the Sheraton, we met John Edwards again, drove to the airport for the flight north to Darwin.

"Darwin has sixty-five thousand people," John told us. "The fastest-growing city in Australia. It only had forty thousand when we came in 1974."

John's wife, Elaine, a slender, cheerful woman, and Drew—who had stayed in Sydney overnight for a friend's birthday party—met us at the hot, crowded Darwin airport. People shuffled about in shorts. The atmosphere was of an old Asian airport in the 1950s, before all international airports became pressed from the same cookie cutter.

Drew said, "This is great! It's hot again. Is there a beach where we can swim?"

John said, "Sure, but watch out for the crocs."

When we arrived at our hotel, Will said, "Ho boy, another Sheraton. They have the best room service! I'll just stay right here the whole time." But when he saw the video promo in our room, he said, "Oh, drats! I've seen it."

Sheravision was offering the American movie *Marie*, and was promoting it this way: "Based on Peter Maas's best-seller about a scandal in the Tennessee correction system—a scandal that ultimately toppled the political structure of the state. Stars Sissy Spacek and Jeff Daniels. Rated M. 112 minutes."

I said, "I know the story. I think I'll pass."

John said to Honey, "Rest well tonight. Tomorrow Elaine will show you and the children Darwin and the crocodile farm while Lamar and I visit with the educators. Then we'll go on to the real 'Crocodile Dundee' Country. But first, I have promised one interview with Lamar. It won't take long. The reporter should be in the coffee shop."

I was not prepared for the reporter who waited in the Sheraton coffee shop.

"Why are you Americans flagellating yourselves?" He savored his words, tasted his question, as if he had been anticipating my visit.

"I represent the *Northern Territory News.* And I am Basque, which is one reason I am blunt. I have been a historian all my life but, this year, at fifty years of age, I have changed jobs. And I like being a reporter."

His questions—which were more like opinions—practically tumbled over each other.

"Why is there so little talent in your presidential race?" This character must have understudied Sam Donaldson in the White House press corps, I thought.

"But what really fascinates me is, why does your country, with so much power and prestige, spend so much time destroying itself? First Watergate, then Irangate, then this [Gary] Hart affair. It's hard to understand from here."

"Well, I have not kept up with it much during the last few months. I haven't read an American newspaper since January twenty-sixth," I said lamely, almost wishing I had stayed with Will to watch "the crumble of the Tennessee state government" on Sheravision.

"Surely you must know about the Hart affair," he pressed.

"Well, yes," I said.

"If it had been in Australia, everyone would have said, 'Good on you. Wish it was me!' "

"And why"—he had obviously been tasting this one for some time, too—"why do you Americans become angry with Japan for making better cars than you do, cars that people want and like? And why do you preach to the rest of the world about open markets and free trade, and then *you* throw up trade barriers against your friends, such as Australians, with whom *you* have a trade surplus?"

I could see my options: Either settle in for a two-hour argument or find some way to encourage a merciful ending to the "interview."

I said, "Let's talk about Australia."

"It's a country searching for its identity," he said.

"These days, what country isn't?"

The Basque said, "Australia is searching more than most. Australia clings to British history, but its vulnerability is to

Asia. Australia's an odd mix of American values and British institutions."

"And Japanese cars," I added.

He let that pass. "And this part of Australia—where we are—many foreigners think this is the *real* Australia. This is a nearly inhospitable jungle. In our wet season we cut grass twice a week. Palm trees grow thirty feet in five years. But nothing we *try* to grow will grow. Art Linkletter and some developers from your country have spent millions trying to grow rice in the Northern Territory. But the buffalo ran through it. The magpie geese ate it. For seven years they kept trying to grow rice, and now it's a bird breeding ground. The developers just walked away from it."

"That's awful!"

"And the bugs eat anything we plant. Fertilizer is too expensive for the leached soil. We get fifty inches of rain in the wet season. There are crocs and sharks and box wasps—which float in the ocean and are the deadliest of all—and snakes. And it is a vast, vast country."

The Basque was starting to sound like a reporter who could care. I said, "What impresses me is that most Australians don't live in the *real* Australia, but the aborigines learned to live all over the continent, even in the most inhospitable parts. European Australians just cling to a toehold on the edge."

The Basque didn't really respond but continued enthusiastically with his new line of thought. "Many things are alike about our two countries. Only twice in history were continents successfully colonized: the Americas and Australia. And our countries are the same size, both have British institutions, both have aboriginal natives. The difference was what explorers found on the other side of the great dividing range. We both got across it about the same time, although we were quicker about it. It took you from 1620 to about 1770. It took us from 1788 to 1813. Your explorers found a country on the other side of the dividing range. Ours found a desert. If we had sent Lewis and Clark west across *our* mountains, they would have come back and reported nothing there."

"Interview over?" asked John Edwards.

The Basque finished his coffee, and seemed also to have

satisfied his appetite for questions—and for giving answers, too. I finished my juice, said good night, and went back to our room just as the Tennessee state government crumbled on the Sheravision. Will lay on the couch where he had fallen fast asleep.

CHAPTER 2 7

''THOSE CROCODILE DUNDEE PEOPLE!''

//

Yes, indeedy! If *I* ain't an American
there *ain't* any Americans, that's all.
　　　　　　　—MARK TWAIN
　　　　　　　A Tramp Abroad

John Edwards had arranged for a plane to fly Drew and me to Smith Point on Cobourg Peninsula, the second most northerly point on the Australian continent. This was Arnhem Land, occupied for at least forty thousand years by aborigines, some of whom still follow Stone Age customs. We had spent the day in the only boat ever licensed by the aborigines for fishing the northern coast along Arnhem Land, and we had caught so many barracuda and trevally that by four o'clock we were exhausted when we came back to the campsite on the peninsula. We cooked and ate some of the trevally, and suddenly the sky everywhere was filled with stars that had not been there the last time I had looked up. The Milky Way spread across the southern sky, and the Southern Cross stood straight up at the top of the sky. We had traveled to twelve degrees below the equator, and were closer to China than to our new home in Sydney.

A mozzie or two tried me several times during the night and the breeze was a bit warm, but I slept until the birds began to sing. Then the generator rumbled, and the lights made patterns of dancing leaves on the sides of the tent. I reached for my boots and found my watch. It was six-fifteen.

I walked fifty yards east to a clearing. The trees formed a black-green outline against the sky's faint blue. I saw one morning star, and then another straight above it, and then pink spreading beneath the blue.

An airplane passed low over our cooking fire, red wing lights flashing, startling us even though we had been expecting it. By seven o'clock the plane had landed and stopped its motor, and Ivan, the pilot, was sitting with us eating breakfast. The sky was all blue now, the generator was silent, and the artificial lights were off. We listened to the birds and felt the warm breeze, and our anticipation grew for traveling into Kakadu National Park, because everyone had been telling us it was one of the world's environmental wonders.

We said good-bye to our fishing companions, and, within minutes, Ivan, Drew, and I were flying toward Wild Man Station on the East Alligator River, deep in aboriginal territory. From four thousand feet I looked down at Van Diemen Gulf and wondered how many big-toothed characters might have me for breakfast if we should fall.

Ivan had flown Australian film star Paul Hogan in this same Piper Saratoga, searching for locations for the movie *Crocodile Dundee.*

"Were any of your sites in the movie?" I asked.

Ivan rattled them off. "The waterfalls, the billabong, Oberi Rock, the water buffalo in the middle of the trail. You remember where the croc attacked the bird [young woman], that? All those places. You'll see most of 'em."

"What was Hogan like?"

"Hard to say. He slept most of the time."

"For ten days?"

"Right. He played pretty hard all night at the casino in Darwin. The next day I'd fly him low over the crocs, he'd take a quick look, pull down his hat, and go back to sleep."

The trips with Hogan had made Ivan something of a celebrity among other bush pilots and had earned him the nickname "Cut-the-Bullshit Ivan."

"What kind of name is that?"

"Well, whenever I would try to talk to Hogan, maybe to point out a film site or some crocs or something, he'd raise his hat, open one eye, and say, 'Cut the bullshit, Ivan, just fly.' So I would fly. And he would go back to sleep."

We had left the bay, which was muddy at low tide, and were flying much lower, at about five hundred feet. There were clumps of light green grass where the buffalo had been wallowing. White birds rose in a circle. "Pelicans and brolga," Ivan said. White egrets stood in the marsh. Black-and-white magpie geese flew below and to the side of the plane. These were the wetlands. This was Kakadu country.

"This is where all the barra are, where the crocs are, too, but don't you worry about that," Ivan said.

"At the end of the wet, the river floods, and when it retreats it leaves billabongs with barramundi in them. The billabong shrinks, so there is more and more competition for food," Ivan explained. After nearly five months in Australia I had almost no trouble understanding Ivan's Aussie English, even mixed in with the noise of the engine of the Piper Saratoga. "The barras are a bit off the bite now. It gets best round the end of the dry season when there is the most competition for food."

I had been seeing smoke and began counting bush fires. Ivan explained that for thousands of years the aborigines had been burning off the spear grass. The fires open the land—spear grass can grow six feet in six months during the wet season— flush lizards for food, give an extra early spurt of dry-season growth to the prairie grass. And smoke drifting over Darwin creates magnificent "Top End" sunsets. "I reckon those sunsets have a bit of renown," said Ivan.

A young aborigine man stood near where we landed at Wild Man Station. His job was to clear the airstrip of animals,

Ivan explained. "Quite often we get wallabies and buffalo and large birds. They can be quite a problem." We walked past termite mounds. They occurred every twenty feet or so and some of them were six feet high, sticking up like little Matterhorns at Disney's Magic Kingdom. We carried our gear into the main house at Wild Man Station.

There we met Lew Balinger, the manager, and his wife, Faye, who had fixed breakfast for us, and so we ate again. The Balingers had been married for forty-one years and had lived in the Northern Territory "on and off" since Lew was "on the other side" (in the Middle East) during World War II.

Lew introduced Drew to Buffie, a sleek pet water buffalo. Lew explained, "She has a good life. She sleeps, moves a few times a day from shade to the shed to stay out of the sun. Sometimes she gets up and knocks on the door and I spray her for mozzies. She gets eight meals a day."

While Lew spoke, Faye Balinger sat quietly. She was draped within a flowing red dress and crowned with white hair, and she was wearing a bemused expression that suggested that she was not likely ever to say anything unless Lew asked first. But after a while, the red dress and white hair began to tremble and the face became animated and Faye Balinger erupted.

"Those Crocodile Dundee people! Those Americans that win prizes on the radio stations. They ring up and if they win a prize they come here, all the way from some big American city halfway around the world to this billabong. *They are terrible.* All they want is air conditioners and drinking. I have to dig cigarette butts out of the floor when they leave. They break out screens and put their feet on the table. I wanted to smack one of them.

"Now they's *some* nice ones. One woman from Texas, she was about six feet two, was real nice. She would sit here at the table and all she'd say was, 'Oh, my God!,' just like this, at everything anybody said, 'Oh, my God!' But when a busload of 'em went to Oberi Rock, only two of 'em would get out and look.

"Now most of the other Americans we meet, they are nice. There was a Georgia cracker who called and wanted a fishing trip for himself and '*mah* baby boy'; and I thought, 'Oh, my God, I'll have to baby-sit some Georgia cracker's baby boy.' He didn't tell me his baby boy was a two-hundred-fifty-pound gridiron player that ate us out of house and home. They were nice as they could be. But at dinner, Daddy would sit across from the two-hundred-fifty-pound gridiron player and just say, 'That's *mah* baby boy, that's *mah* baby boy.'

"But those Crocodile Dundee people—they came back from the trip to Oberi Rock, put the music on full blast, and took their glasses of wine into the bunkhouses and stayed there. Now, why do you suppose they came halfway around the world to Wild Man Station to do that?"

Lew walked with us about fifty feet to a dock at the end of what seemed like a very narrow river filled with water lilies. He said, "I've got a bush council meeting, so Graham will go with you on the billabong. The barra were biting like buggers at half past five this morning."

Graham, a young aborigine man about Drew's age, stepped into the dinghy, and Drew and I stepped in after him. Graham began yanking the engine cord without success. After a dozen tries, the engine began sputtering and the propeller began to move and the dinghy drifted down the billabong. The black water disappeared into thick bullrushes along the banks. Bridi-kin ducks and magpie geese with black necks flew by. Drew and I popped out two lines and began trolling for barramundi. I wondered what might be under the black water.

"How long have you been a guide?" I asked Graham.

"I'm not a guide. Guide is off today," Graham said. He turned to yank some more on the outboard engine, which had stopped.

"Any crocs around here?" I asked, after Graham had resuscitated the engine.

"Twenty or thirty," he said.

The engine stopped again and while Graham pulled up the propeller to examine it, the dinghy drifted into the bullrushes on the bank.

"Where are the crocs?" I inquired uncomfortably.

Graham swung his arm toward the bank. "In there. You can see them best at night, on the bank, chewing a barra. At night along the billabong you can put a spotlight on them. One night I counted twenty-six in sixty yards."

"How big?"

"The smallest one would be about twelve feet."

"What do they eat?"

"They like barra. One tried a horse last week, tore his leg nearly off. They don't do much, so they don't eat much. They don't chew much either because their jaws aren't that strong. They stick what they want to eat in the mud and wait to eat it so it will go down better."

Drew said, "At the crocodile farm they only fed them two chickens a week."

I was grateful when finally the engine started again and the dinghy floated back out into the center of the billabong. Two small green kingfishers flew overhead and an egret meditated in the bullrushes. We let our lines drift, and we lay back to enjoy the sun beating down. After two hours, having caught nothing, we sputtered back toward the dock at the end of that long, thin body of water and walked up to the station where Lew and Faye and Ivan waited.

Lew was talking about his bush-fire council meeting with the aborigines, which he said would last all afternoon. I had counted eighteen such fires on our flight from Cobourg Peninsula to Wild Man Station. "This station is on aboriginal land, so we have lots of discussions with the abos," he said. "What's said is not so important as the ceremony." Like dealing with legislators, I thought.

Drew gave Buffie, the pampered water buffalo, a good-bye rub on the back of her neck. "She's nearly fifteen months old," said Lew.

We walked through the termite mounds toward the airplane, and I asked, "By the way, Lew, how many crocodiles would you guess are in that billabong?"

"Oh, two hundred, three hundred, at least that many. Put a spotlight on the bank at night and all those croc eyes look like a city. I don't worry about 'em. You have to be very unlucky to be taken by a croc," Lew Balinger said.

FIFTEEN

//

The problem is that your daughter
has given her heart to a
fifteen-year-old boy, and a
fifteen-year-old boy does not qualify
yet as a human being.

—BILL COSBY
Fatherhood

We had escaped to Australia in order to establish a more "normal" life, but it was hard—especially for the children—to know which was real, life at the Tennessee Governor's Mansion museum or life in Australia or something else. Leslee, who had been the most outspoken about wanting to seek a "normal" life in Australia, especially began to run into difficulties with her parents about the definition of "normal."

These difficulties demonstrated that as a family we had not been communicating well. And when we began to communicate, the discussions sometimes rubbed old sore points, such as how I had spent my time swiveling in the governor's chair instead of watching Leslee show-jump her horse, Spring, in competition. These discussions were painful, but I was glad that we had them and that I was around the house more to hear them because Honey, Leslee, and I all said some things that needed to be said and then we had to be there to comfort each other after they were said.

Leslee said, "I wanted you to be around more."

Honey said, "We *were* around, more than you might remember, and we wanted to be around more than that but we didn't want to be in your way."

Our most difficult discussions were about what "normal" freedoms might be for our fifteen-year-old daughter in Sydney, Australia. These discussions came to a head one Saturday morning, the day before we were to leave for our last family excursion from Base Camp Sydney, for a week's vacation on Dunk Island in Australia's sunny "Deep North." "We only went out to watch the sun rise," Leslee explained wearily.

"And what time was that?" inquired the lioness.

"I can't remember," Leslee confessed.

"Was it before or after your father and I went to bed at midnight?"

"After."

"And you didn't come home until you called at about nine the next morning to see how much trouble you were in?"

"Mom, it was only to watch the sunrise. It was really beautiful on the beach."

"Who else was watching this sunrise?"

"Oh, just some friends."

"Why didn't you wake us up and ask us?"

"You might've said no."

"That's correct," I said, entering the interrogation. Honey's stern countenance suggested that she already was weighing a smorgasbord of punishments that might be applied to Leslee either during our last week in Australia, or after we returned to Tennessee, or both.

Honey said, "Your father and I need to talk. We'll call you in fifteen minutes."

Leslee left and the talk began.

I—the wise conciliator and struggling assistant mother—suggested, "The problem is that after a sweet little girl has been locked up in a big mansion and guarded for eight years, it may be hard for her to set limits for herself, especially in a place as much fun as Sydney. Maybe we could have a little constructive discussion with her."

Honey—the accomplished setter of teenage limits and herself once a fifteen-year-old girl—replied, "Like what?"

I explained. "You and I will take turns suggesting some hypothetical situations and Leslee will tell us how she would conduct herself in each situation and then you and I will make our comments and then we all won't be surprised the next time something like this happens." I felt very proud of my plan.

Honey suggested, "Why don't you let *Leslee* make the suggestions if you really want to avoid surprises. You'll never think of what she can think of."

I puzzled over this, but agreed and said, "I guess you know what goes on in the mind of fifteen-year-old girls and I don't, although when I was fifteen, I remember it was one of my major objectives in life to find out."

We invited Leslee to rejoin the discussion, explained the procedure, and she leaped to the challenge.

"Well, what if one of my friends gets drunk on the beach and asks to spend the night?" asked Leslee, who doesn't use alcohol.

"One of the *boys?*" I asked, holding the arms of the chair.

Honey looked at me, and then at Leslee, and then said, "Now, Leslee, you answer your own question. How would *you* handle it?"

"I would help him up the hill to our house and give him some tea or coffee and then put him to bed. It would be dangerous to let him drive home."

Her mother admonished, "It's not your responsibility to minister to boys who are drunk on the beaches of Sydney. You might loan him a quarter to call his parents, or the police, or whatever is the Australian equivalent of 'free rides home for people who have been drinking too much,' or you could call them yourself, and then you should walk home with your friends who haven't been drinking, or call us—no matter what time it is or where it is—and we'll come pick you up."

"Well, that's probably a good idea," said Leslee, who was warming to the discussion of horrible dilemmas in which she might find herself. "Here's another one."

We continued in this vein, Honey learning only what she had already suspected, I learning more about the mind of the fifteen-year-old female than I had ever wanted to learn from my own daughter, and Leslee, we hoped, learning something about reasonable limits for an adventuresome spirit. We analyzed several more dilemmas Leslee presented that I could never have imagined, and established a punishment—but postponed it until we got home to Tennessee. We did not want our daughter to miss the last few days with her Australian friends—which she told us she genuinely appreciated. She rushed out to meet friends for a day at the beach, "I'll call by five o'clock—promise!"

Will, who had celebrated his eighth birthday only three weeks earlier, came from the kitchen, where he had been playing with his toy train and cars and trucks—as well as listening illicitly. He said, "Leslee is one of a kind with her going-out habits. She could be one of the best of her age."

I told him, "This was our private discussion with Leslee, Will. You're *not* supposed to be listening to other people's private discussions."

Will persisted. "But Leslee may be in for some trouble. She'll probably have about twenty kids and she won't know how to stop and she won't have enough money to have that little operation—the one Molly, the cat, had—and she'll just keep on having them. Leslee's in for some trouble."

I yelled, "For heaven's sakes, Will!"

Nothing Will said seemed to disturb Honey.

She turned to him. "I suspect we'll be having some similar conversations with you when you're Leslee's age." Will went back to playing with his train and cars and trucks, and I went for a long Saturday morning walk.

CHAPTER 29

THE WILL OF THE FAMILY

//

I have five children and I love
them as much as a father possibly
could, but I confess that I have an
extra bit of appreciation for my
nine-year-old.

"Why do you love her so much?"
the other kids keep asking me.

And I reply, "Because she's the
last one."

—BILL COSBY
Fatherhood

We had spread ourselves around the little airport lobby
the way families will do when they've been living

close together for a long time and want space. This was the Townsville airport and we were waiting for a flight to Sydney after a rainy week on what should have been sunny Dunk Island. The doors were open and everyone was in shirtsleeves and wearing bright shorts, except for two men in the center of the lobby talking and looking uncomfortable in suits and ties. The clock over the door by the TAXIS sign said six-fifteen—thirty minutes until our flight—and outside the streetlights had just come on.

Older brother Drew walked over to me and he seemed genuinely anxious.

"Something's wrong with Will," he exclaimed. "He's talking funny, not making any sense. He doesn't seem to know who anybody is."

I guess the reason I wasn't so concerned at first was that I had just been thinking how lucky we'd been. After nearly six months of far-flung adventures nobody had fallen off a cliff or swum too close to a shark or stepped in front of a car or on top of one of the world's most poisonous snakes. No monster croc had "taken" and stuck one of us to "ripen" in the mud of some billabong. I was thinking what a miracle it was that we were all still in one piece.

Drew talking to me and looking so uncharacteristically anxious brought Honey right over. Leslee and Kathryn saw us and came too, and suddenly the whole family's attention was focused on where Will sat in the middle of the lobby's main floor. He was talking loudly, practically at the feet of the two uncomfortable-looking men, who were still carrying on their own conversation. Will's backpack was beside him, his books were dumped out, and he was arranging them in patterns.

I said, "He's OK. That's just Will." I was thinking of the Will who just yesterday had been so proud of himself: "I've done some 'new first things' in Australia, Dad. Galloped on Harry the horse and helped feed a chicken to the crocodiles, and rode the train all night to Melbourne. When we go home I think I'll walk to school by myself *every day*."

So I tried to reassure Honey. "He's carried on loud conversations with himself plenty of times."

But Honey, Will's guardian angel, said softly, "I don't know. I'm not so sure," and walked away toward him. I followed, watching her careful approach to our son, her eyes appraising—and then I saw the worry when Will paid his mother absolutely no attention and began talking even louder and then fell over on his side, laughing uproariously.

Honey was incredulous. "He acts like he doesn't even know me!"

The airport lobby abruptly echoed with an announcement that our flight to Sydney was boarding. Honey and I made a spot decision: The two of us would stay and try to handle whatever this emergency was with Will. The rest of the family would go. We gave taxicab money to Drew and Leslee and Kathryn and they ran to catch the plane.

Then with the help of Australian Airlines' Tom Davey—to whom we'll be forever grateful—I telephoned the local hospital, and next I called a taxi and dashed outside. Honey waited at the airport entrance, holding Will's hand.

Standing there, it was impossible for me to imagine our family without Will. On our way to Australia, when we had been touring around Fiji, Honey had asked who wanted to see the World War II "Guns of Momi" installation and Kathryn did and Will didn't, so Leslee suggested a family vote and instead of casting my usual five votes, I made the mistake of saying, "I'll follow the will of the family," and Will had ended the discussion by announcing, "I AM The Will of the Family and I want to go!"

This proud little growing-up boy clutching his mother's hand tries so hard to keep up with his bigger sisters, I thought, and how he idolizes Drew. That is why Drew's anxiety had so quickly captured Honey's attention. Usually the older-to-younger brother message was all hardline: "No whimpering, bub. Act your age," which only made Will try even harder—to talk like Drew, and to wear rock T-shirts like Drew and to act older than eight. How frustrated Will had become this past week trying to hit a tennis ball and kick the soccer ball straight. Last month, when we'd climbed Ayers Rock and Will was afraid to go all the way, afterward all he would talk about was what would Drew say.

A taxi approached. I flagged it waving my arms like a dervish—it was not ours. I ran over to tell Honey it might be a few more minutes and found it was taking all her strength to manage Will. He was alternating between wildly delirious loud talking and intermittent rational moments. I wondered whether to call another taxi, but I was afraid I would miss the one that was on its way, so I ran back to the main road and waited. Another taxi passed, again not ours.

At last, our cab arrived, and fifteen minutes later we were at the emergency room of Townsville's hospital. The sign said: PLEASE RING ONCE FOR THE SISTER. RING TWICE IF URGENT. I rang twice. And then two more times.

"Just one parent, please, with the youngster," said the white-clad nursing Sister. There was no question about *which* parent. Following the Sister, son and mother disappeared down a long hall, walking close together, touching each other the way they had been yesterday walking on the Dunk Island beach in the rain collecting shells, and Will had said to Honey matter-of-factly, "I saw you last night looking at babies."

"I love babies," his mother said.

"Does that mean we're going to have another one?"

"No, Will, you're the last."

"So I'm lucky. I'll always be the littlest one. The littlest one gets more care—and he gets more mads at, too."

"But you're getting bigger. You're learning to play tennis and even squash."

Will thought about that. "Mommy, I'll stop playing tennis if I can stay little longer."

Will was never sure when he wanted to remain little, or when he wanted to be thought of as bigger and older. Once when he was sitting in Honey's lap, she had told him, "Soon you'll be too big to sit in my lap. You won't want to."

Will had looked dumbfounded. "Why, Mom?"

His mother had explained carefully, "Because you'll grow up."

How grateful I was for every day of this special six months off together watching our children grow and change—before it was too late.

I thought about what a big change for *all* of us it had been, leaving behind, half a world away in America, our familiar ruts and crutches and orbits and all our friends. Especially it had been a big change for Will. "Maths is impossible," he had complained one day walking home from Balmoral Infants School. And then he had said, "Dad, John Austin could be twice as big as I am when we get home. He was already bigger when I left. He will probably grow a lot while we're gone and I might not have grown at all living in Australia. And he was my best friend and he might have a better friend now."

We had all been grabbing for anchors trying to deal with the big changes in our new lives in Australia, and Honey had always been Will's main anchor. On our first nights in the rented house in Sydney with the dusty locked-up smell, and the big clock's unfamiliar loud clicking downstairs, and the surprising sea breezes *whooshing*, it had not taken our brave-acting Will long to come scrambling in the dark from his room to find and nestle in a warm secure place for sleeping between his mother and me.

The hospital clock showed 8:00. A full hour had passed, and there was no word, no messenger, no nothing, no nobody to bring me any word of what was happening. Unable to stand it any longer, I walked down a long hall and found the room where the Sister and Honey had taken Will.

He was supposed to be lying on an examining table, but in fact it was all Honey and two male nurses could do to keep him from leaping off the table.

"There's the airplane!" Will shouted, pointing wildly to the ceiling. Just as he was about to jump, one male nurse picked him up.

"Hey, Dad," Will hollered in the direction of his mom. "Take my picture with this totem pole," he demanded, referring to the male nurse.

"Well, thanks a lot," said the male nurse.

By now there were no more rational moments. Will obviously didn't even recognize his mother, who was standing squarely before him. He grabbed her arm and began swinging it like a tennis racket, shouting, "I can play, Drew. I can play!" It was clear that spilling out were the innermost thoughts of a very frightened youngest son growing up in a strange place and under a lot of constant pressure to act older and keep up. He was so pathetic and the situation so frightening, and we were so far from home and familiar medical care, that I felt tears of hopelessness in my eyes and saw them in Honey's, too. She said softly, "I've never seen anything like this before."

Honey gave an international operator a frantic trans-Pacific call to our family doctor, John Sergent, in Nashville. Will's temperature was 103 degrees, and it was almost impossible now to translate any of his wild gibberish. All I could think of was what I'd read about LSD users hallucinating. I didn't recall how long such a condition lasted, or if it ever stopped, or if it permanently damaged the brain—and once that thought had entered my mind, I wished to God that it had not, but suddenly I felt reassured: Surely God also must delight in the magic of such an eight-year-old mind, one that can so precisely instruct the clerk at the "Lay-go Cen-tah" in Sydney: "Tanker car number seven seven seven four five, city electric express train; twelve volts, in the new catalog, not in any other store in town, and it might not be here." A mind that has just discovered God's purpose for fish: "That's awful how the hook and barb work in the fish's mouth. I'm glad nobody's trying to catch us. But I believe fish are *supposed* to be caught. I believe God put one half of the fish for us to look at and the other half for us to try to catch."

Sometimes this working-so-hard-to-keep-up eight-year-old thinking machine would catch up and pass us. Like when Will and I were riding "home" to Sydney on the overnight train from Melbourne, and he had wanted to know, "Will Mom like the pig book I bought her, Dad? I think she likes pigs, doesn't she?"

"She'll like that you got it. It's always *better* to give something than to receive it."

The pause was only a couple of seconds. "Then will you buy me a toy, Dad? It'll be *better* for you."

The telephone's *brrrng, brrrng* interrupted my thoughts. The nurse who answered the phone looked at us. "Your doctor, John Sergent?" John was the inexhaustible best-friend doctor, the one we always called when we really needed help at an inconvenient time—when Kathryn broke her ankle or Leslee had a midnight fever or, once, on vacation when I hurt with the flu. Now we needed him again and we had found him, but he was as far away from us as he could be and still be on earth.

Honey talked. "John, could it have been the seasick pills? We took a cruise ship this morning to the Great Barrier Reef. The wind was strong and for an hour and a half we rolled through nine-foot waves. Will saw his dad and sister throw up; in fact nearly everybody on the boat got sick. There were packets of seasick pills lying around in little bowls everywhere, and

Will ate some—they must have tasted OK. We don't know how many pills he ate. I think then the rolling of the boat scared him and he may have eaten even more because of that. Drew said he was eating them like candy. Now he's been bouncing off the walls!"

John said, "If that's what it is, he'll probably be OK by morning." It was the first encouraging word we'd heard, and what an enormous relief!

The Sister said it had been too long since Will had eaten the pills to make pumping his stomach worthwhile, so the Totem Pole tried to persuade him to drink a cup of liquid charcoal to absorb whatever might be in his stomach.

"C'mon, William. The Aussies don't believe you can swallow this," said the Totem Pole. Will drank, then splattered charcoal all over the white gowns of the Totem Pole and three other attendants and nurses—and grabbed for my arm. Through all this my own son didn't even recognize I was the one standing there by him. He acted as if he thought my arm was some kind of pump, and he tried to use my hand as a water cup. About midnight I walked with Honey and Will to the hospital room, where they climbed in bed together to sleep.

The next morning when I returned to the hospital main anchor Honey was exhausted. She told me that she had done her best to stay awake, but had dozed once and barely awakened in time to catch Will just about to take a running leap from the bed into midair. "Look at the ships!" he had cried. "His arm was stiff and he just kept waving it at the wall," his mother said. But the night had settled Will down. He looked tired, too, but apparently he was going to be OK.

"It *was* the seasick pills," confirmed a different doctor who examined Will. "It's happened before. The kids see them lying around and eat them. It makes them mad as a hatter, crazy as a loon, and hot as hell. I've already warned those cruise-ship people twice not to leave those pills lying around where kids can get them."

We said a grateful good-bye to the doctor and to the Totem Pole and to the Sister, and the three of us took a taxi back to the Sheraton, and by the time we got back to our hotel room we could tell from the way he was talking that our eight-year-old was coming back to normal.

"I had the worst dreams I ever had and I remember them all," Will said. "In one I was going to school and before I went I looked at the calendar—it was a calculator calendar and it said seven/seven—and I said, 'Today's going to be a lucky day,' and then when I got to school I forgot the teachers' names and I failed all my work and they were real mad at me and then when it came to French class I couldn't even count to four. See, Daddy, all my Australian friends knew how to count to twenty at the very beginning and I couldn't even count to four and I felt awful. Then I remembered that it was all a dream and I tried to wake up and I couldn't wake up and so all the teachers were still mad at me."

Another sign of Will's rapid coming back to normal was when he pushed the button to see what Saturday morning Townsville television had to offer. He found some familiar cartoon characters and began chuckling, and we laughed, too. He scurried on top of the bed where Honey sat, pulled the blanket up around his neck, snuggled close against his mother and looked over at me and said sadly, "Dad, this hasn't been my best day."

The yellow sub at the Great Barrier Reef: Everything was thousands
of miles in every direction.

The Olgas at sunset

It will "take" you and stick you in the mud of some billabong to "ripen."

Northern Territory termite mounds stand six feet tall.

With Malcolm and Tamie
Fraser at Nareen

Honey and Kathryn, a very
special relationship

Ready for reentry

My Honey, in Xian

Birthday #47: Kathryn and I had arrived at that delicate point of equilibrium where it was not clear who was the custodian of whom.

Setting an example

Drew

Rebellion outside the
Kremlin

When we got home,
Kathryn didn't leave her
dearest friend Torie's house
for a week.

This place of all the
places in this whole world
where we fit best.

GILBERT M. GROSVENOR

CHAPTER 3 0

FIRST
COUSINS

//

When a stranger from America steps
ashore in Sydney . . . the thing that
strikes him is that it is an English
city with American trimmings.

—MARK TWAIN
Following the Equator

You would have thought the Sydney taxi driver, who
was English, was speaking of his barely grown-up step-
children.

"They hate the English, the Australians. Why? Because
they realize we're superior. Minute they find out you're from
England they've got a chip on their shoulder. It's the convict
thing—you know they came from convicts. It's the darndest
thing I've ever gotten meself into. I've been here four years and
now I've got a superiority complex."

The taxi paused at the entrance to the harbor bridge, but no one was waiting to take the toll. I had read in the morning *Herald* how toll-takers were striking in support of the postal workers, who had stopped carrying mail while they bargained for a pay increase. We sped on across without paying and the genealogy lesson continued. "Master the little quirks of living here and you know it's not a bad place, but the Aussies still need convincing of the fact. They'll find their own identity one day. Then they won't have to come on so strong. Over the years England ruled a bit too heavily here, but the Aussies are their own people now. They don't have to always prove themselves to anybody, but they do."

The Grand Ballroom of the Sheraton Wentworth Hotel was crowded with guests, black-tied and long-gowned for the Australian-American Bicentennial Dinner. Honey and I found our places and introduced ourselves and found that the other ten who were with us dining at large round table number 27 were all Australian. We sat down and then were immediately invited to rise so that the American ambassador could toast the queen of Australia. The governor-general of Australia responded with a toast to the president of the United States, and we sat again.

"He is the only man in Australia for whom everyone will always stand," explained the lady on my right, as the governor-general began speaking so gently that the raucous table talk in the ballroom quieted.

"It is a happy accident of fate that the Constitution of the United States was being signed in 1787 just as our first fleet was sailing eastward across the Atlantic from Rio to Cape Town on the third leg of its ten-months long voyage. The fleet carried a cargo of convicts who would have been on their way to Georgia had not the American Revolution succeeded and denied the British the opportunity to send their prisoners to America."

The lady on my right, who wore a white dress and dangling gold earrings, whispered, "It's the 'in' thing now, you know, to trace back to see if your ancestors were on the first fleet. A lot of people have always known they were descended from lawbreakers, but very few had been willing to spend money to prove it."

The governor-general was proceeding toward a triumphant conclusion. "The links between our two nations have evolved from earliest times. Our pioneers, like yours, were as unlikely a band as one could conceive. Your gold rush spilled into ours. Our constitution has been built on yours. Our soldiers have died together and we have shared freedoms of speech and of association and of laws and of humanities and of civil liberties—and now both of us are a melting pot. We read your prose, we speak your poetry and watch your plays and films. We even watch your terrible TV dramas!"

Applause and generous expressions of affection erupted all around, and the governor-general smiled, cautiously retreated, and sat, and Dame Leonie Kramer of the University of Sydney rose and strode to the microphone and spoke bluntly.

"We *are* profoundly interested in one other, but we are more profoundly ignorant. Americans, for example, are enchanted that this is the land of the crocodiles but they don't seem to have enough sense to stay out of the water when they are here."

Dame Leonie Kramer then sat, and our table plunged into grilled fresh fish and boiled asparagus tips and hot conversation.

The car dealer on my left said, "When I was in America, they thought we had roos hopping in the streets and crocs in the swimming pools and abos behind the fences." His short-cropped hair and narrow tie and innocent eagerness would have made him a perfect candidate for the role of father in a 1950s American family television series.

His plumpish wife agreed. "Most Americans can't find Australia on the map, and even when they do you always have to prove to them it's as big as the United States."

Her husband laughed. "One bloke coming to the America's Cup almost went back when he found out Perth is as far from Sydney as L.A. is from New York."

A tanned young blond woman, sitting between the car dealer and me, said, "I was skiing in Denver once, was on the lift, and an American man was in the next seat and he was trying to come on to me, and so he asks me, 'In Australia it's summer, isn't it?,' and I say, 'Right.' and then in a minute he says, 'And what *month* is it in Australia?' "

The Australians especially enjoyed that, which encouraged the blonde, who turned to me and asked, "How do *you* like Australia?" She asked this in the same worried way Californians used to question visiting New Yorkers.

I said, "It's beautiful and friendly, but what surprises me is how much like America it is. Sometimes I think I'm at a family reunion on another planet."

The blonde said, "It *is* another planet, orbiting in sight of the big ones but never to be one."

The plumpish wife of the car dealer agreed. "We always seem to be missing *something.*"

I said, "But, for an American, coming to Australia is almost better than going home again. When you try to go home again it's a disappointment. It's only *nearly* perfect. But when you come to Australia it's such a pleasant surprise how nearly perfect it is."

The car dealer said, "I reckon everyone in America must have heard about your family reunion. Three hundred thousand of 'em coming this year. That's what the telly said."

The lady in the white dress and earrings on my right asked, "Isn't Australia just the flavor-of-the-month in America? Couldn't we just as well be Timbuktu?"

"It's more than that," her thin and red-faced husband said. He was a member of Parliament.

Honey, who was sitting on the right of the member of Parliament, suggested, "Some Americans come here looking for 'The America that Was.'"

The M.P. said, "Some of *us* hope America is the 'Australia that Might Be.'"

The car dealer leaned across the table and said to them, "And you'll both be disappointed. Australia's the land of bushmen and sheepshearers and croc hunters in about the same way America's the land of Hopalong Cassidy and the cowboys."

His plumpish wife supported him. "*Crocodile Dundee*'s a fairy tale, isn't that right? And America's not *really* like *Miami Vice.*" She didn't seem entirely sure.

I said, "Sometimes we don't know so much about ourselves. Sometimes we're visitors in our own countries."

Waiters arrived with plates of an Australian dessert called a Pavlova—whipped cream and fresh papaya in meringue shell—and exclamations over its fluffiness only temporarily diminished the conversation.

"Well, we're mates, all right." The car dealer could not

tolerate a lull. "The English may be our ancestors, but you Americans are our cousins."

"*First* cousins," said the thin, red-faced member of Parliament, whom I sensed correctly was preparing to make a statement. "We started out the same kind of people, underprivileged, a long way from home, doing the same sort of thing, looking for a new life. Found a hard life. Hoped it would be better for the children. Each wave of new ones lifted up the last ones. A pioneering spirit in the countryside here. In America, too."

"I love America!" exclaimed the wife of the Australian bicentennial chairman who was sitting across the table. Her cheerful face had been hidden behind an enormous centerpiece of flowers. "When they sing 'New York, New York' I get excited with the best of 'em. It's our second home. It opens your eyes a bit, doesn't it, to get out of your own country."

"When you do, we look awfully small." The speaker was a dour bald gentleman sitting next to her, who might have been seventy, a plywood manufacturer who was rather obstructed by the centerpiece. For the moment, he held the floor. "Our GNP is about the size of the GNP of Los Angeles."

The blond woman said, "Australia's a village, same names always popping up."

The plywood man said, "Americans have got a head start and size and location and better education, and they have more self-confidence."

This resonated with the blond woman's male guest, whose name I never got in all the din and who now decided to talk to me. "We follow America. You regulate the stock market, so we do it, too. You change school curriculum. We do it, too. Don't think about it. Just do it."

"We'd have been better off to start with pilgrims and a revolution, instead of convicts," said the plywood manufacturer.

"We could have used an Alamo," suggested the car dealer.

"We *had* Gallipoli," said the blonde's friend.

"Wouldn't it have been nice to have something in the center besides a red desert?" sighed the plywood man's wife.

The last of the fluffy Pavlova had been scraped from the plates, and coffee and mints arrived.

The young blond woman suddenly turned to me and insisted, "I reckon I ought to have a quarter of a vote every time you elect a president. I should. After all, we sit here half our time waiting for America to do something. *Our* prime minister can't make a deal with Gorbachev. No one's wondering what *Australia*'s trade policy will be. We have to depend on you."

"We already do," said the member of Parliament.

"Do what?" asked the blonde.

"Depend on America. For defense. For things we really enjoy. Ask any of our school kids. I've done it. 'Where would you like to go on this planet?' and nine out of ten say, 'Disneyland.' The script for every Australian *Tonight* show was prepared by an American until recently."

The car dealer was saying to Honey, "We never can have anything like the things that you have in America. There're not enough of us Aussies. Disneyland and interstate highways—things that are ordinary to you—are a wonder to us. Space stations. All the museums in Washington, D.C."

"Another reason we can't is what's happening on Pitt Street," intoned the plywood manufacturer.

"The esplanade work?"

"The *lack* of it. Did you hear the workers complained about passers-by harassing them for leaning on their shovels? And that yesterday the arbitration board awarded them a twenty-seven-cent wage increase because of the harassment!"

The blond woman's date said, "Watch them on MacQuarie Street, at the restoration, the workers smearing on suntan oil. It would make a good frame for 'still life.' I watched them from my club window yesterday at lunch."

The car dealer said, "Sunday's *Herald* said United stewards work twice as much as Qantas stewards."

I said, "You see that on flights to Tokyo. The same Qantas crews going up on Monday and coming back on Thursday. And last month the Bridgestone Tire Company president told me his tire plants work three hundred forty-five days in Japan and America, and the Bridgestone plant in Adelaide works only two hundred ten."

The plywood man looked positively funereal. "We're unusual, all right. We pay double time for afternoon work, for overtime, for vacation. We pay for days off on a butchers' picnic and on a bakers' picnic—*everybody* has a picnic and we pay for that. How are we going to compete with the rest of the world when we're on a picnic?"

Now the men were enjoying long cigars and the ladies were doing their best to survive the haze, and my watch said the dinner had already lasted three hours.

Honey said, "I see a lot of Japanese cars and American fast foods, but I don't hear much proper English. Is it because I'm American and just don't notice it?"

"It's because we've changed," said a lady across the table who up till now had been mostly listening. "We moved here in 1978. We decided Sydney winters were better than English summers, so we sold our house in London. Then, Australians still spoke of 'going home' to England. In everything we did we seemed to compare ourselves to England. Now, no one talks about 'going home.' Australianness is coming out all round. We're more American, too, but mainly we're prouder of being Australian."

The wife of the member of Parliament said to Honey, "Read our children's books. I'll send you some for *your* children. Instead of stories about English hobgoblins, there are more about aborigine spirits and stories full of the sounds of frogs croaking and of the didgeridoo, hostile and growling like the belly of the earth."

Honey said, "The new Sheraton in Yulara was lovely, brown like the desert and built like sails."

The wife of the M.P. said, "Our Australianness came out all right when they tried to kill the brumbies in the Snowy Mountains. Put a stop to that."

Honey said, "We've seen a lot of Australia in David Williamson's plays and Mary Gilmore's poetry and Ken Done's bright splashy painting . . ."

". . . and Fred Elliot's old marine watercolors even if he was drunk a lot," I added.

The wife of the plywood manufacturer said, "And I believe *we're* learning that our harsh vast spaces and distance from everyone sometimes can be a wonderful advantage." Those were the first words she had uttered in nearly two hours.

From behind the centerpiece of flowers came the cheerful contribution of the wife of the bicentennial chairman. "Eight hundred ten of our eight hundred thirty shires have bicentennial committees."

The member of Parliament added, "At least now we toast the queen of *Australia* instead of the empire."

His wife, on my right with white dress and earrings, asked me, "Have you tried the wichety grubs, the moth larvae the abos used to eat? They're all the rage. Large and crispy and in all the best restaurants."

"No," I said, "but I *have* been to the beaches and I *have* thought about those convicts who were laughing at the aborigines standing there sandy and naked and greasy. Now, the descendants of some of those first-fleet convicts are on the same beaches, sandy and naked and greasy."

The member of Parliament had arranged himself into speaking position. "Remember. The English left *us*. We didn't leave them. They joined the Common Market. Gave us five years to adjust our exports."

This roused the car dealer, who said, "It goes back to the last war. Churchill said, 'Let them have Australia. We'll win it back.' Our boys were on the other side, fighting in North Africa and in Europe and the Japanese were bombing Darwin four times a day. The Americans saved us."

His wife, who was finishing off his mints, too, agreed. "Two Christmases ago there were ten thousand American sailors in Perth and some family took every one of 'em home for the holidays."

The lights dimmed and the official bicentennial film began. Trumpets heralded the arrival of the first fleet of "settlers" on Australia's Identity Day, January 26, 1788, and violins moved the story quickly along into the nineteenth century, and then lingered amid the excitement of the gold rush at Ballarat.

I whispered to the wife of the member of Parliament, "It didn't mention that the 'settlers' were convicts."

"No worries," she said. "The first bicentennial logo forgot Tasmania. Had to make a new one. But it's a good thing, our bicentennial. Helps us remember important things."

CHAPTER 3 1

QUESTION TIME

//

Are these our people's leaders? These
Whose babbling voices
Sound in familiar keys,
Like farm-yard noises?
The world churns like a maggot-pit,
Turmoiled in strife,
While the mice-minded sit,
Nibbling at life.

—MARY GILMORE
"These" (Australian)

For several weeks we had been talking about driving to
Canberra to see Question Time, the almost daily episode
in Parliament when the opposition quizzes the prime minister.
Will was skeptical. He wanted to know, "Do they ask hard

questions, or do they ask questions like 'How many wheels does an eighteen-wheeler have?' and 'Where is the blown-up house?' "

Canberra, diplomatically located between Melbourne and Sydney in the Australian Capital Territory, is a lovely inland city of American design, with Australian birds and European trees. At 1:45 on a cool and sunny June afternoon, Honey, Kathryn, Will, and I entered Parliament House through King's Hall. Five minutes later we were sinking into the green leather seats in the dark-paneled speaker's gallery. A few members of Parliament were rising sleepily to offer to one another those exaggerated gestures of respect that legislators come to expect when they are away from home.

At 1:55, bells rang and two white-wigged individuals entered on our left and occupied seats in front of what turned out to be the speaker's throne. The chamber filled quickly, members performing various politician's rituals. I thought, This must be a tighter than usual little political community. I already knew it was too *remote* a place for some tastes. "Canberra stinks!" a European ambassador had whispered the night before at dinner. "The only way to survive is to take a flat in Sydney."

Suddenly through the hubbub trudged a woman carrying a huge mace. "THE SPEAKER!" she screamed, and the speaker, who also was a woman, entered and ascended the throne, and things began happening. It was not until then that I noticed the prime minister, Mr. Robert Hawke. He was sitting in front of the speaker's throne, grinning and gossiping and swiveling first in one direction, then in another. The opposition leader, Mr. John Howard, sat sternly across a table—closer to the prime minister than I had imagined would be the case—looking like a schoolboy who had just learned that his girlfriend had been stolen and whose prime suspect was the prime minister himself. Members of Parliament were now pouring in through all three doors and bowing to the speaker. "Just like karate class," observed Will.

At two o'clock the questions began. The first one came from Mr. Howard, who delivered a speech in which it was difficult to discern a question. The prime minister nevertheless rose with the eagerness of a thirsty camel at an oasis, and presented his answer—an answer for which the only possible question could have been, "Will you kindly enumerate for us, Mr.

Prime Minister, many examples of how your extraordinary leadership has caused Australia to prosper so?" I was certain that was *not* the question that had been imbedded in Mr. Howard's speech.

Next one of Mr. Howard's cohorts asked a question about U.S. import quotas on Australian wheat, and then there was a wrangle about an unsuccessful search for someone lost in the bush. Occasionally a lesser minister would respond for the prime minister, the most notable of these responses coming from Senator Barry Jones, who was reputed to know everything and who nearly proved it on that day by reciting astronomical amounts of information about the newly sighted supernova. After an hour of such back-and-forthing, the prime minister left the chamber and answered some of the same kinds of questions from the capitol reporters.

Australian observers said afterward that it had been a well-behaved Question Time. Certainly it was no match for the occasion when another opposition leader had leaned across the table and tossed a pitcher of cold water in the face of the then prime minister, shouting: *"Theah-ah.* That ought ta cool ya off!" But even during a well-behaved Question Time, there was constant murmuring among the members—of the kind that goes on between plays at an American football game—and occasional roars of support from the prime minister's side, which in turn provoked groans of disrespect from Mr. Howard's side. There were interruptions, too, some egregious enough to cause The Speaker to stir on her throne, and on a few occasions The Speaker turned out to be more The Referee.

Kathryn and Will talked later about how hard it had been to tell who was the prime minister.

"I thought he was the guy asking the questions," Will said.

"It looked to me like the speaker lady was in charge of everything," Kathryn said.

"It was tons of noise," Will said.

"They have no respect for the people who lead them," Kathryn said. "Everyone else should have shown more respect for the prime minister. When he was trying to read a letter, they kept yelling "no" on one side and the others kept saying, "Read it, Bob. Read it!"

* * *

A week later I was looking forward to finding out more about why Australian politicians endure such unmerciful rudeness. Honey and I were on our way to visit with a Question Time veteran, the former prime minister of Australia, Malcolm Fraser.

I almost lost my chance to ask my question because I had promised to telephone Fraser at his home in Nareen, but had written down the wrong number. Since I was not sure even in what Australian state Nareen was—or even *what* it was—I tried Melbourne information. Fraser, I had heard, kept an office in that city.

"The number for Malcolm Fraser, please?"

"I'll have to have an address," the Melbourne information operator said.

"I don't have an address."

"Have you ever been to Melbourne?" asked the operator.

"Yes."

"It has three million people," said the operator.

"Have you ever been to New York City?" I asked.

"Yes."

"There are eight million people in New York City, and the operators there try to help you find the telephone number even if you don't have an address."

"Not here," said the Melbourne operator, and hung up.

Not even for a former prime minister.

Or, perhaps *especially* not for a former prime minister in Australia, where "Tall Poppy" politicians are cut down to size almost before they sprout.

"Why are you surprised?" consoled Honey. "It's the same with the garbage. They barely pick it up—one small can, no trash, twice a week. They don't deliver mail on Saturday and don't pick up mail at all."

I recalled my first visit to the Mosman Post when I had innocently asked a clerk why, in Australia, is the mailman, who thrusts his hand within my home mail box to deliver the mail, unable to withdraw in that hand a fistful of mail I have placed there for dispatch?

The clerk stopped sorting mail and wrinkled his forehead. "Now *what* would you want me to do? Let me understand this. I should stay awhile at your mailbox everytime I put some mail in—and then I should sort through this outgoing mail of yours piece by piece and decide into which country and into which city and into which box it must go so that when I come back to the post office I can dispatch it into its proper slot? *That* is the way you do it in America? You are *sure* of this?"

Before he had finished I wondered whether during my eight-year absence from the real world the U.S. postal service had stopped picking up mail. Perhaps I had only *dreamed* that American postmen picked up mail. Certainly Australian postmen did not.

Fraser solved my wrong-number dilemma by telephoning me, and we agreed to meet in Nareen in time for a late lunch on Wednesday, June 10.

The Fraser home was an old sheep station at the center of the best sheep country in Australia, four hours' drive west of Melbourne, the capital of the state of Victoria. I knew very little about the former prime minister except that he was a distinguished member of the more conservative Australian political party (the Liberals), that he was tall, serious, and very well intentioned, almost too perfect for some Australians.

Driving to Nareen, we traveled through a softer Australia than we had been living with in New South Wales. Century-old European trees lined the driveways of English-style houses and of long-established farms. The winter sun rolled across the bottom of the sky, slanting light against the sides of brown sheep that seemed to grow out of the brown grass. After four and a half hours, some of it spent getting lost on deserted roads, we drove between a double row of huge pines to a long, low white country house. A cedar hedge, thirty feet high, hid the side of the house closest to us. The former prime minister's wife, Tamie Fraser met us and explained, "The hedge tries to stop the north wind from drying out the camellias and azaleas in the front yard."

For a long time that afternoon the former prime minister drove us in his four-wheel-drive Toyota around the Fraser sheep station and rumbled about dread grass fires and cockatoos eating plants and opossums chewing trees.

"I used to have a Land Rover. Most Australians did," he said. "Now Toyota has eighty percent of the business. Out here you must have a vehicle that makes the fewest mistakes."

We stopped and I got out to open and then close a gate.

When I climbed back in, Fraser said, "Let me propose some-thing to you. What if some country, say the United States, invited other countries to join it in a new trade association? There would be only two rules for members: one, no more trade barriers, and two, no more subsidies."

I asked, "What if just the United States and Japan did this?"

"That would scare everyone else. But the United States and Japan could do it and invite in anybody else who wanted to live by the same rules and then do things step by step."

I asked, "How do you think the United States would do in that kind of competition, with no subsidies and all the barriers down?"

The former prime minister parked his Toyota by the cedar hedge, climbed out, and said, "I cannot believe that the Japanese are intrinsically capable of making a better product than the Americans are."

Later, at dinner, I asked, "Who has been America's best president?"

"Nixon," Fraser answered immediately. "Nixon knew why he was president. He thought about how to make the world a safer place to live on down the road. He knew he had to make a deal with Russia and to open China and he did both."

An Australian woman, sitting at our table, said, "I never trusted Nixon really, on the telly. Something about him. Now *Reagan* is different. Let's put it this way: If Reagan told me something, I'd believe it."

Tamie Fraser said, "Reagan restored your country's re-spect in itself after the Nixon-Carter years. I felt awful visiting my American friends. I never went *anywhere* that Americans didn't apologize for Watergate—I'm talking now from the point of view of a visitor to America for thirty years. I just *hated* to see how Americans looked at themselves."

After the meal, as we sank in big soft chairs in the living room by a hot fire, it seemed like a good time to ask my question: "The other day in Canberra we saw Question Time. The chil-dren were astonished by how things went. Why is everyone so rough on Australian politicians? You're even hard on your-selves."

Tamie Fraser said, "We have no respect for politicians here. It is a tradition of lack of respect for authority—first for the British, then for the police, and then for the government. It is the larikin in us."

I said, "You toast the queen and stand up for her governor-general. That leaves your politicians standing there naked. We toast our president and play 'Hail to the Chief' and stand up when he walks in. Ours can wrap the American flag around them. To kick our president, you have to unwrap him first."

She said, "The president's your king, but our way is healthier. We don't shoot each other. We take it out on the politicians."

I said, "It's hard to imagine our president at Question Time. He needs to be arguing with the Russians about nuclear weapons a lot more than he needs to be practicing answers to questions about daily crises. What if he slips up? Every stock market and every capital and every missile trigger finger in the world quivers when our president makes a mistake—and we're not so good in America at living with his mistakes, either."

The former prime minister of Australia said, "Sometimes standing up there every day helps keep small mistakes from becoming big ones. Iran was a big one. Swapping hostages for money with Iran was a serious American foreign-policy mistake. And it never would have happened under the Australian system."

CHAPTER 32

A LAST DISCOVERY

//

I left the woods for as good a reason
as I went there. Perhaps it seemed to
me that I had several more lives to
live, and could not spare any more
time for that one. It is remarkable
how easily and insensibly we fall into
a particular route, and make a beaten
track for ourselves.

—HENRY DAVID THOREAU
Walden

Dogs turn on a master who gives up
the chase.

—Japanese adage

Been There. Done That.

—Australian adage

Suddenly we were ready for another ending, our second in six months. But this one would be different. There was more time to pack and to visit and to think about the memories that already had made so special what we were about to end. There were the usual good-bye things to do—visits with many new friends, thanking principals and teachers who had gone out of their way to help, taking last long walks, disconnecting phones and closing accounts, paying the electric bill and arranging for the water bill to be sent to America, selling the Holden car and—finally—packing. The two suitcases apiece, which had carried our life's essentials to Australia, had miraculously grown to seventeen, and I am embarrassed to say how many boxes we shipped home by air freight.

And for Drew, it was time for a haircut. For this fateful encounter he had waited until after his farewell party. "You've got me this time," he said on Tuesday morning while eating his scrambled eggs before heading to the barber shop. This haircut was the consequence of his losing a hard-fought tennis match one rainy morning two weeks earlier during our Dunk Island vacation. I remember the morning well, because I had sensed something in the air when Drew and his visiting Nashville friend Patrick Keeble were the first to appear on the wet outdoor courts. The boys practiced for more than an hour, then showed up early for the official match, so that by the time the opposing team, Honey and I, arrived, they were well warmed up. They were bouncing on their toes the way television tennis players do and were dressed smartly in whites instead of the usual wildly colored rags. Something was afoot, but still I was not prepared when Drew elevated the match stakes to nuclear proportions by announcing, "We'll play for my hair. When Patrick and I win, Dad, no more talk about my hair."

I had recovered quickly enough to blurt out, "What about Patrick? What will Patrick do if you lose?"

Patrick had caught the spirit and took only seconds to respond, "I'll cut my two-day growth," and the mighty battle was on.

As the contest began, I had terrible mixed emotions. Honey and I lost the first two games, but then we won two sets, 7–5, 7–5, and won the match. I felt like a Philistine competing for Samson's locks.

"We can keep playing," I offered, trying to imagine the consequences to Drew of such a high-stakes loss. Honey looked at me sternly. I realized she would never have made such a second offer. A commitment for Honey is a commitment. It had started raining, so we moved to the indoor court for the second match. Even indoors, every ball was wet. We squeezed them and put them in our pockets in a vain effort to dry them so they would bounce higher.

Honey and I won the second match 6–2, 6–2. It was no contest, but its pathos was worthy of national television in America. Drew's knee dripped blood as a result of his having slipped earlier on the wet outdoor court. As his fortunes worsened, the knee's supply of blood seemed inexhaustible. Then, during the second set indoors, Drew turned his left ankle. (A few weeks earlier in Sydney, he had cracked a bone in his right foot walking home from a night out, or at least that is what we heard.) The newly turned left ankle also began to bleed. During the second-match set, Drew tied a kerchief around his head to keep hair from flopping in his eyes, and he and Patrick began diving desperately after balls. When the contest ended, we noticed that even Drew's racket handle was cracked, but the ending was solemn and the boys made no excuses.

All this went through my mind as Drew consumed four breakfast eggs. He said, "Actually, I'll be glad to see again. Can I have ten dollars for the barber?"

I gave him the money and said, "Just tell the barber what you want. He'll cut it the way you want." It had been so long since his last haircut I was afraid Drew might not remember how to talk to a barber.

He said, "They're all the same. They all give bad cuts."

After Drew had gone, I said to Honey, "I really don't care if he cuts his hair."

Honey, who was filling the dishwasher, said without turning around, "Oh, you're about to grow out of that stage?"

I said, "I thought it was *his* stage."

She turned around. "I think it's *yours.*"

On Wednesday Honey and I caught the 11:15 city bus two blocks from our house and arrived seven minutes later at the ferry wharf below Taronga Zoo. Fishermen yanked in their lines just before the ferry bumped the pilings at 11:30. Riding the ferry took the hurry out of the day and gave us a last look at Sydney's astonishing winter light. The sun in Sydney's winter does what floodlights do along the edge of a stage. It makes the street signs glare and the poinsettias and red-tiled roofs flame. Summer light seemed to come from everywhere, but winter light was rarer and clearer and slanted in from the side. This was so breathtakingly different I always wanted to stop and look.

On the city side of the harbor, we lingered over sandwiches and soft drinks at a waterfront café behind the concrete sails of the opera house and watched sailboarders in wet suits skimming the water, and we wondered why, during nearly six months, we hadn't done this more often, why we hadn't taken more sailing lessons or picnics, spent more time together, just the two of us. Where had the time gone when there was "nothing to do"?

On Thursday Honey and I left the children and drove two hours north for an overnight visit in the Hunter Valley vineyard country. Early Friday morning, when we were walking along the valley roads, we saw all the familiar signs of winter—a gray horse wearing a blanket, pruned grapevines like sticks, porches stacked with new firewood, and the sun rolling low in the sky. But we also saw gardenias and camellias, and there were yellow and white flowers blooming in the fields. In Australia there is always a feeling that at any moment winter might disappear.

It did disappear—for an afternoon—the next day on Saturday, when we played a final tennis game with an English couple who were living for a year in Sydney. The wife had said to us, "Australia is a sunny England. Even the nastiest winter day in Sydney is likely better than any day in England." And as we played that winter day it happened. White clouds parted and the sky became blue. Sweaters came off. After tennis we walked along Balmoral Beach. Footprints had appeared again in the sand, couples strolled along holding hands and eating ice cream, and families sprawled under the Morton Bay fig trees enjoying picnic lunches—and swimmers splashed once more in the harbor, even though the shark net had been taken down for the winter, and sea gulls perched expectantly on the DANGER NOT SHARK PROOF sign watching swimmers the way racing fans watch for a wreck. Sails suddenly were filling in the harbor. There were even people working in their gardens, and my shirt was soaking when we came home again. It was winter, but for an afternoon it had become Real Sydney Weather again.

On Sunday, our last night, Honey and I walked to Balmoral Beach for one last taste of grilled John Dory at Mischa's Restaurant. Afterward, it was so cold and we walked so fast home that we neglected to say a last good-bye to our new friend, the Southern Cross.

We awoke at six on Monday, June 29, our last morning in Australia. Red streaked across the bottom of the sky. I reached for the top shelf of the table by our bed, but it was empty. That was where the coloring pencils and sketch pad had been. I had wanted to learn to use them, but they were gone now, packed, unused, except for the time when Honey had used them along with Will's Crayolas to try to identify the many brilliant colors of Australia. This was why I wanted them now. Was that red or a kind of orange across the water just above the black city buildings? Dots of light speckled the outline of those buildings, and the water was also black, and the sky still slept.

Outside the kookaburras laughed and ravens cried and a few car engines began warming up, and we heard the warbling and gurgling and squawking of the rest of the symphony. The sky began to come alive and the water borrowed the hue of the sky, and we could see the sailboats' lonely masts rocking and waiting in Mosman Bay, and beyond, the stately ferries churning and the hydrofoil walking, and beyond them the gray, sloping sandstone heads that protect the most beautiful harbor in the world. Within minutes the sky burst white yellow, and then the sun rose red and big, and Honey and I pulled our blanket up to ward off the cold breeze spilling through the bedroom windows, and we marveled at this land down under the sky blown blue. It seemed impossible that our plane for Bangkok, the first stop on the way home to America, would leave in six hours.

I asked Honey, "What did *you* discover in Australia?"

She looked at me and smiled and it didn't take her a second to answer: "That I'm about ready for *my* six months off."

C H A P T E R 3 3

R E E N T R Y

Odysseus goes through hell on his
way home—as most of us do. And he
does so in a different spirit from those
underworld journeys taken by
younger mythic heroes. His journey
is not another exploit and not a test
of his manhood, for Odysseus
journeys into hell humbly and
because it is necessary to his
homecoming. He goes to learn what
he needs to learn.

—WILLIAM BRIDGES
Transitions

"No kookaburras, no ravens calling, no telephone bird.
And no red sky." Honey had awakened first and was

standing on the third-floor porch of our room at the Oriental Hotel in Bangkok, Thailand, listening to the morning and watching the river below.

Yesterday we had been in winter, below the equator living at Base Camp Sydney. We had put on sweaters, paid last bills, settled with the landlord for damage to two lamps and one rug, rushed to Mosman to buy Ken Done T-shirts for nieces and nephews, then stuffed ourselves and seventeen suitcases into one taxi and two cars belonging to friends. We had cast a last glance at our Australian home and waved good-bye to the harbor bridge when we crossed it, and finally at the airport had maneuvered our bags and ourselves to a place in line and waited. As the line advanced toward the ticket counter I realized that some teenagers who were not ours were materializing and moving with us. I recognized Simon, the drummer, and Martin of the hearty appetite and Mark and Sturt, and Leslee's friends Bec and Catriona and Caitlin, and there were several other familiar faces, but neither Honey nor I knew the pretty brunette who stayed close with Drew.

When we reached the counter, a jovial Qantas agent admired our number—six, our bags—seventeen, the length of our proposed trip—twenty-one days, our itinerary—Bangkok to Hong Kong to Guangzhou to Beijing, then Moscow to Paris by train, and then home to Nashville; and the agent especially admired the crowd of extra teenagers, which by then had grown to at least two dozen.

We moved to the center of the lobby, where our friends surrounded us until Honey said, "It's time." We hugged our first friends in Australia, Graham and Barbie, and Sam and Jackie, and shook hands with our newest acquaintance, Peter Aboud, the travel agent, whose normal business must have been demolished while he helped invent such an elaborate scheme for riding trains and airplanes and cars through ten countries. Drew and Leslee and Kathryn hugged their friends, kissed them, and tried to laugh, and exchanged tentative last touches, and as we walked away, the Australians began shouting good-byes, "See ya, mate. See ya lay-tah!" and I wondered whether Drew would ever separate from the pretty brunette. But when Drew finally came through the gate, he turned and shouted, "I'LL BE BACK!" and Leslee screamed, "I'M COMING

BACK, TOO!" and the waving crowd of friends disappeared behind the security walls. We walked along the corridor to our gate, and it was several minutes before Drew could say to me, "Trisha. Her name is Trisha. I met her at my farewell party," and he was as unhappy-looking as I had ever seen him.

His sad look reminded me of summer camp when I was sixteen, and of a very special athletic girl from Florida and how painful teenage good-byes can be. My good-byes then had only been from Tennessee to Florida. I tried to imagine what good-byes now must mean to our children, who were leaving for the other side of the world. Such distance must have made even more frantic their good-bye words: *We may never see each other again.*

Qantas Flight 7 lifted off at 1:30 P.M., bound for Bangkok. Red-tiled roofs, that beautiful harbor, and five months of memories disappeared beneath the clouds and into our thoughts.

Drew said, "I *am* going back. I think I'll go to college in Australia."

Leslee said, "I'm going to get a job and save fifty dollars a month and go back when I'm eighteen."

We all laughed when she said *ate-ain*, the way an Australian would have said it.

Honey asked, "Do you remember when we first got to Australia? Will was looking for McDonald's, Leslee for surfers, Kathryn for the first plane home. Drew was looking for himself, your father was looking for a place to hide, and I was looking for the Laundromat."

Our conversations and thoughts were a mixture of planning ahead to home in America and looking back to home in Australia. For Drew and Leslee, making plans to return to Australia someday made the leaving and the long flight more bearable. They would have been glad to stay another six months, and if they had, it might have been a real struggle to take them home. The older children especially had swapped eight years of a structured, publicized, restricted life at the Governor's Mansion for a delicious time off in Australia during which they experimented with being themselves.

Will busied himself with drawing first the harbor, then the clouds, then the window itself, and, as the flight wore on, the airline magazine cover and the seat handle and the ashtray. His mother was teaching him to draw anything he could see, and that it was OK if it didn't look just like it *really* looked. His homecoming plans were simple. "I'm going to John's and play games."

Kathryn read. Her plans were simple, too. "I want to see my friends. I'd like to be home tomorrow."

The fourteen-hour flight to the top half of the world was the beginning of a three-week reentry, the sort of suspension in time that makes coming back to earth easier for underwater divers and astronauts. I had hoped that experiences in big cities on the way home would help us to absorb the wonder of our time away and to move more gradually back to reality. But I found myself wondering *which* reality? Australia? In Australia we had rented our own house, bought our own car, made friends, eaten meals together, argued, stored up memories, talked to each other, explored, read, walked to school and to the store and to church, rarely dressed up, created our own little environment—of a world coming into order—instead of being transfixed by the world on the evening news. Or was reality Nashville, where all the children had to compare with the Australian experience was living in a ceremonial house, restricted opportunities for friendship, family occasions interrupted by a thousand duties, troopers enforcing rules, other people always around, someone other than parents driving them to school, chefs shopping for meals, a father with blue suits and red ties and white cards that listed events scheduled every fifteen minutes? Were we flying away from dreamland or back into it, or would there be some new one?

And what have *I* learned during these six months off? I asked myself. Mostly little things about living: to focus on the day, to start each day with a few quiet minutes instead of a sprint. My exercise is walking now instead of running, and I stand more than I sit. I eat less. I have lost twenty pounds without trying. I have discovered that in a family it is important just to be there, physically and mentally. I know now that there is plenty to do in life besides what I was doing, that it is good somehow to do the most basic things for yourself, to be on your own. Trying to simplify life seems more and more like a good idea. And it is absolutely true that it is good to break out of ruts for a while every now and then, even if they are good ruts, just to see the ruts from another view and understand them. I left America searching for answers. I'll be home in three weeks without many, and still searching for how to live better with other people. I left America expecting to learn about the world and Australia. I'm going home having learned the most about America, our family and myself.

Will said about the plane trip, "This is long and slow, like a fly buzzing around the world." To pass the time, I suggested that I would like some help making a list of what was different about Australia.

Will volunteered, "McDonald's is bigger, and the fries tasted like fish."

"They call fries 'chips' at Kentucky Fried Chicken," said Kathryn.

"They call fries 'chips' everywhere in Australia but McDonald's," said Will.

Drew said, "You need a nutcracker to unscrew the top of an Australian Coke. And teenagers smoke more."

Honey said, "The children *mind*. If a mother at Balmoral Beach says, 'Come 'ere, Michael,' Michael comes."

Leslee said, "The song lyrics are worse. I couldn't believe some of what they said."

Drew said, "The way they talk is what's so different. They think *we* have an accent. Everything's half a word."

"When we left, Mom was starting to say that everything was *lovely*," Leslee said.

"And you were saying boys were *beautiful*," Drew said.

Kathryn jumped into it. "Leslee had an Australian accent after *one day*."

Will said, "Maths were harder."

Honey said, "I liked the village shops instead of the supermarket. And it was nice that the azaleas and rhododendron were confused and tried to bloom almost all the time."

Drew said, "The bacon's no good. Pigs must be different in Australia."

Will said, "Venus is the morning star, and we don't have a Southern Cross."

* * *

Traveling from Sydney to Bangkok was more than crossing the equator from winter to summer. It was going from European to Asian, from "Do the Right Thing" litter-pickup containers to garbage floating in the river, from sidewalk cafés to dinner on sidewalks, from sailboats to long-tailed houseboats, from red-tiled roofs on brick houses to wood-thatched houses on stilts, from ocean breezes to the stink of gasoline and spoiled food.

Bangkok is the capital of Thailand, old Siam. Our tour-bus guide explained, "There are five million residents of Bangkok, and another million in the dry season when there is no rice to grow in the countryside. There are one thousand meters of highways for every two-thousand-meter lengths of cars." No one disputed that fact. We had begun our drive to Puchong's Rose Garden on the outskirts of the city before nine A.M.—a time of day when trucks were banned in the city—but it still took us one and a half hours to travel twenty-five kilometers. The only really successful motorists were motorcyclists, who would weave recklessly in and out of lines of three-wheeled scooters, speed in front of taxis and occasional Japanese cars, and somehow squeeze between buses so close that their window mirrors almost touched.

At Puchong's, tourists could experience in two hours many of Thailand's best-known traditions: sword fighting, beautiful dark-eyed dancers with long fingernails, a Thai wedding, elephant rides, cockfighting, and Thai boxing—in which the contenders fight like cocks and have all the spontaneity of Saturday-afternoon wrestlers in the United States.

"Celebrating traditions helps keep your identity," I said to the Thai manager of the Rose Garden, who seemed to be about my age.

"Yes, but it is not good to keep traditions too much," replied the manager, looking at our four children. "These children have to be more international now, have to learn to grow up in the whole world. It is true that if we forget our roots, we forget who we are. But if we sink too deep in our origins, then we cannot communicate with anyone else."

We walked from the exhibit center toward the elephant rides and stood for a while among the roses, talking. He continued. "My son, he has been at school in London since he was ten. He comes home three times a year. I came home from school in New Zealand every two years. Air fares are much cheaper now. I want him to go to the United States for two years of high school and then come back home. Britain. The United States. Thailand. That's about right. Anyway, that's my plan. I don't know what the outcome will be."

I asked him, "Why do the Thai people all seem so happy? I have never been anywhere where people are so helpful and friendly and seem so genuinely at peace with themselves."

He answered, "Our religion, I suppose. Almost everyone is Buddhist. The Thai heart opens easily, but there are many compartments, doors, and turns inside. The western heart is harder to open, but there is only one door and it opens wide and deep."

We took turns riding elephants and having our photographs taken with a white cockatoo who liked to sit on people's shoulders, said good-bye to the Rose Garden manager, and boarded the tour bus for the slow ride back to the Oriental Hotel. After a while, Drew moved to the seat next to mine.

"I'm having some radical thoughts," he said.

"Like what?"

"I'm not going back to school in New Hampshire. I want to finish in Nashville and then come back to Australia."

"American colleges are better than Australian colleges," I said cautiously.

"Maybe I'll just take a year or two off in Australia."

"You've worked awfully hard to be readmitted to school. They really want you to come back. That's quite an achievement."

"But everybody there knows what they want to do. They want to be a lawyer or a doctor. I'm not ready to get on the ladder."

I asked, "How does that square with what you said a few weeks ago about your Australian high-school friends, about how so many of them want to do nothing but drink at parties, have a good time? You said no wonder Australia was going downhill."

"I still think that, although they've got some pretty good

ideas about how to live, too. I just don't want to go back to a prep school and be like everybody else—right hair length, right schools, just to get on the right ladder. I know you probably think I'm weird but that's how I feel."

I thought for a while. Then I said:

"This may be hard for you to imagine, but I've been having a lot of the same thoughts you're having. Taking six months off for me at almost age forty-seven has been about as unusual as it has been for you at seventeen to think about changing schools and spend another year in Australia. Some of *my* friends may think *I'm* weird for some of the same reasons you're afraid I'll think you're weird. I don't believe you're weird at all. I hope you keep on thinking about things. You're almost eighteen and eighteen is a good age to *start* thinking, not to stop. I hope you try to figure out what's really important to you and just be yourself. This trip came at a very good time for you. In a way, you grew up in Australia. I can remember a little of what it was like at eighteen. I taught canoeing at camp that summer. Had a flat stomach. Even some muscles. Every so often I thought I caught the girls taking a look. Eighteen can be a very good time."

"*Ate-ain.* That's how the Aussies would say it." Drew laughed.

I looked out the window at the traffic and at happy Thai children pushing toy trucks on the sidewalks, and I thought, Drew is a chip off the part of me that doesn't often get to do what it wants to do. To him, personal friendships are the most important thing. He practices and composes on his guitar hours a day. He lets his hair grow. He follows his feelings. I could learn something from him. I organize my feelings so I can stay on that ladder he doesn't want to climb. I'm rushing back into a structured life, but I would really like to live about one half of that life still free, but in six months off I have not figured out how to do that and still have a central purpose to my life.

After a long silence, I remembered a call from home that Honey had received just before we left Sydney. I asked Drew, "Did your mother tell you that Art Gaiser died?" (Art was our always happy neighbor when the children were young.)

"Yes," he answered. "I remember how when we were little

we would pick flowers in the summer with Mom, and take them next door to him through the hole in the brick wall."

"I don't remember that," I said.

"You were always busy," Drew said.

Riding a jumbo jet into Hong Kong's airport reminded me of the time Drew and I rode a single-engine Piper Cub to the floor of the Salmon River Canyon in Idaho. We had flown down through the clouds in the canyon, then below the clouds, lower and lower, until out of the windows we could see only canyon walls, and then suddenly the plane landed on the river's edge, just when we were wondering if there would ever be a place to land.

Leslee said, "Hong Kong is pretty. Maybe I'll come back here on my way to Australia when I'm eighteen." Tall white buildings grew with trees on mountainsides, and more boats than we could count moved slowly across a huge harbor whose beauty rivaled Sydney's.

Friday night was my birthday. The girls presented me with a tailormade tie. Honey had found two elephant-decorated walking sticks. Drew played "Happy Birthday" on his guitar. And Will had spent half his spending money on four tiny ivory elephants. Leaving the children in the luxury of the Holiday Inn Harbourview, Honey and I enjoyed a long, quiet dinner alone. Saturday was all shopping.

The next morning Will said, "It's a yucky day." Rain was splashing on the big hotel windows facing the harbor. We slept late, washed clothes, and counted the different kinds of ships in the harbor. It was the seventh day of our reentry, a sort of breakpoint, a day for laziness and reading before visiting for eight days in China and Russia, and four days in France. Already Australia was not on my mind. But Drew had left dinner early the night before to develop the photographs we had taken while saying good-bye to everyone at the Sydney airport.

The vote was unanimous for Sunday evening dinner: real hamburgers and real french fries, ordered up from the Holiday Inn room service. Between gobs of real American ketchup, we talked about my visit in 1985 to the interior of China when at a banquet the provincial governor had served in my honor birds' feet, whole sparrows, ox tendon, the intestines of something and even sea slugs. I had become too ill too eat, and Honey had expertly carried on the necessary diplomatic conversation.

Drew said, "In China, I'm going to fast."

"I'll eat rice," said Will.

"I'll lose ten pounds by France," said Leslee.

Honey said, "I have a jar of peanut butter for your father, and some crackers."

N O G R A T E - F U L D E A D T - S H I R T S I N T H E K R E M L I N !

//

Broad, wholesome, charitable views of men and things cannot be acquired by vegetating in one little corner of the earth all one's lifetime.

—MARK TWAIN
Innocents Abroad

"U S. money feels good," Drew said.
For nearly six months Drew had not seen United States dollars; now he watched as twenty of them paid for the extra charges on the seventeen bags on the train from British

Hong Kong into Guangzhou, inside Communist China. The train station was efficient in a crowded sort of way. English was spoken. Long lines moved steadily, and after a while we found ourselves comfortable in seats on an air-conditioned train.

As we moved across the countryside, Honey wrote the last of her Australian postcards, Kathryn read to Will, Drew read a travel book on China, and Leslee listened to tapes on her Walkman and looked out the window.

Drew began looking, too, and said, "I thought China was wall-to-wall people." The train had left behind the concrete roads and new apartments of Hong Kong, and was traveling through fields of banana trees and rice where there were dammed-up ponds with high paths alongside. Workers hoed outside wide bamboo huts and others drove water buffalo and some pulled carts with wooden wheels along the new concrete highways.

Honey said, "The real green of the trees is nice to see again after seeing only gum-tree green for such a long time." The countryside was wet and green and rolling like North Carolina countryside and no more crowded.

In the Guangzhou train station, an eight-clock sign told the time for San Francisco, Pyongyang, Frankfurt, Cairo, Tehran, Karachi, Honolulu, and Bangkok—a different list of cities than we were accustomed to seeing. I felt disoriented, and realized that the British terms Americans use to describe the world are most confusing. For example, what the British call the "Far East"—China, Japan, Singapore—is for us, in fact, the "Far West," a natural extension of the pioneer drive beyond California. And for the United States, the "Near East" should be Europe, and "Down Under," Argentina and Chile.

The other family members sat on the bags under the time clock while I searched for a lost visa. Finally Leslee said very carefully, "Dad, if visas hassle you so much, why do you insist on keeping up with them?"

I answered, "I'm not doing so badly."

Kathryn said, "This isn't the first time you've lost one."

"It's the *fifth* time," Will said.

Honey said, "Why don't you let me take the visas and the passports from here? You won't be hassled and I won't be nervous about one of us getting tossed off a train in a Communist country because you've lost a passport."

Seated around a long table, we eyed our first real Chinese meal, then nibbled and stirred it with our chopsticks so the food would look as if it had been eaten and our smiling hosts and eager Chinese guide would not be insulted.

That evening we flew north to Xian, a dusty ancient city of two and a half million in southern China, home of the Big White Goose Pagoda and the two thousand-year-old marching warriors.

Elena, our guide, told us, "You will live more than twelve hundred years if you climb to the top of the Big White Goose Pagoda."

"I'm already in paradise," Will said, racing up the pagoda steps. "I crawled through that thing in Japan."

Some Chinese asked Elena whether Will was a boy or a girl. And many put their hands on his blond hair. Elena explained, "We only see Chinese, so we think American children are very pretty. They have different hair."

I thought, And there are not nearly as many cute eight-year-old Chinese heads to pat. Will was born in the year that China started its new policy of one child per family. China has become a country of one family, one bike, one child. These only children have become China's most admired and—authorities have complained—most spoiled assets.

"Qin became emperor of China in about 2000 B.C.," Elena explained as we drove along a new concrete road through dusty fields toward the site of the emperor's marching warriors. "He was thirteen, about the age of Kathryn, and he immediately began to unify the warring sections of China and to build his mausoleum. He accomplished both before he died at age thirty-nine."

Will said, "He was important like Dad was important."

"Isn't Dad still important?" asked his mother.

"Everything's important, but a long time ago Dad was more important than lots of people," Will said.

Elena continued, "To keep the mausoleum secret, Qin built it underground and, when it was finished, buried the craftsmen—perhaps as many as twenty thousand of them—with his secret. None of this was known until 1974 when farmers digging in fields west of Xian uncovered bronze hands, and legs and arms, and then chariots and parts of horses, too."

After four excavations archaeologists unearthed a marching army: 8,000 clay figures, all majestic and powerful, up to 1.96 meters tall. All were different. Some were thin-faced, some had wide faces; some had hands that grasped bronze tools, some, weapons. But all stood erect and faced east with their hands straight down and their feet apart at attention. Their long-tailed horses—straining, open-mouthed, ears forward—pulled chariots. The figures had been fashioned so expertly that it seemed that, if you were to blink, they might march away.

Riding back to Xian in a new bus, we saw wheat that had been spread to dry along the outer lane of the concrete highway. Our modern tourist bus competed with hand-pulled carts for the remaining space. Farmers in the fields were using primitive hand tools not so different from the ones the marching warriors carried, not even much different from some we saw in the excavation of a six thousand-year-old Chinese city near Xian. Many farmers had new stone houses, paid for with money earned from their own creeping capitalism—encouraged by policies that within a few years have turned once-hungry China into an exporter of food. But in those nice new farmhouses, water supplies and toilet facilities were still like they were when Qin's warriors were marching.

In Beijing we—including the children—enjoyed a two-hour lunch with the American ambassador, Winston Lord, and his author wife, Bette Bao. I said, "There is such a steady, pleasant flow about China. My image of China is of a long, weaving, never-broken line of bicycles. The line will bend and adjust to accommodate whatever may come, but it never breaks and it never seems to stop."

Winston Lord said, "China is a confident country. The Chinese attitude is, we were number one for thousands of years and that has been interrupted relatively recently, within the last couple of hundred years, and there is no reason for us to expect that before too long we won't be number one again. Having such a strong sense of themselves gives them self-confidence and makes them pleasant to deal with. They're hard bargainers, but you don't have to wade through all sorts of preliminaries dealing with their insecurities as you must, for example, with the Soviets."

* * *

Russia is best in the winter when the snow is so deep that farmers talk about how much better the crops will be in the spring. It is the best time because the deep snow covers the gloom. For me, Russia has always been a melody in a minor key. Part of this could be American propaganda; most Americans arrive at the registration desks of Moscow hotels already angry. But I think it is much more than propaganda. Our children, who even in pleasant China began making lists of what they could not do there that they *could* do at home in America—such as marry whom they wish, go to school, take a job, and live where they want—found that the lists grew even on their first day in Moscow.

Kathryn said, "You can't travel unless you're important."

"Or buy a Walkman," said Leslee.

Will said, "All the cars are the same and not that good."

Kathryn said, "They do you a big favor to give you a table at the Nacional Hotel."

"They have special stores for special people," Leslee said.

Drew said, "I asked the guide what if somebody tried to form a new political party, and she just walked away."

For an American the music of Moscow is especially sad because of the pervasive sense of order. I am always surprised at how quickly and easily I learn the rules around Red Square. Rules change and barricades move and the places where you are not supposed to walk often change, too. But the brown-suited soldiers blow a whistle at your first step toward the wrong place, and you sense instantly that that whistle is for you and you quickly step back into line. In Moscow, every third person seems to be a brown-suited soldier and someone always seems to be whistling to keep someone in line.

So much order knocks life out of tune, stirs in those who know freedom a powerful impulse to return to it. When I first visited Red Square in October 1985, I felt swelling within me this urge suddenly to break through and run across the square where the barricades and soldiers made clear I was *not* supposed to be. I wanted to do this shouting at the top of my voice. I wanted to defy the restricted space, perhaps in the same way the young German Mathias Rust flew his small plane from West Berlin to land just outside the Kremlin walls.

When Honey jogged around the Kremlin early on the second day in Moscow it had been raining and it was still windy and chilly, more like March in Tennessee than July. And later that morning, even though the sun burst forth, she and I and Kathryn and Leslee wore sweaters and windbreakers as we waited outside the Nacional Hotel for an Intourist guide. We were going to visit the Kremlin.

Then out of the old hotel strolled Drew. He was wearing his loudest, most awful-looking Bermuda shorts and an outrageous purple, green, and yellow Grateful Dead tie-dyed T-shirt. On his feet were Technicolor tennis shoes, and he wore no socks. Around his head he had looped a spotted bandanna to harness hair that at that time was more scraggly than long (because of that fateful tennis-match on Dunk Island).

He said, too hopefully, "Bet they don't let me in."

"Yeaahhh," said Will, who emerged out the same door, right behind his older brother. Will had sought to match Drew's bravado in each detail. He wore *his* bright-colored Australian shorts (the red ones with yellow palm trees), no socks, and his smelliest tennis shoes. And Will wore something arguably finer even than a Grateful Dead tie-dyed T-shirt: his prized white T-shirt imprinted with flags of the United States and a picture of the U.S.S. *Midway*, the American aircraft carrier we had visited in Sydney Harbor. These rebellious American brothers slapped hands like two National Basketball Association guards after a three-point shot, and leaned against the wall of the hotel, defiantly. Drew crossed his arms, so Will did, too; then Will announced, pointing to his U.S.S. *Midway* T-shirt, "That ought to keep 'em off of me when I'm in the Kremlin!"

The guide arrived and said the expected, "The boys can't go into the Kremlin like that. The older boy can't wear that shirt and the younger boy may wear shorts but not *those* shorts."

"I don't like the way they do things here," Will said as he marched away with Drew to change clothes. "Everybody here has to wear normal things. For little people like me it's regular shorts and shirts, and then when you're big you probably can't wear shorts."

After the Kremlin tour, we returned to the Nacional Hotel to repack our suitcases. Tomorrow we would board the train to Paris, our sixth big-city visit since leaving Sydney. Each visit had squeezed the last one deeper into our memories, making Australia an even more distant dream.

"Tomorrow, tomorrow, we're leaving tomorrow. How lucky can we be," sang Will as the elevator creaked to the third floor of the old hotel.

We left Moscow on Monday evening, July 13, at 8:15, lodged in car 10, berths 1 through 6. Our Soviet train was headed west. It went through western Russia, and then through the Polish countryside, which looked golden and clean like Kansas in summer. We traveled approximately the route Napoleon had used in 1812 to invade Russia, the route that Hitler also took when, in the winter of 1941, he got to within twenty-four miles of the Kremlin. As the train inched toward Berlin, on the second night, we woke one another just before midnight and hung out the windows in the cool air for so long that I was sure we had missed it until Drew said quietly, "There it is," and we saw blazing lights and barbed wire and bare ground and guards marching with guns, and then the train moved on into West Berlin, and the Berlin Wall disappeared as quickly as it had appeared, but seeing it had been another special long moment on our six months off that would remind us again of what we could do that millions of others could not.

Our bargain-basement round-the-world travel tickets required us to get to either Paris or London to catch a plane to America. We opted for Paris, because we learned that some of our best friends would be there at the same time and we had never been there. After Moscow and the Soviet train, Paris was unexpected dessert, a delicious four-day blur.

We arrived coughing, tired, layered with Communist dirt from the Moscow milk run—and hungry; there had been no dining car from Moscow to Paris. After I bought some francs, somehow we stuffed ourselves and our bags into two taxis and located the American embassy, where we were to be the guests of Ambassador Joe M. Rodgers and his wife, Honey, also friends from Nashville. The eighteenth-century embassy residence is one of the finest residences in all of Paris—and our rooms measured up too.

"Mom, this is about as good as an all-suite hotel," said Will, inspecting a box of corn flakes, and then he proclaimed, "Hey,

these corn flakes are made 'Only in Battle Creek, Michigan.' "
He put down the box and said, "I can't wait until I get home
to eat some good old Cap'n Crunch cereal."

Drew said, "I want to see some American TV commercials.
I haven't seen any in six months. And I'm going to a different
fast-food place every day."

Will said, "I'm ready to go to Captain D.'s right now—and
Wendy's. And I haven't had any doughnuts of the good old
American kind in six months."

Leslee and Kathryn squealed when they discovered friends
from Nashville and sat for most of the afternoon beneath the
trees in the embassy backyard, hungry to find out everything
that had happened at home during the last six months. Drew
met a group of Nashville students who had been hired for the
summer to wait on tables.

Honey and I unpacked our bags, then we met Carole and
John Sergent, in whose Nashville home we had stayed for three
days after leaving the Mansion and before our twenty-one-gun
getaway. They, Honey, and I walked along the boulevards, and
by the Arc de Triomphe, and the Louvre and the Cathedral of
Notre Dame. Standing on a bridge over the Seine in the sun at
5:00 P.M. infused us with the joy of some new stolen adventure.
For an hour we sat at a sidewalk café with our good friends and
relaxed and talked. I didn't want it to end. That evening, after
perhaps the best-tasting dinner I could remember, it was still
light out. The mellowness of Paris, the ease of the living, the
excitement of the colors and the food, the softness of the evening
light—life in such harmony—made the end of that summer day
at 10:30 P.M. as poignant as saying good-bye to Sydney three
weeks earlier. I thought, what a different feeling from when it
is 10:30 in Moscow and the summer light is still there and you
wish it would go away so the day could end. Even the black-
caped policemen with tommy guns did not spoil the feeling of
the richness of life in Paris.

On Sunday, the day before our flight home, Will had set his
watch seven hours back to Nashville time. And I had begun to
experience a feeling of tiredness, even of moroseness, of readi-
ness to end this stage of life. It made me more than a little angry
at myself that I could not just enjoy this wonderful city. I sat
down at the desk in our bedroom.

"What are you doing?" Honey asked.

"Making a list of things to do," I answered, hating to admit it.

The next morning Honey told the Sergents. "It's a short good-bye. We'll be at your house for the next two weeks while ours gets finished. Who knows when that will be?"

Drew asked John Sergent, "How long are you staying?"

"In Paris? One month." Dr. John Sergent said proudly— this was the same physician who six months earlier had told me it would be "unprofessional" to take off more than three weeks.

"A month! You can't do *anything* in a month," Drew said. This was the same boy who a year and a half earlier had announced he could not possibly go to Australia, that even two days away on a family vacation would be "boring" and "embarrassing."

On the way to the airport, Drew slept.

When he awoke, I said, "It looks like you enjoyed your nights in Paris."

He said, "People had told me this was the best place to go in the world, but I didn't believe it. Now I do. I met a girl from Nashville I went to school with for nine years."

"Cute?"

"Well, she wasn't, but she's changed."

"Maybe you have, too," I said.

BOOK III

NEW BEGINNING

The God within mankind is the
spirit of purposeful and creative
adventure.

—René Dubos
A God Within

CHAPTER 35

OUR HOME-COMING

//

We shall not cease from exploration,
And the end of all our exploring
Will be to arrive where we started
And to know the place for the first
time.

—T. S. Eliot,
Four Quartets

The pilot's voice sounded as excited as we were. "We're about to begin our descent into Detroit Metropolitan Airport. We should be on the ground in thirty-five minutes. Please complete your customs declaration form, one for each member of the family."

WELCOME TO THE UNITED STATES

The words spread across the top of my customs form, the way a rowdy American welcome ought to. There would be none of this laid-back "G'day" Australian-style, no Bangkok happy faces, no Beijing distant smiles, not one Tokyo bow or Moscow scowl, not a touch of Parisian disdain.

I was ready for *America!* A thump on the chest. Slap on the back. A push. An arm over the shoulder. Soul brothers slapping hands. "How ya doing?" "Where ya been?" "Wha's happenin', brotha?" "Hey, mannn . . . WELCOME TO THE YEW-NITED STATES!"

What if I were a first-time visitor coming into the United States? What would I be thinking about thirty-five minutes before landing in this huge, cocky, magical, lurching land of ours? I thought about what I had heard overseas about America during our six months off.

Just how dangerous is it? would probably be the first-time visitor's first question. *How many people wear guns?* The streets of most cities in the world are safer than ours. *How many people are rich and what are they like? How many are poor and what does poor mean in America? What about black people? Do you still mistreat them? Will anyone be friendly? Are the Americans who don't travel noisy like the ones who do?*

Is anything in the middle of America, in all that space you never hear about between New York City and California? There must be a different fast-food place on every corner, a television-production studio on every block. Where does Bill Cosby live? Who thinks up all the amazing things Americans invent? Can you visit the National Geographic? Does almost everybody who helps really wait for a tip, and are the tips really sometimes twenty dollars? Can we see Disneyworld and the Grand Canyon on the same trip?

We had three hours to wait in Detroit before our flight left for Nashville. Leslee nearly exhausted her month's allowance making phone calls to John and Angie and Ann and "everybody in Nashville" as she arranged for them to meet her at the airport. With the little money she had left, she bought a box of Oreos and shared them with Will. Kathryn called the friends she had missed so, reaching Torie in Nashville. Her friend Liz was at Torie's house, so Kathryn said, "Call Caroline and bring everybody," and the three called Shad and Chad and Liza and Tiffany, and they all made plans to go to the Nashville airport at 7:00 P.M.

Drew bought a great big red cup of Coke and a hamburger and U.S. magazines. Will "chowed down on about five and a half hot dogs of the good old American kind," and then trying to keep up with Leslee and Kathryn called *his* best friend, John, to see if *he* would come to the Nashville airport. Then Will read all the airplane signs ("Dad, I haven't seen an American Airlines sign since maybe Denver!"), and bought two packs of Juicy Fruit gum, "big ones with like twenty-four in them and I think I'll have about twenty," and he saved the other four for the flight to Nashville. I sat by myself, guarding the seventeen bags, and watched—gawked would be a better word for it—*gawked* at a airport lobby busy with my fellow Americans. They are, when you have not seen them for six months, a wondrous sight!

Sitting there gawking, recalling China as a long, continuously weaving and unending flow of bicycles, I tried to imagine what would best describe America, and this is what I came up with: one of those New York City Fifth Avenue intersections where the pedestrian signals say WAIT, and everyone waits and waits and waits until street corners full of impatient people are spilling over the curbs, and then ALL THE LIGHTS AT ONCE SAY "WALK" and everyone explodes in every direction, jamming the intersections, scrambling across—some people walking straight, some edging sideways, some stumbling catercorner, some weaving in and out, some dressed properly, some a mess, some helping, some pushing, some strolling shoulder to shoulder, every which way. If China is a flow of bicycles and sameness, then America is the scrambling intersection and nobody the same.

On July 21, 1987, Detroit Airport looked something like a New York intersection with ALL THE LIGHTS SAYING "WALK." My thought was, how much bigger Americans are, and—there is no delicate way to say this—how well fed we are. Bellies and thighs and jowls and cheeks and rear ends must stick out more in America than in anywhere else in the world. Most of us are so relatively oversized and relatively well-off and well fed. And we are such a bunch of scramblers—everybody so busy, heading fast in a different direction, head up, going his or her own way. No flow to it. No stopping anybody, either.

And the clothes. If you have been away for six months, you cannot possibly remember the festival of hats and undershirts and shorts and jams and floppy shoes and windbreakers and T-shirts and bandanas, and all the wild-colored combinations of everything. There must be nothing like it in any airport or on any street in any other country in the world. We Americans do our own thing—we talk it, look it, act it.

On the radio in the courtesy car, riding to the domestic terminal: Mattingly had hit another home run, Willie Randolph was injured, Tigers were rolling in Motown, Mets catcher had fallen into the dugout, breaking his leg, every detail.

Continental Airlines, purple Federal Express planes, giant yellow construction machines pushing around airport earth— American progress; ninety-two degrees and hot this afternoon.

In the terminal: more to buy, pay phones everywhere and people using them, English spoken with every kind of American accent, nine newspaper stands and more papers and magazines available in the gift shop, every headline blazing the latest worst about Irangate.

Flying to Nashville: Great Lakes below and big farms.

Nashville: Will had calculated from his watch that from the time he left the embassy in Paris all the way until he went to bed in Nashville he had been awake for twenty-three and a half hours.

I was awake at five the next morning at the Sergents' home on Whitland Avenue in Nashville. Drew and Kathryn and Leslee had all spent the night with friends who had met them at the airport. Will's best friend, John, met him, and John's sister, Susan, drove the boys to Wendy's for some fries and Will's first burger since Tokyo. Then John came over to the Sergents', where the boys played a few games of chess, all of which Will won, he remembers. The four children had disappeared within minutes after we landed. Kathryn, who was positively beaming, didn't leave her dearest friend Torie's house for a week.

The Sergents' morning newspaper had arrived, but it didn't tempt me. I watched the sun rise instead. For eight years I had read five newspapers front to back each day. Now for six months I had been without them and was nearly weaned. And I thought I understood better what newspapers by their nature must do, which is selectively to create an addictive environment of several-day stories about the world whirling into minor key. Understanding this meant that I also understood that newspapers, or at least most of them, did not help me much to understand the world I *really* lived in. For example, it is not "news" if I drive safely down the street to work. It *is* if I have a wreck. Since most of us make it safely down the street, most of us live in a world that is mostly in order, or one that we busily try to bring into order, into the naturally happy major key melodies of life. What is so confusing is that communications technology continues to devise more and more ways to assault us with more and more "news" from everywhere, and that "news" of a world out of order becomes so powerfully absorbing that we think *most* lives must be tumbling irrevocably out of order, too. This "news" contradicts our own experience with our own lives. Living with that contradiction is something many of us have not learned how to do.

I walked up the Whitland Avenue sidewalk and then, on West End Avenue, I found more sidewalk. I had never thought much about there being so many sidewalks in Nashville. But then I had never done much walking before in Nashville. I was wide awake. It was noon, Paris time. But what could be better? Wide awake at sunrise, dressed in old pants and tennis shoes and T-shirt, walking with no real destination, no need to go to any office.

In Australia the early morning had become my favorite part of the day. Now as I walked down West End Avenue, I studied the Nashville morning. Only a few cars were warming up for the drive to work. Hardwood trees protected dewy lawns. Spider webs had been spun on moist ivy. Had I ever before noticed that when you are on West End, the sun rises over West End School? There were birdcalls, not the raucous, laughing kookaburras or bawling crows, but a quieter warbling and singing, the sounds I had grown up hearing. A few early-morning walkers said hello. Workmen were busily putting together a new home, starting early to avoid the heat of the day. Election signs decorated clipped front lawns. There had always been everything to see in Nashville, but I had never really been looking before—nor even feeling. Nashville was *hot* in July. Hot like Bangkok. Stickier than I remembered.

A few days later, on Sunday, I drove to Westminster Presbyterian Church for the eleven A.M. service and was grateful for the air conditioning. The Reverend K. C. Ptomey preached a good one, and I thought about how in America, instead of brown-suited Soviet soldiers blowing whistles, someone is almost always rallying somebody else: preachers, athletic coaches, salesmen, broadcast announcers, auctioneers, politicians. A good American feels shortchanged if someone doesn't stir his juices real good two or three times each day.

The choir and the preacher had marched out, and people were filing out of the pews, when the lady who had been sitting behind me felt my arm and observed, "You're skinny, like an Australian."

Her friend said, "Look at his hair. Your hair is long."

A third said, laughing, "A haircut's all he needs, and a few good meals."

As I was leaving, I heard the first woman whisper, "He *does* look thin."

When I returned to the Sergents', Honey had returned from early service at Christ Episcopal Church and was making lunch. She said, "You drove to church? It's only two blocks. Why didn't you walk?"

"Well, I guess for sure I'm home again. I didn't even think about walking."

The whimpering began when we neared Miller's Cove. Their undersides quivered and their tails circled and wiggled. I let the cocker spaniels run where the gravel road begins, and they raced the car through the creek to the cabin. I went immediately to the back porch and sat rocking and watched the day disappear, when suddenly the air changed. It was that long late moment in a mountain summer day when the cool brushes your face and the temperature drops at least five degrees.

After six months away, Honey could not resist inspecting the house, but soon we were rocking together and reminiscing about when we used to sit on the car hood in the high grass and dream about building a cabin in this very place. We wanted always to be able to feel the breezes rolling up the hill, wet and cool and full of the sounds of the cricket orchestra and the cattle mooing and all the mysterious cove smells and noises. The sky grayed and the hills turned black. The only light against Chilhowee Mountain was at the farmer's gate across the hill, except when headlights occasionally darted through the woods on the Foothills Parkway.

The next morning it was my turn to inspect the outside of the place. Will was already riding the thick rope hung from the lowest branch of the biggest oak, and when he saw me he wanted pushes, *big* pushes—well, not *too* big. No high wind had conquered the two-century-old oaks during our six months off. For these venerables it had been a wink of time. The tulip poplar had outgrown its hole in the porch. I would have to cut the hole bigger. There were ashes in the fireplace—and no trash bags either, Honey declared, inspecting again. *She* would take care of that.

The log cabin and the rope swing and the old oak trees and our rock dam in Hesse Creek—they all fit here. And so did we. Will and I cautiously rearranged the rock dam, and I tried to imagine it—it seemed almost impossible—we had traveled all the way around the world, safely, the six of us on this six-month adventure, and we had found out about the world and ourselves and found our way back home again to our place, this place of all the places in this whole world where we fit best.

J O N A H

Jonah is my kind of missionary.
Reluctant, withdrawn, stubborn.
Never quite ready to go to Nineveh.
—THE REVEREND DR. WILLIAM J.
CARL, III
Preaching Christian Doctrine

A man knows when he has found his
vocation when he stops thinking
about how to live and begins to live.
—THOMAS MERTON
Thoughts in Solitude

I t was breezy that April morning in Sydney and I had closed the door, but still I heard the mailman's double whistle. I was sitting at my basement desk planning our trip to Japan when Honey came downstairs with the letter. I opened it.

Dear Lamar,

We miss you but hear that you are enjoying your time off. I am writing to ask whether you would serve as chair of a national Presbyterian campaign to raise $175 million. Your role would be to give the campaign visibility. A staff would do most of the work.

Please do not say "no" until you have re-read the book of Jonah!

(signed) K. C. Ptomey

The Reverend K. C. Ptomey was pastor of Westminster Presbyterian Church in Nashville and my preacher. So I read Jonah, all four chapters and forty-eight verses. Then I laid the Bible and the letter aside and the next day went to Japan with the family for nearly two weeks. I hoped that while I was gone someone else would get the call for this job.

After we returned from Japan, I was working again at my desk when the phone rang. I picked it up and heard a familiar American voice. "Lamar, how are things?" My hometown preacher had my telephone number in Australia!

I said, "K.C., you must be calling to say that storms are coming and a great whale is in Sydney Harbor waiting to swallow me unless I will go raise the hundred seventy-five million dollars."

Then, gathering my courage, I said, "Jonah doesn't say anything about raising money for the Presbyterian Church. It's just about a missionary God calls to go to Nineveh, and keeps cooking up excuses. That's about the way I feel. I'm ready to go, to do the Lord's work. Just send me. Send me any place but off to raise that hundred seventy-five million."

I was especially proud of what I said next. "K.C., just how sure are you that it's *God* calling me to do this? Being chairman of big committees *for anything* is what I'm trying to get away from. I'd rather do something down my own street, in my own church, in my family."

K.C. surprised me. "You're in luck. I'll cancel your trip to Nineveh if you'll make our annual stewardship address on October 12. That's the one your brother-in-law, Bill, preached last year. It's when the whole church gets together to decide what each of us will give back to God. How about it?"

"You should have been a horse trader. You've got me," I said.

K.C. said, "That's great, and I understand how you feel about a big campaign. It's more important now to think about what to do with your life. Your life is a gift from God, and not that many people take time off to think about what to do with it."

I had forgotten all about the speech until September when the church bulletins began touting my October 12 appearance. K.C.'s sermons hinted that I might have interesting revelations to make. The youth group mailed to every church family fake one-dollar bills with my face pasted where George Washington's face was supposed to be. Elders stopped to talk and my Sunday school teacher made a fuss over me. Saint Paul coming to report his conversion would have received no finer promotion.

"I'm afraid to go to Sunday school," I said to Honey exactly one week before the event. "They'll have posters up saying, 'Swam with the sharks, pulled from the belly of a crocodile, stopped on the road to the deep Red Centre—come and hear Lamar's revelations!' I've got to get to work on this speech!"

After church that day I told K.C., "This is not exactly fair. It is one thing for you or my brother-in-law to make the stewardship speech. You two are red-hot preachers. Good at it. Paid to do it. That's what you're for! How would you like it if someone called up and wanted *you* to stand on some courthouse steps some Saturday morning and holler about Republican principles while two hundred citizens gossiped and whittled and jingled change and spit tobacco and paid no attention—unless you stopped hollering. I can holler a political speech like you can make a stewardship speech. But I believe it would be easier for me to make the keynote address to the Democratic national convention than it will be to make this stewardship speech!"

The next day, Monday, I called the other red-hot preacher, my brother-in-law, Bill Carl, and asked for help.

Bill said, "We don't have stewardship dinners at First Presbyterian in Dallas anymore. Each year we just ask everybody to increase their pledge by one percent of their income, moving toward tithing."

"If you'd told K.C. that, I wouldn't have had to make this speech," I said.

Bill said, "You'll have no trouble. Just remember, it's *how* it's given that counts. Tithing's our response to Christ's grace, a divinely inspired suggestion about how to live. It's basics—something like John Wooden's basics when he used to win all those NCAA basketball titles coaching at UCLA. He didn't show game films of other teams. He told his team, 'Work on basics, and your game falls into place.' The idea is, do these things—tithing, praying, good deeds, worship—and you move toward a whole and more balanced life."

I said, "Sounds a little eastern to me."

"Well, it does. But I believe salvation is moving toward wholeness. Something that you do the best you can your whole lifetime."

I said, "Sometimes I think I have more in common with Jonah than Paul."

Bill said, "Sometimes I feel that way, too."

"I wonder why that little Jonah story is so fascinating."

"Because Jonah resists God's call. Something holds him back. And Jonah never changes. Does that sound familiar?"

I took notes furiously as Bill went on.

"It's really the story of any believer in the Judeo-Christian tradition. It's the story of sin, of forgiveness, and of the beginnings of new life. Jonah's the classic human being, for he had a flaw in his character and on his own he couldn't erase it."

"And that is . . . ?"

"He wanted to control his own destiny. Jonah forgot about the mission in life that God had given him."

"Things turned out all right. He got out of the belly of the whale."

"Only because God never gave up, called him again to go to Nineveh. That was Jonah's big chance to begin a new life. He sort of took it. But notice he didn't jump up and say, 'Okay, Lord, it's off to Nineveh I go!' There is no dramatic turnaround like Paul had. Off Jonah went, halfheartedly, stumbling, half hoping that no one in Nineveh would pay any attention to him, and that God would have to find someone else to do the job."

"Still, in the end, things worked out."

"Not as well as they might have. Jonah stayed the tragic figure. He never opened up. He kept resisting God's calling. He completely blew his chance to become a new person."

I said, "Thanks. I'm on my way to see K.C."

"Give him my best."

K. C. Ptomey was relaxing in his study.

I said, "I'm wallowing around in things I thought I already knew. It's just really dawned on me that a stewardship speech isn't just about giving your money. It's also about giving yourself, what you do with your life."

K.C. said, "They're the same—stewardship of your possessions and stewardship of your life. What you do with your life is your calling, and Presbyterians believe that everyone has a calling. It's just a matter of discovering the one that's yours."

I scooted uncomfortably in the chair, and said, "That's the most joy—and the most misery, too—finding my calling, figuring out what to do with my life."

I remembered a Sunday morning in Australia—it seemed a very long time ago—and I told K.C. about it. "There is one way out of this dilemma that sometimes tempts me. Once in Sydney, at our little Uniting Church in Mosman, a young missionary spoke. He was thin and wore plain glasses and a white gown and sandals and he had an easy manner. He told about his plans to go to Argentina to work with the Indians and he was full of a sense of mission. I'm sure that was no bed of roses, working with the Indians. But his decision—just the *decision* to give it all away and go do God's work—sounded so much simpler than deciding what *part* of our lives to give, which is what most of us have to figure out."

K.C. said, "Hold on. What you do with *your* whole life is just as important to God as anything the missionary did. *Everyone* has a calling. Missionaries in Argentina, preachers in Nashville, woodcarvers, conservation leaders, mothers, teachers, all have a calling. You've probably seen politicians who really knew why they wanted to serve. Didn't *they* radiate the same sense of purpose that you saw in that young missionary? The important thing is that you keep searching for your calling and keep trying to give your life to it."

I got up. K.C. got up, too, and smiled and said, "We already have seven hundred reservations for Sunday night, the biggest stewardship dinner ever. And we expect a couple hundred more."

I turned to leave and then I stopped and said to K.C., "You'd better build a bigger back door on the church."

"What for?"

"People are going to be wandering in that way, people who've started searching for the meaning of life somewhere out in the wilderness, and whose journey pulls them to God. They'll come stumbling through the back door and be standing in the middle of the sanctuary without even knowing how they got there."

"I'm not sure I've ever thought of it quite that way," K.C. said.

I went on. "Change will cause it. So much change running over people. Look at the people who change jobs every few years. People are going to start figuring out that the way you deal with so much change is to learn to take it *on your own terms.* And that means a lot of hard and uncomfortable and inconvenient thinking, questions like who you really are, and what is really most important to you. It requires a continuous sort of personal renewal. That's why you'll need a bigger back door. Most people won't be on their knees when they start down this road. But when they figure out what they are doing—that the purpose of their journey is to discover the truth about themselves, and about the world they live in and about God—that's when they'll find themselves stumbling in the back door of the church."

I had one more stop to make, to have breakfast the next morning with Mickey Miller, a seminarian turned lawyer who taught Sunday school class nonstop with his notes on big posters taped to blackboards so that even the slowest could keep up.

Mickey sliced two hard-fried eggs and started talking immediately about my stewardship speech. "What you give to God is more than a tip left over. Your whole life is giving and growing. That's the pilgrimage we all have."

I said, "You make me think of my eighth-grade confirmation class, the one Kathryn is in now. What always stuck with me from that was the First Catechism: 'Man's chief end is to glorify God.'" Then I blurted it out: *"How do you know how to do that?"*

Mickey missed a bite of egg. "That's an unanticipated question," he said and laid down his fork. "Sometimes you find out in all the hustle and bustle of whatever you're doing. It's not always clear before you start, but after a while you just have to start anyway. Some people use the hustle and bustle as an excuse to put off doing what they know very well they ought to be doing."

And he asked me, "When was the last time you read Jonah?"

EPILOGUE

A NEW
AMERICAN
HOMECOMING

//

I'm old
Botany Bay
Stiff in the joints
Little to say.

I am he
Who paved the way,
That you might walk
At your ease today.

Shame on the mouth
That would deny
The knotted hands
That set us high!

—MARY GILMORE
"Old Botany Bay" (Australian)

In 268 well-chosen words he gave
America a chart and a compass . . .
demonstrating that our nation's
strength lies in rededication to those
beliefs to which it was committed at
its birth . . .
—BENJAMIN P. THOMAS
Abraham Lincoln

O ur six months off turned out to be a homecoming,
even while we were half a world away from home.
Now that we are *really* home again, in America, we can see
the results in each of our lives. The Will of the Family is almost nine now and much more on his own, entertaining his
fellow second-graders at lunch with stories of fantastic adventures in Australia and making big plans one day to be an ar-
chitect. But he still hasn't warmed up to bubblegum
milkshakes, and just yesterday he was parading around in one
of those awful purple and green Grateful Dead T-shirts, like
older brother Drew.

Drew's own transformation has been most amazing. At age
eighteen he has emerged self-confidently from the teenage Period of the Perpetual Frown, and now always has something
interesting to talk about. During family "discussions," he remains the calmest. He has had a good senior year in Nashville,
has been waiting on tables, when not practicing the guitar, and
made all his own arrangements about becoming a freshman this
fall at Kenyon College in Ohio.

When Kathryn returned from Australia, her eighth-grade
classmates—the friends she missed so much—nearly consumed
her. They elected her captain of her class team, and she responded by winning several track-team races, and then by
breaking her wrist playing soccer, almost at the same time she'd
broken her ankle the year before. She is growing taller and, her

mother and I think, very pretty and she has decided to become an actress.

Leslee is sixteen and off on another adventure, this time at the same school in New Hampshire Drew once attended. "Dad, I'll never know what I missed if I don't go," she said, and off she went. She is happy there, but we all miss her. When she's home she works at Miss Daisy's Restaurant and has more friends, especially boyfriends, than I can count. She wants to go riding horses in the Wyoming mountains next summer or "something like that." Leslee still needs a harness every now and then.

Honey became busy again the minute we arrived home. Fixing up our new house took a lot of her time. Then, being ringmaster and lioness keeps getting even more complicated as our thirty relationships age and swirl. But Honey is managing to squeeze out a little more time for her own ventures. She works part time with the child-care company she and I helped to start. President Reagan has appointed her to the Corporation for Public Broadcasting. She dreams of going back to school, to study archaeology, and every now and then, just as she is about to fall asleep exhausted, she turns over and wonders, "Is it time yet for *my* six months off?"

Looking back, I realize that I jumped into some pretty deep water during our time off and then came back up about where I jumped in, which surprises me a little. I'm not sure what I expected: some different direction, maybe a big new idea, answers to deep questions. About the most I can say is that now I understand the questions better. I understand, too, that this life will end before the search for answers ends, but that I can't stop searching—because I might miss the joy of discovering some adventure that suits me right down to the ground, and feeling its compelling purpose, and pouring into it every creative ounce I have and that may be life's real joy.

We Alexanders haven't been the only ones in the world feeling the need for a homecoming. In fact, the year before we went to Australia, in 1986, our whole state of Tennessee had one that got completely out of control. The Forest Brook neighborhood in West Knoxville, for example, invited every family who'd ever lived there to come home for the annual Fourth of

July party. Every house was open. Old friends and children who had grown up and hadn't seen each other for a long time, were hugging on the sidewalks and playing ball with their children in the yards they knew. There were baby-carriage and bicycle races like there used to be, and they cooked old-favorite, good-smelling foods and sat around some of the same kitchen tables and on the porch swings in the warm evenings looking at old photographs and laughing about how they once used hoses to spray the lawns and sometimes each other, and how the children would put fireflies in jars and how they would worry about the children—and that night a few even slept in their old beds. They talked about the things that were really important and when it came time for everyone to go away again a lot of eyes weren't dry.

The Forest Brook neighborhood homecoming was only one of 5,000 celebrations in 540 communities during Tennessee Homecoming '86. Families in Hickman County made a huge Heritage quilt with a patch for each of the sixty-three places with names in the county, and began to remember how places like Aetna and Lyles and Bon Aqua and Minnie Pearl's Grinder's Switch got their names, and where they came from and what was important about them. In Finger, Tennessee, they needed a fire hall, so volunteers built one. A library went up the same way in Selmer. In Newport, people started cleaning up the Pigeon River because Homecoming reminded them that the river was why Newport was there in the first place. Henning put up a sign showing the way to Chicken George's graveyard and made a museum out of the house where a little boy named Alex Haley once sat by the front porch listening to his snuff-dipping Aunt Liz spin the tales that eventually became *Roots*. Children began interviewing their grandparents and using their tape machines to record what people knew who had lived for one hundred years.

Tennessee Homecoming '86 started quietly in January 1983, when I asked every community to do three things:

1. Look at its roots.
2. Find something there to celebrate and to build on.
3. Invite everyone who ever lived in that community to come home to join in the celebration.

Nobody in the state capitol gave anyone permission to do any of this. The government spent very little tax money. And there was almost no "news" of it—because Homecoming was a celebration of lives coming *into* order, not tumbling out of order. But by 1986, Tennessee Homecoming had spread like a prairie fire. "It's the 'in thing,' " said Dorothy Wood, who was busy helping Jonesboro celebrate being our state's oldest town.

You could see the results by the time we were packing for Australia. For instance, General Motors arrived with its new three-billion-dollar Saturn car plant. We fed the General Motors people country ham, and we asked Charlie McCoy to play the harmonica. We were becoming less embarrassed to sound and act like how we had grown up. We were also becoming more comfortable with our own company; so much so that we were busy welcoming company from everywhere. Newly confident Homecoming communities set higher goals for themselves, such as improving their schools. The state jumped to tops in the Southeast and third nationally in job growth. There were lots of reasons for all this success, but most Tennesseans will tell you today that of the things we could have done *to help ourselves,* Homecoming did more than anything else.

The first book I packed for Australia was the one my home county of Blount published, tracing every community back to when the Cherokee Indians lived there. You can imagine my surprise when we arrived in Sydney and found the same sort of thing going on. "The archives in Sydney are full of people trying to prove that they are descended from convicts." I heard again it was the "in thing," as in Tennessee. It was the wife of a member of the Australian Parliament who told me. Everyone was busy getting ready for the two hundredth anniversary of the arrival of the first fleet of British convict settlers. The results of Australia's search for identity were everywhere: television broadcasters speaking less British or American—and more Aussie; higher prices for Australian paintings; packed houses for a long-running reading of Mary Gilmore's poems; more sheepshearers' ballads on the government radio; no one feeling put down when artist Sydney Nolan observed, "Camels are right for most of Australia, not cars and trucks."

I suppose that what made me think most about how much

a new Homecoming might also help all of America was when
I saw the television antennae in Cessnock. Honey and I were
driving through the Hunter Valley vineyard country, two hours
north of Sydney. It was our last week in Australia, and we had
rolled down the windows because the winter felt so good. The
farther we drove from the city, the higher the television antennae reached, until when we arrived at Cessnock, they were
desperately, grotesquely high. They seemed to be futilely trying
to connect with all the other tall antennae and satellite dishes
one now sees in almost every part of the world. Looking at them,
I tried to imagine how much disturbing news of the world those
antennae must be pulling into the homes of Cessnock, news of
lives running out of order globally—starving babies in Ethiopia,
peasants losing their freedom in Afghanistan, someone else
jumping from a window in New York City. Tragedy and dis-
order everywhere heap in on us. We must know it. We are all
one big community.

But, I thought, we are not—even though the Holiday Inns
in Beijing and Memphis look the same, as do almost all the
international airports, and even though there is a McDonald's
in Hong Kong and a Kentucky Fried Chicken in the Northern
Territory of Australia, and Western business manners dominate
Tokyo boardrooms, and maples turn orange and red and yellow
about the same time in Nikko and Nashville, and there is creeping capitalism in the Chinese countryside. There are all of those
things, but we are not the same. Neither do all the sophisticated
antennae bring us together. They only are symbols of marvelous
changes in communications technology that mostly we have not
learned how to handle. So the antennae reach out desperately
and we stare at our televisions, sometimes left feeling so confused and helpless that we can do nothing—like John and Elaine
Edwards's twelve-year-old child who saw famine for the first
time in New Delhi. The child had food for herself and there was
enough for her family but not enough to help so many people
dying of hunger in the streets. She didn't know what to do. So
she simply stopped eating.

Instead of desperately reaching like the antennae in Cessnock, the more natural thing for each of us to do—at least at
first—is to respect the natural impulse to help our own lives

come into order and then to try to reach for *those around us in our family and community.* This first requires being an optimist—believing that the world and its inhabitants naturally *want* to come into order instead of out of it. I believe this more firmly now after spending so much time in the Australian out-of-doors, feeling the wash of the waves and the breezes and watching the sky blow blue and the big stars burn at night—all that has helped me understand more clearly what a perfect melody God's music is. When the melody turns sad, it must be because *we've* caused it, because after that doesn't the melody always struggle to become happy again? The minor chord wants to become major. Things try to flow naturally into order—the way things are supposed to be.

Australia's bicentennial celebrators are busy reminding themselves of a Stone Age lesson about this: that communities are the best places to conduct individual struggles. For 50,000 years Australian aborigines have spent almost all of their time finding ways to live in harmony with one of the world's harshest environments. As René Dubos has written, these people have always hunted in families or groups of twelve or so, and have banded in groups of fifty or in entire communities rarely exceeding five hundred. Through trial and error they have discovered that living works out best in relatively small groups. Many anthropologists believe it is a pattern of man's distant past that has not changed much, and that this pattern is one reason why communities and families are such an integral part of the formula for successfully practicing the art of living.

The next president of the United States should call for a New American Homecoming. Community by community, family by family, from Kitty Hawk to Long Beach, from Brownsville to Niagara Falls, in every crossroads, village, and big-city neighborhood, there should be a yearlong celebration of what is most worth holding on to in each of the one hundred thousand places we Americans call home. You should expect a politician away from America for six months to come home bursting with some Big Idea, and that is mine.

This is not the only kind of leadership that's needed in a dangerous world. But such a Homecoming would be the first thing to do. Imagine tens of thousands of communities rediscovering and then celebrating American values! We would become more comfortable with ourselves and learn better the difficult art of self-criticism. Our goals for living would become clearer and probably bolder, and so would our striving for those goals. *How* we would be living would become our most persuasive claim for real leadership in a world filled with people hungry to know how to live.

Our New American Homecoming would help us learn to deal with the enormous changes we face—and do so on America's own terms. We would be doing it in the way America works best, community by community, family by family.

Now we Alexanders have supper at a different table in a different breakfast room in our old Green Hills neighborhood in Nashville. Honey sits at one end. I'm at the other. The children still perch two on each side. (I hope it's not my imagination, but I do believe their chairs are turned a little more my way than they used to be.) We seem to have more to say to each other. What's most surprising is how often our talk is about Australia. We measure the passing time by those memories.

One day just like that bright blue day a year ago when Honey and I slept in the sun after picnicking on North Head above the Tasman Sea, Honey and Kathryn were admiring the new maple leaves and remembering how happy they'd been to be in Japan last year and not miss spring. Will nearly chuckled himself to sleep last night reading *Thrump-O-Moto* again and imagining the Forty-Headed Fu the way he and I did when we took our overnight train trip to Melbourne. Leslee was home from school, and she and her mother were discussing curfew times, and I hadn't said a word, when suddenly Leslee exclaimed, "Dad, you'd better not even say one word about when I went to Palm Beach to see the sunrise and got in so much trouble!" and we all laughed. And when thundering rock music in the living room interrupted the curfew discussion, all I could think of was Billy King and Simon, the drummer, and Martin of the hearty appetite and the rest of the jam-session crew in the basement of our home in Base Camp Sydney.

Honey and I took a long walk last night after dinner. In late March it stays light in Nashville until about 7:00, and the evening was pleasantly cool, about like it is in Sydney, although the seasons there are moving the other way. We were enjoying the coming of spring and wondering how much of our time in Australia we would remember ten years from now. Here's what we decided: We'll never forget the adventures, but what we'll treasure the most is the memory that we were important enough to each other actually to manage to do it—to take six months off, while we still could—together.

ACKNOWL-
EDGMENTS

//

Didn't Governors used to be more
vivid?

—Roy Blount, Jr.
Not Exactly What I Had in Mind

When I decided to write this book I enlisted as my
agent Peter Jenkins, who is known as the author of
best-selling books about walking across America. When Peter
and I went to New York City, he introduced me to some publishers in roughly this way: "Lamar would like to write a book
about what a great governor he's been."

"His mother might read it," the first publisher said.

"Boring," said number two.

I forget what the third one said, but number four asked,
"Anything else you could write about? Doing anything interesting *after* you leave office?"

"Not really," I told him. "The whole family's moving to

Australia for six months off. I'm going to do absolutely nothing."

"Six months off . . . now, *that* might be interesting," number four said.

"Six months off . . . that's *exactly* the book we had in mind," Peter Jenkins said.

So, first I want to thank Peter for grasping the idea for this book and for constantly encouraging me.

Next, thank you, William Morrow, for providing a nice advance and the perfect editor. The advance helped pay for the six months off, and Pat Golbitz's patience and skills and relentless red pen purged the book of (most of) my speeches and kept it a family story. Thanks, too, to Morrow assistant editor Jill Hamilton for moving things along so expertly, and to diligent copy editor Sonia Greenbaum, and to Morrow president/CEO Al Marchioni and all the talented and creative Morrow publicists and salespersons who have taken such a personal interest.

In Nashville, Marc Lavine's research and Sondra Morris's organizational skills have been indispensable. I am especially grateful to Belmont College president Bill Troutt and to Dean Wayne Brown and his assistants, Nancy Rainey and Carol Dunn, of the Jack C. Massey Graduate School of Business, and to Mr. Massey himself for providing such a hospitable place for my writing and study.

Late in 1987, *Roots* author Alex Haley invited me to join him on the S.S. *Wellington,* a cargo freighter, as it sailed from Long Beach to Auckland, New Zealand. For sixteen days, while Alex worked on his newest book, I wrote the basic parts of this one. Alex read most of those early drafts and made welcome suggestions, but his gentle encouragement was more help than he can know.

Honey and Drew and Leslee and Kathryn and Will all want to add their thank you's, too, to those people who helped make our six months off possible. Australian Ambassador to the United States Rawdon R. Dalrymple and his wife, Ross, visited Nashville twice to make certain that we were making our way easily to Sydney. Christine DeFrance, our neighbor and Kathryn's scout leader, helped arrange departure flights and introduced us to our first Australian friends—her parents, Elma and Max Goode, and brother, John, in Melbourne; and Barbie and

Graham and Sam and Jackie Crawford in Sydney. We owe them all thanks, but to the Crawfords especially because Sydney became our base camp. Barbie and Graham were expert volunteer housefinders, school arrangers, car buyers, and crisis managers. They shared their friends with us and also gave us plenty of room to be on our own—which was just what we needed.

There is no possible way to express our gratitude to every new Australian friend who helped us, because almost everyone we met tried to help—from Mosman Village's ANZ banker Brian Loundar, to Mike Connell at the Baronia Art Gallery, to Peter Rose at the milk bar. We must mention Bob Winder, the director-general of the Department of Education in New South Wales, and his able assistant, Allan Ruby, and all the teachers and, especially, the three principals—Mrs. Pitts at Drew's Mosman High, Mrs. Wheeldon at Leslee and Kathryn's Queenwood School for Girls, and Mrs. Locke at Will's Balmoral Infants School. They helped our children gain new memories and friendships and confidence in themselves. We are grateful to the Barry Labaleisters for renting their home in Mosman overlooking the most beautiful harbor in the world, and to Bridget Alonso, who, while looking after their house, became our friend. Sydney Holden dealer Barry Smith would be our candidate for small-business man of the year in any country, and IBM's Phil Singleton was just plain thoughtful. The New South Wales Minister of Heritage and Environment, Bob Carr, and his associates opened up for us the Real Australia, as well as meetings of the Chester A. Arthur Society, during which Australian politicians demolish any American contenders in trivia contests about the U.S. presidency. And if all America's professional foreign service officers were like U.S. Consul John Dorrance in Sydney, and if all spouses were like Mary Lou Dorrance, then our diplomatic adversaries might as well surrender.

Many old and new friends made unusual efforts to make our traveling a greater joy: Rosalyn and John Rudd at Reynella in the Snowy Mountains, John and Elaine Edwards in Darwin (and the Education Department of the Northern Territory), the Teruhisa Tabuchi family in Ashiya, the U.S. Embassy staff in Tokyo, former Japanese ambassador to the United States Yoshio Okawara, and the Mitsuya Goto family in Yokohama, Tamie and Malcolm Fraser in Nareen, Mike Rose and Rudy Koppen, and all the Holiday Inn people in Hong Kong and Beijing, Jean and Ambassador Bill Lane in Canberra, Bette Bao and Ambassador Winston Lord in Beijing; and Honey and Ambassador Joe Rodgers in Paris. Peter Aboud in Sydney deserves a medal for arranging our complicated trip home to America.

There are some very important other friends who gave crucial help: Houston Goddard kept the goldfish and cactus; Molly and Bob Weaver put up with Molly, the cat; Jan Talley gave Corfe and Lady, our cocker spaniels, a country home for *their* six months off; and a crowd of friends—Carol Elam, Dana Sherrard, Flem Smith III, Sam Sanders, Bernadette and Gary Doyle, and Delmar Caylor—made sure our home was ready when we returned. Our families at home let us put so many responsibilities on hold, and Tom Ingram and Lewis Lavine helped make sure a barrage of mail and official responsibilities did not follow us to Australia.

Many, many thanks to all and to everyone else we wish we could mention; and to all our new friends in Australia a very special hello, and a Happy 200th Birthday from this family of admiring first cousins half a world away in America!

NOTES

//

There are two fictional scenes in this book. The first is the table conversation at the Australian-American Bicentennial Dinner in Chapter 30, "First Cousins." The second is the last portion of my "interview" with the Basque reporter in Chapter 26.

The dinner scene in Chapter 30 actually occurred, and all the dinner table comments are *someone's* accurately quoted words, mostly gathered from the people who attended the dinner. I believe the spirit of the conversation is an accurate representation of Australian-American feelings. But the exact line of conversation is my own invention, and I hope no one (except the delightful wife of the Bicentennial chairman James Kirk) imagines he or she is one of the characters. The governor-general and Dame Leonie Kramer's remarks are as they said them.

As for the Basque reporter in Chapter 26, there *is* such a reporter, and the first three quarters of the episode are presented exactly as it occurred at the Sheraton Hotel coffee shop in Darwin, but the reporter's comments in the last quarter, mostly those describing Australia, are not his, but instead are accurately quoted comments made by the administrator of the

Northern Territory and by Department of Education employee John Edwards.

Other than those two instances, this is a true story. The scenes are as they happened. At least I have tried hard to recall things accurately, although the memory does get rusty going back twenty or thirty years. Sometimes I have had the aid of my notes. Some of the quotes from Australia came from Honey and Drew and Leslee and Kathryn and Will, who kept their own journals and who consented to be "interviewed."

I do not think much of people who violate private confidences, so I have followed a rule that has seemed to work well in my other books. If I think someone will be embarrassed by my printing his or her private comment, I have not used that comment. If it seems even a close question, I have either not used the comment or have asked for permission from the person to be quoted. For instance, I asked Honey and each of our children and the Edwards family in Darwin to read what I wrote to make sure they were comfortable with what I included about them. With the private statements from public figures, I have tried to be especially careful. For example, I have asked for and received permission from President Ronald Reagan and Vice-president George Bush, and from former Australian Prime Minister Malcolm Fraser to use brief portions of our private conversations.

One might say the information in Chapter 8, "Prelude in D Minor," is not especially flattering to former Tennessee Governor Ray Blanton, but all of those facts have been published before in newspapers. The only thing new is what was going on in my mind during those extraordinary events, and I have waited ten years to describe it.

In the legends between the title and the beginning of each chapter I have tried to give the reader an idea of some of the books I enjoyed during our six months off. Ideas from many of these books—as well as others—work their way through my pages. I should acknowledge the influence of four of these. One is an old friend, *A God Within* by René Dubos, which I have tried to read once a year since the early 1970s. Another is *Transitions,* by William Bridges, a book I did not discover until late in 1987 after I had completed a first draft of this book. From these two especially I have borrowed ideas and even references to other writers.

Two other books, written twenty-four years apart, are crucial texts for anyone interested in how best to deal with the enormous changes facing us. The first is John Gardner's *Self-Renewal*, first published in 1963. The second is Robert H. Waterman's 1987 book, *The Renewal Factor*, which uses Gardner's thesis to show how successful businesses stay successful. The times are so fast-changing that Waterman argues the new Rule of Life must be "If it ain't broke, *fix it anyway.* " Since "the only true source of renewal . . . is the individual," Waterman's lessons apply to everyone.

The words "Sky Blown Blue" are Mary Gilmore's, and I cannot write about the Great Smoky Mountains without borrowing something from Carson Brewer.

DATE DUE
